KU-414-637

THE DREAM HOME

T.M. Logan is a *Sunday Times* bestseller whose thrillers have sold more than two million copies in the UK and are published in 22 countries around the world. *The Holiday* was a Richard and Judy Book Club pick and was adapted into a four-part TV drama, as was *The Catch*. Formerly a national newspaper journalist, he writes full time and lives in Nottinghamshire with his wife and two children.

Also by T.M. Logan:

Lies
29 Seconds
The Holiday
The Catch
Trust Me
The Curfew
The Mother

Praise for

T.M. LOGAN

'Smart, intense and with a humdinger of a mid-point twist. I loved it'
GILLIAN MCALLISTER

'Taut, tense and compelling. Thriller writing at its finest'
SIMON LELIC

'T.M. Logan's best yet. Unsettling and so, so entertaining.
The perfect thriller'
CAZ FREAR

'A tense and gripping thriller'
B.A. PARIS

'Assured, compelling, and hypnotically readable – with a twist at
the end I guarantee you won't see coming'
LEE CHILD

'A compelling, twisty page-turner, and that's the truth'
JAMES SWALLOW

'Outstanding and very well-written . . . so gripping
I genuinely found it hard to put down'
K.L. SLATER

'A terrific page-turner, didn't see that twist!
A thoroughly enjoyable thriller'
MEL SHERRATT

'Another blistering page-turner from psych-thriller god
T.M. Logan'
CHRIS WHITAKER

'Even the cleverest second-guesser is unlikely to arrive at
the truth until it's much, much too late'
THE TIMES

THE DREAM HOME

T.M. LOGAN

ZAFFRE

First published in the UK in 2024 by
ZAFFRE
An imprint of Zaffre Publishing Group
A Bonnier Books UK company
4th Floor, Victoria House, Bloomsbury Square, London, WC1B 4DA
Owned by Bonnier Books
Sveavägen 56, Stockholm, Sweden

Copyright © T.M. Logan, 2024

All rights reserved.
No part of this publication may be reproduced,
stored or transmitted in any form by any means, electronic,
mechanical, photocopying or otherwise, without the
prior written permission of the publisher.

The right of T.M. Logan to be identified as Author of this
work has been asserted by him in accordance with the
Copyright, Designs and Patents Act, 1988.

This is a work of fiction. Names, places, events and
incidents are either the products of the author's
imagination or used fictitiously. Any resemblance to
actual persons, living or dead, or actual
events is purely coincidental.

A CIP catalogue record for this book is
available from the British Library.

Hardback ISBN: 978-1-80418-132-4
Trade paperback ISBN: 978-1-80418-133-1

Also available as an ebook and an audiobook

1 3 5 7 9 10 8 6 4 2

Typeset by IDSUK (Data Connection) Ltd
Printed and bound in Great Britain by Clays Ltd, Elcograf S.p.A.

Zaffre is an imprint of Zaffre Publishing Group
A Bonnier Books UK company
www.bonnierbooks.co.uk

For my amazing children,
Sophie and Tom,
who make me proud every single day

FLINTSHIRE SIR Y FFLINT	
C29 0000 0929 577	
Askews & Holts	12-Mar-2024
AF	£16.99
FLIFLINT	

The dead keep their secrets.

—Alexander Smith, *Dreamthorp*

PART I

You never get used to it. Not really. It hangs over your head, always waiting, a debt that's never been settled. The knowledge that it's waiting somewhere to trip you up – and that you need to be ready in case the past comes knocking. Hoping that day will never come. Knowing what will have to happen if it does.

1

SUNDAY

It's towards the end of moving-in day that I find it.

A day full of lifting and carrying and making cups of tea for the removal team, of going up and down the broad staircase a hundred times, of unloading boxes, building bedframes and giving the children small jobs to keep them occupied. A non-stop day bringing this old house back to life.

It still doesn't quite feel real, even as Jess and I are debating where to start with the decorating. None of the rooms have seen fresh paint or new carpet for decades. A *fixer-upper*, the estate agent had said with a hopeful smile. But we had fallen in love with the place on the first viewing, had both known it was something special, this rambling Victorian house with its high ceilings and tall windows, its soaring chimney stacks and half-timbered gables, the date in delicate raised stonework over the big front door: *1889*. Six bedrooms, three bathrooms, two reception rooms, a cellar, a pantry, a snug – there was so much *space*.

We knew it needed a lot of work, that was one of the reasons we'd been able to afford a house in this part of the city. The Park, first named for the old deer park next to the castle, maintained for the king's hunt – now an enclave of grand nineteenth-century houses and wide-spaced streets, a tree-lined oasis of walled gardens and leafy calm right in the heart of Nottingham.

By late afternoon, I'm clearing left-behind rubbish from the second floor. My legs are heavy, my back starting to ache after going down two flights of stairs carrying stacks of old newspapers, an ancient put-up bed that had been left on the landing, a broken bookcase, boxes of tiles and bin bags of musty clothes. In the smallest of the top-floor attic rooms, where the air is stale with neglect, the carcass of an old fitted wardrobe hangs off the wall. Its chipboard shelves are splintered, one door is jammed shut and the other has fallen off its runner completely. Nails and screws protrude from the broken frame, ready to catch small hands. The whole thing looks like it might collapse at any moment, and it doesn't take me long to prise it away from the wall with a crowbar, flattening the nails and breaking the whole wardrobe apart, stacking the broken wood in the corner.

Every room in this house seems to have some quirk or curiosity that we hadn't anticipated.

And this room is no exception.

Because the wall behind the fitted wardrobe is not painted plaster, or wallpaper or brick. Instead, it's panelled in dark wood like the hallway on the ground floor. Panels of walnut or teak stretch floor to ceiling across the width of the room. It's a big improvement on the fitted wardrobe, a shame to have hidden away this handsome facade behind something so ugly. The whole thing is seven panels high and a dozen or so wide. The workmanship is very fine, each piece seamlessly fitting into the next, the only blemishes a handful of holes where the wardrobe had been attached.

I run my hand over a panel, the grain of the wood smooth under my palm. Standing back to admire it, I snap a quick picture on my phone to show Jess what I've discovered. The late afternoon sun coming through the skylight makes the wood almost glow, like burnished bronze, as if carved from a single piece of—

I look again at the picture, then back at the panelling. Comparing the high-definition image with the reality in front of me.

The way the sun catches it in the photo, at just the right angle, I can see the workmanship is not *quite* perfect. Not all the way along. Perhaps there's been some movement over time, the house shifting its old bones slightly in the years since this wall was added. In the phone image, there is a very fine vertical line running between two panels at the far end of the wall.

But with the naked eye, I still can't make it out. I run my hand up and down the right side of wall, between two of the panels. I don't see it. I *feel* it. My fingertips brush an almost invisible join, a seam in the wood. I run my hand up higher, then down to the floor. Up again, across, down.

Not just a seam.

It's the outline of a door.

Perhaps there was old pipework behind here, the wood panelling a smart solution to disguise it, with discreet access if there was ever a problem. Or perhaps a little extra attic space beneath the eaves of the sloping roof.

There doesn't seem to be any kind of keyhole, or lock, or latch, or anything that will open or close it. I spend a minute feeling all the way around the seam again but there is nothing at all to give any leverage, to pull or push or turn. No button or handle.

In frustration, I place my palm flat against the middle panel and push.

With a reluctant *click*, the door opens towards me. Just half an inch. I pause for a second, taking a breath, then pull it open all the way on silent hinges.

Over the threshold, there is total, perfect darkness. The air is musty and stale, a blunt spoiled smell of old bricks and slow decay that has not been breathed in a long, long time. My heart beating a little faster, I take the phone from my pocket and flick the torch on, white light throwing leaping shadows over an armchair, a side table, a dresser pushed up against the wall, all of it thick with dust and cobwebs.

It isn't just a panel to hide ugly pipework.

It isn't extra storage space either.

It's a whole new room, hidden behind the wall.

2

I *knew* something about this top bedroom wasn't quite right.

The dimensions seemed a little too small, the wall didn't quite match the one in the bedroom next to it. This hidden space is small and cramped like a hide, a priest hole – but the house was nowhere near old enough for that. According to the stonework over the front door, it was built in 1889 and I knew it had been extended at least twice since. On my phone, I pull up the floorplan from the estate agents' website and zoom into the top floor layout, checking the dimensions of this bedroom – ten feet by twelve, give or take a few inches. That looks about right to me. No indication of more space to the side, of a hidden annexe that must have been built into the fabric of this place so long ago that people forgot it was even there. An extra four feet of width that had been turned into something else.

Ducking my head, I step through the door.

The air is thick with years of dust, smells of old timber and crumbling brick that catch at the back of my throat.

A floorboard creaks beneath my feet and I freeze. There is the weird sense that I'm somehow intruding on someone else's private space. I know it's ridiculous. We own this house now – and everything in it. From the swirling 1970s carpets on the top landing to the stack of rust-crusted paint pots in the cellar, the fading cookbooks abandoned in the pantry and the stippled Artex ceiling in the sitting room, stained a dull yellow from years of cigarette smoke. All of it left behind by the elderly previous owner. All of it belongs to us now.

The bright light from my phone throws dancing shadows as it sweeps over the room, cobwebs filling every corner. Old rugs nailed to bare brick on one side, the slope of the eaves on the other. There's a low, tatty armchair with a tiny side table next to it, a brown ceramic coaster where someone long ago might have placed their cup of tea. A battered Welsh dresser crammed against the wall, the wood dark, almost black.

A bare bulb dangles from the ceiling. I pull on the cord but nothing happens; the bulb is long dead.

The dresser has a single large door on the right, with eight small drawers to the left, in two columns of four. I pull the handle of the door and it opens with a rusty creak.

Empty, except for more cobwebs and the cocooned carcasses of dead insects. I try the top drawer. Locked. As is the one beside it, and the one below.

Curiosity piqued, I feel a small spike of frustration added into the mix – a dangerous combination for me ever since I was a child. A locked dresser, a hidden door, a secret room. Now I *definitely* need to see what's inside. Maybe there was something valuable hidden here, money or jewellery, a stash of gold coins or the key to a safe deposit box at a private bank. All of which would come in extremely handy, especially now.

I'm pretty sure I can lever the drawers open if I use a little brute force and ignorance. I bend to duck under the low doorway and back out into the main room, to my toolbox on the landing, where I find the biggest flathead screwdriver

I've got, an old chisel and then – as a last resort – my crowbar, the steel smooth and heavy in my hand. Dumb, dumber,
dumbest.

I start with the chisel, sliding the blade into the gap between
the top drawer and the wooden frame. Levering the handle
back, putting my weight into it—

With a dull *snap*, the blade of the chisel breaks off.

I'm left with just the old wooden handle in my clenched fist.
I pull the broken blade free and study the dresser with a new
curiosity.

This old thing was *really* well made. Before I mangle this
antique with the crowbar, I should at least have a proper look
at it.

I make my way down both sets of stairs to the Minton-tiled
hallway on the ground floor, taking a sixty-watt bulb from one
of the boxes labelled '*MOVING SUPPLIES*' in Jess's neat capitals. In a bowl on the windowsill are a bunch of house keys
handed over to us on the day we exchanged contracts, for the
front and back doors, the garage, the shed and some others I
haven't identified yet.

I take them back up to the hidden annexe and go through
them one by one, trying to fit them into the locks by the light of
my phone, perched on the edge of the old armchair.

None of the keys work.

None of them are even the right size to fit into the eight
identical keyholes of the small dresser drawers.

I let out a sigh and shove the bunch of keys back into the
pocket of my jeans, the pulse of my curiosity beating stronger
now. In all likelihood the right key was lost forever in a box or
a cupboard or an old jar of odds and ends. Or buried beneath a

ton of rubbish on some landfill site, separated forever from the drawers to which it belonged.

Or . . . maybe not. Would you go to all this trouble to create a hidden place, but then keep the key in plain sight? Where it might be easily found?

I replace the bulb and pull the light switch again, blinking against the glare for a moment while my eyes adjust. The room seems older, less grim and more functional in the wash of white light. Everything is more unnerving in the dark, I suppose. Using the torch on my phone for extra illumination, I play a beam of light all around the dresser, on the wall behind it, the wooden door frame beside it.

A floorboard creaks beneath me again and I crouch down, testing each dusty plank to see if one might be loose. Studying the rows of bricks, I run my fingers over rough mortar to seek out any gaps. The bricks are flaking, the mortar unevenly applied, but I can't find any obvious place for a key to have been tucked away. The exposed wooden frame around the doorway is like the back of a stage set, the side of the wall that no one ever sees, the timber raw and unfinished. But it's very solid and it *is* wide enough to accommodate a key.

I reach up to feel around the top of the frame and almost immediately there is a sharp stab of pain in my index finger.

Pulling it back with a curse, I see a dark orb of blood rising from the skin of my fingertip.

Shining the phone torch directly onto the frame I can see what I'd missed: nails that have been hammered through from the other side. Half-inch points showing through around the door, on the wooden panels, some above my head in the sloping ceiling. A dozen at least dotted around the small space, tiny traps for the unwary.

I stand back, sucking the blood from my punctured finger, staring at the dark wood of the dresser, the untouched layer of dust on every surface. Each of the small brass handles on the drawers taunting me, goading me.

They're probably empty. But that's not the point.

There's something else weird about it, I realise: it's too big to have fitted through the doorway into this little room. It's not a huge piece of furniture, but it's still too large, too tall to have been manhandled through such a small opening – the angles are all wrong. Ditto the old, low armchair I'm sitting in. So they were put in place *before* the extra wall was built, bricked in here with no prospect that they would see the light of day again. Stuck in here for good.

I heft the thick steel crowbar in my hand, ready to wedge it into a gap in the drawers and crack the wood, break the lock to force it open.

This old thing was not going to beat me.

I jerk up at a sound behind me, banging my head on the low ceiling.

'You going to smash that up, Dad?'

Behind, me, silhouetted in the light from the bedroom, is a slight figure in jeans and a T-shirt, ducking her head under the wooden door frame. My eldest daughter stares around the small space, nose wrinkling at the smell.

'Hey, Leah.' I put the crowbar down. 'How's your unpacking going?'

'Slowly.' She peers into the gloom. 'What *is* this?'

'Some sort of storage room, I think.'

'Storage for what?' she says. 'Stuff you never want to see again?'

'Perhaps,' I grunt. 'I think maybe it was just forgotten about, years ago.'

'Creepy.'

'I know, right?'

'Maybe we could put Callum in here,' Leah says with a mischievous smile. 'When he's naughty?'

She leans in further and I hold a hand up. 'Don't come in, there are nails sticking out of the wood all over the place.'

'You're bleeding,' she says, pointing at my hand.

'Just a nail.' A thin red line of blood tracks through the creases in my palm and drips from my wrist, dark drops spotting the floor. 'There's some kitchen roll on the landing, could you grab me some?'

She disappears for a moment and returns with a couple of sheets.

'Probably better if you don't come in here for the time being, OK?' I wrap tissue around my bleeding finger. 'Not until I've flattened these nails and made it a bit safer. And we need to make sure your brother and sister don't either.'

'Sure.' She nods, already losing interest. 'Oh, Mum says what are you doing and can you come down to sort out the thing-amajig.'

'The what?'

'The thingy, you know. The boiler, or whatever. She just said to come down.' She flashes me a grin. 'When you've finished smashing the antique furniture.'

She turns and is gone, the lightness of her footsteps receding onto the landing.

I turn back to the old dresser. Now this weird little room has drawn first blood, maybe I *will* break it open with the crowbar.

But not yet.

I nudge the tools out of the way, making space so I can kneel down and reach behind the dresser – feeling my way carefully to avoid any more sharp surprises – and heave it towards me. It's heavy, the feet making a loud scraping protest on the bare floorboards as I shift it away from the wall. A whisper of something on my skin as a spider runs over the back of my hand.

I kneel down and pull again, opening up a gap of about a foot between the bulky dresser and the brick wall it has stood against for years, batting away a new cloud of dust as it rises into the musty air. The back of the dresser is not a single flush piece of wood but sunk slightly into its own frame, solid right-angled thicknesses of wood that are nothing like IKEA furniture: no MDF, no fibreboard, no tiny panel pins to keep the back on. I lean back to allow the light from the bulb to shine on the back panel, the wood thick with old cobwebs and the curled remains of desiccated insects waiting for the spider's return.

Something else, as well.

In the bottom of the frame, an inch-long trench has been gouged out of the wood with a chisel or a blade.

Nestled in the shallow indentation is a key.

3

The key is short and thick, a stub of dull, dark iron barely two inches long. Brushing cobwebs out of the way, I lever it out of its hiding place and blow on it to shift some of the dust. It looks like the key to an old jewellery box or a desk drawer, the metal cold and surprisingly heavy in the palm of my hand.

Almost as if it's been waiting for me, all these years.

From far away down the stairs, I can hear Leah calling for me. But tucked away here on the top floor, her voice is hardly audible at all.

I'll go down in a minute.

I slot the key into one of the top drawers, on the left-hand side.

The key slides in smoothly and turns in the lock with a dull *click*.

Pulling on the little brass ring, I ease open the top drawer. It's stiff, but it gives to a little bit of pressure, the wood scraping. At first, all I see is the faded floral lining paper just like my grandma used to have in her Welsh dresser, crinkling and curling at the edges. But then I see it: an old wallet, brown leather curled and creased with age. I pick it up, my fingers tracing the initials *DF* stamped in the corner. It's empty. In the next drawer is a scarf of purple-checked wool, folded neatly. I turn it over in my hands, the wool still soft to the touch. The faintest smell of perfume catches in my nose – the ghost of a scent, like a flower pressed flat between the pages of a book. The soft fragrance is a delicate counterpoint to the dry, dusty air.

The next drawer down holds an old black leather dog collar without a lead. The small circular tag is scratched and worn, a name etched into the metal. *Woody.* On the flipside is *167 Sumner Street*, above a landline phone number without an area code. I don't know the area well enough to know how close we are to that address, and presumably dear old Woody is long gone.

Another drawer rattles slightly as I open it to reveal a couple of rings, a plain gold band and a slim signet ring with a black stone inlaid. Neither of them look particularly fancy. Each of them is threaded onto the key-ring loop of a single brass key, a door key by the look of it, attached by a thin metal chain to a key ring in the flat shape of a two-dimensional tennis ball. Maybe a key to our own front door? I need to get another set cut but it will be handy in the meantime to have an extra one for my brother. I pocket the key, making a mental note to try it later.

I pull open the fifth drawer. This has become like some strange, badly lit version of an old TV game show. *What's in the Box?! Deal or No Deal.* Or a weird *Antiques Roadshow* in which none of the exhibits are actually worth anything. In this drawer is a pair of glasses with slender tortoiseshell frames and rectangular lenses, the arms folded as if someone has just taken them off for bed one night, put them in the drawer for safekeeping, and forgotten all about them. One of the lenses has a thin crack across the bottom half, like a single strand of hair laid across the plastic. I take them out and extend the arms, peering through powerful lenses that have the dull patina of age and dust and old grime like everything else in here. I fold the glasses back up and put them back as I found them, checking for a glasses case I might have missed. But there is nothing else.

The next drawer down appears to be empty at first. Angling the phone torch inside, I see a dull edge of metal and glass. A watch, its thick brown leather strap dappled with age. I shine my light on it to make out the words in the centre of the dial, below the symbol of a crown. *Rolex Explorer*. I don't know much about watches but I know Rolex is an expensive brand. Somebody probably hunted high and low for this watch. But judging by the dust covering everything, probably not for a very long time.

I take it out of the drawer and lay it in the palm of my hand, smooth metal cool against my skin. The hands frozen at ten past eleven of some long-ago day. A year ago? Ten? Twenty? Squinting in the dim light, I can just about make out the date window, digits stopped on the twenty-fifth of the month. Engraved initials on the back above a date. *EJS 29–11–75*. A treasured possession that no longer did what it was designed to do and probably cost too much to repair, but nevertheless was too precious to throw away – and so it had ended up here, forgotten and lost, in limbo. I knew what that was like. Our old garage had been full of similar bits and pieces, old bikes and gadgets and toys with sentimental value.

Or *junk*, as Jess called it. Most of ours had only gone to the tip when we came to move house and Jess finally put her foot down.

I give the watch a shake. Nothing. But it certainly is a handsome piece of precision timekeeping, a real classic. Whoever *EJS* was, they had been a lucky person to have owned such a beauty. Absent-mindedly, I wind it up and – to my amazement – the watch starts ticking again. It works. *Not broken. Just abandoned, then*. Put in here for safekeeping and forgotten about.

There are only two drawers left. Something small and solid rattles when I open the one on the left. The light from my torch beam bounces off dull silver plastic and it's a moment before I realise what it is: an old mobile phone, its silver casing dulled with age. My very first phone had been similar to this one, a flip phone with a clamshell design, back when I'd thought it was *so* cool. Now it's obsolete, discarded in a drawer and forgotten about like millions of others. Somewhere I had three or four old phones too, each one upgraded at the end of a contract and kept, *just in case.* Jess always sold hers on eBay but I liked to keep my old handsets in the event my new one got dropped or lost or stolen – even though that has never happened.

The little Motorola feels small and dense compared to my iPhone, more like the size of a small chocolate bar. It flips open with a satisfying spring, the screen on the inside blank and tiny, barely bigger than a postage stamp. Below it, an old-school twelve-button keypad and a handful of other buttons, phone icons for accept call, hang up, four arrows pointing up, down, left and right. It can't be that old but it feels like a museum piece, a relic of a simpler time when these things were meant only for making phone calls and sending the occasional text.

I shake my head and smile. *God,* I sound like my dad.

But it's a novelty to handle a mobile with any buttons. This style of handset was so old, so out of fashion that it had actually come full circle and attained a kind of retro cool, like vinyl records and Polaroid cameras. One button on the right-hand side even has the on/off symbol, a short vertical line enclosed in a circle. Curious to see the display, I hold it down with my thumb.

Nothing happens. The little screen stays black. Of course it does – it's probably not been charged in years, the battery drained flat long ago. The charging socket is small and circular but I reckon that somewhere, packed away in a box, I probably still have an old charging cable that will fit.

The last drawer is empty except for the faded floral paper liner. I reach all the way to the back, a little dip of disappointment that there is nothing left to find in this curious corner of my new house.

I sit carefully down in the old armchair, springs squeaking under my weight, and run a hand down the dark wood of the dresser with new-found interest. It's a fairly random collection of items, made strange by the fact that each one has a drawer to itself. Almost like the way a child might arrange a collection of favourite objects; each particular thing in its proper place. I lock each drawer individually and push the dresser back into its original position against the wall. We'll have to figure out what to do with this room, this old stuff, at some point – but not today.

There is a sudden frenzy of noise from somewhere below me in the house, running footsteps on the stairs, my children's voices rising in a competing babble and Coco barking enthusiastically in reply.

I turn to leave and then, without really thinking too much about it, I unlock the bottom drawer again and take out the little flip phone, holding it in my hand for a second, feeling the dense weight of it, a shape familiar and foreign at the same time. The quaint, simple charm of technology that had been cutting edge when I was a teenager, but was now antique.

I slip it into the pocket of my jeans and duck as I head out.

What I *should* have done was close that door and nail it shut. Board over the whole side of the room, cover it with new shelves and forget the dusty annexe was ever there. Because some things are better left buried.

But it was already too late for that.

4

The brass key with the tennis ball keyring doesn't fit the front door or the back door, or anywhere else in the house. I guess it must be from a time before the locks were changed. I drop it into the key bowl by the front door. It must fit *somewhere*.

For our first meal altogether in the new house, I pick up Styrofoam boxes of fish, chips and mushy peas from a chippie on Derby Road. The dining room table is soon spread with paper plates and unwrapped meals, salt and pepper sachets strewn about; the air fills with the tang of vinegar as we eat, mouth-watering steam rising from freshly battered cod and salty thick-cut chips. I hadn't realised how hungry I was; lunch had been half a sandwich and an apple, wolfed down as I worked with the removals guys to bring in load after load from the lorry.

Everyone, it seems, is as hungry as me. Even Daisy tucks in without complaint, dipping chips into a large pool of ketchup as her older sister leans over to cut her scampi into bite-sized pieces. Callum has discarded the wooden knife and fork from the takeaway, holding a piece of cod like a chicken drumstick as he devours it.

Jess stands at the head of the table, holding her phone up to capture a selfie for posterity.

'Come on then, everyone,' she says. 'Cheese!'

Leah pulls a face. 'Really, Mum?'

'First supper in our lovely new home.' She stands with her back to us to take a picture, then another. 'This is a special occasion.'

Daisy gives her best cheesy grin while Callum leans around behind her, his tongue sticking out. I hold up my plastic cup of Prosecco in a toast at the far end of the table.

Jess takes a couple more then sits down and Leah leans over her, index finger swiping quickly through the pictures.

'Not that one,' our elder daughter says, swiping through the images. 'Or that one. That one's *awful*. You can post the last one if you absolutely have to but *don't* tag me in anything.'

Jess smiles and gives our daughter a peck on the cheek. 'I wouldn't dream of it, darling girl.'

Daisy stands up in her seat. 'Let me see, Mummy!'

Our youngest grins at the sight of her own smiling face on the screen, the novelty of a selfie still fresh and fascinating to her four-year-old eyes. The rest of us return to what remains of our fish and chips as Jess types rapidly on the phone before the chirruping *ping* of an uploaded post.

I study a stack of cardboard boxes as I sip my Prosecco, the sweet bubbles fizzing on my tongue. Without curtains or carpets or any decoration, under a single bare bulb, the high-ceilinged room feels echoey and unloved – like a space that has been empty for a long time, waiting to be filled again. Long cardboard boxes stamped with the black and yellow logo of Robinson Removals are piled halfway up the window that looks out onto the drive. Coco, our golden retriever, has made a bed on a pile of old dust sheets stacked in the corner. There is one solitary picture in the room: Jess has dug a framed wedding photo out of one of the boxes and put it in pride of place on the mantelpiece, the two of us looking ridiculously young on the steps of the registry office. Jess laughing in a cream and scarlet silk dress and me in a three-quarter-length coat, waistcoat and red cravat, an outfit that had been volcanically hot on that July day almost a decade ago.

Leah looks impossibly cute in the picture, our little bridesmaid in cream silk, clutching her mother's hand. Our eldest child had been a surprise, conceived only a few months after we first met and already seven years old by the time we got around to tying the knot. She had loved every minute of the wedding and insisted on wearing her bridesmaid dress every day for the following week. Jess had never been able to bring herself to sell it or give it to charity – as far as I know, the little dress is somewhere in the house now, among the dozens of boxes and crates and cases waiting to be unpacked.

Our cat, Steve, jumps up onto the chair next to her, his chin just at the level of the table as he stares hungrily at each of our plates in turn, his ginger nose twitching at the smell of fresh fish. Jess slices off a chunk of cod beneath the batter, holding it out for him as he leaps off the chair to receive it, chewing noisily and purring at the same time.

'I thought the big lad was going on a diet?' I say.

'He's had a stressful moving-in day.' She picks off another slice of the white fish and drops it down to him. 'Haven't you, Stevie? Particularly as he's not allowed to go outside and explore for another week.'

'The vet did say he was chunky enough as he is.'

Jess gives me a mock frown. 'Are you fat-shaming my ginger son?'

'He's going to struggle to get through the cat flap if he gets much wider.'

She scratches the tomcat's big blunt head.

'Don't listen to the nasty man, Stevie. You're perfect as you are.' Steve purrs in response, blinking contentedly under her hand. 'It's bad enough that you make him wear this collar.'

The red collar, with the words 'Please do not feed me' stencilled along its length, had been a vain attempt to dissuade our old neighbours from giving him treats.

I grunt. 'Not sure it made much difference to all the little old ladies he used to visit.'

'In any case,' Jess says, 'he doesn't even *have* a new cat flap yet.'

'It's on my to-do list. Just need to dig the right tools out from whatever packing crate they're in.'

'And how long is your to-do list?'

'Slightly longer than *War and Peace*.'

'Be quicker to tick things off if you spent less time in your new secret room up on the top floor.'

'I've hardly been in there at all,' I say, hearing the note of protest in my voice. 'But it *is* curious.'

'Not a priority though, is it?'

I shrug; it was hard to explain. And I knew my smart, logical, pragmatic wife wouldn't understand, but while the little hidden room was certainly not a priority, it was instead that most frustrating thing: the *unknown*. It was an unanswered question, it was disorder, it was opaque – it was all of these things. With no obvious reason for being there, the obsolete phone offering a tantalising hint of how *long* it had lain undisturbed. It was the very definition of chaos, and it was crying out for me to put it in some kind of order. To make sense of it all. It was just in my nature, I suppose. It was how I had looked at the world for as long as I could remember.

'I'd like to figure it out,' I say. 'That's all. It's our house now, our home, and I want to know everything about it. From top to bottom.'

'I like your cute new mobile, by the way.' She gives me a playful smile, indicating the little flip phone on a side table in the corner. 'Very retro.'

'Found it upstairs.' I'd plugged in the old Motorola to charge earlier, more in hope than expectation. 'It's pretty much the exact same handset I had when I was nineteen. You had one too, didn't you?'

She shakes her head. 'Mine was a Nokia.'

'Thought I'd see if I could get this one working again, show the kids what our old phones were like, although I'm not even sure if it'll switch on after the battery's been dead for so—'

'It does,' she says. 'I powered it up when you went out to the chip shop.'

'You got it working already?'

'Well.' She gets up and fetches it from the side table. 'It switches on, but there's not a lot to see, really.'

Daisy holds out a small hand, sticky with ketchup.

'Can I have a look, Mummy?'

Jess gives our daughter's hand a quick wipe with a piece of kitchen roll.

'Used to love these old flippy phones,' she says, sliding the Motorola over. 'First time your dad ever asked me out on a date was via text from one just like this.'

'Gross,' Leah says. 'Don't need to know the details, thanks.'

Daisy swipes at the screen with little fingers, frowning in frustration when nothing happens.

'It's broken,' she says, tapping and swiping. 'What's wrong with it?'

'It has buttons instead of a screen, Daisy.'

'Why?'

'That's how phones used to be, before your sister was born.'

The handset reminds me of a child's toy and it must be five, six, seven generations old, like the great-great-great-grandfather of my iPhone. An old Ford Cortina next to a Tesla.

Daisy presses buttons at random. 'Does it have Balloon Pop or Numberblocks?'

Jess shakes her head. 'I shouldn't think so. Let Daddy have a look.'

With a disappointed frown, our youngest goes back to dipping her chips in the small lake of ketchup on her plate. Callum picks the phone up instead, flipping it closed and open a few times before losing interest. He slides it between two Styrofoam boxes of thick-cut chips towards me.

The screen on the little Motorola shows a half-full battery icon and the time as 00:29 – the clock resetting when it powered up, presumably. Opening it up, there is a blue backlight behind the buttons that was probably incredibly high-tech when the phone first came out but now just looks quaint. I know the SIM card will have long since ceased to work, but it has a nostalgic aura that I can't quite put my finger on. It's like a little piece of my own history, stumbling across an old friend from back in the day.

There are nine icons arranged in a square on the home screen, basic options for texts, calls, settings and so on. There are no stored messages – sent or received – and nothing shows in the call log. Did these things even have email? Nothing happens when I select the option marked with a blue and green globe; there is nothing in the Calendar option either and no high score recorded in a rudimentary game called Hungry Fish. There are also no bars of reception, no network listed. I assume it's so old it would be 2G, or maybe 1G – far too primitive to connect to today's modern 5G network. If the contract was even still being paid, which it probably wasn't.

'Bit of an anticlimax,' I say, returning to the main menu screen. 'Looks like it's never been used.'

Jess pushes her plate away and comes around the table to sit next to me, perching on a stack of plastic packing crates.

'I did find a couple of curious things on it while you were out,' she says. 'Let me show you.'

She leans over, pushing small silver buttons. The menus are choppy and slow and the home screen display has a lot more in common with the clunky display on our landline than any modern smartphone. The media option shows one picture in the memory, but the screen is so small and pixelated it's impossible to tell what it is. It's slightly blurred, maybe a hand, a thumb, or the side of someone's face? The camera is very primitive and the tiny square screen likewise, barely an inch across and painfully slow to load even this single picture.

'What is it?'

She shrugs. 'Could be the previous owner? Here's the other thing – it's a bit cryptic.'

She clicks buttons to get to the phonebook, which lists a single number. But instead of a name it's simply listed as *USE THIS*. Nothing that suggests who it belongs to.

'Maybe it was an unwanted gift,' I say. 'A backup phone for a grandparent to contact their grown-up children? Just one number to make it as simple as possible instead of them having to scroll through pages of names or numbers.'

Jess nods. 'Mum tried something similar with Grandad.'

Her grandad Eric had refused all efforts to join the mobile era, had never yet sent so much as a text message and only ever turned it on to make a very occasional phone call. After which he'd turn it off again and put it in the kitchen drawer, forget about it for another week or two.

'Perhaps it belongs to someone like him.' She had a particular soft spot for Eric, who had lost his wife long before I'd first met him, and had never remarried. 'Do you think we should ring it and check?'

'Odds are the number's probably out of service.'

She gives me a playful nudge. 'Stop being so *boring*. Maybe it'll still work.'

'How much do you want to bet?'

'Loser clears the dinner and puts the kids to bed?'

I raise an eyebrow. 'High stakes. You're on.'

She lays her own mobile flat on the table next to it and taps the number in before pressing the green *dial* button, switching it to loudspeaker as we both lean in to listen.

I'm expecting an automated message saying the number is not available.

Instead, there is a pause. A click.

And then it starts to ring.

5

The number rings six times before there is another click, another pause, and I'm not sure if we've been cut off.

'Hello?' Jess says into the silence.

A robotic female voice asks us to 'Please leave a message after the tone.'

'Hi.' My wife shoots me an awkward look. 'My name's Jess, I just found an old phone with this number in it and I wanted to return it to the owner?'

Callum chooses this moment of distraction to lean over and grab two of his little sister's last remaining chips.

Daisy's voice is squeaky with outrage. 'He stole!'

I point a finger at my son. 'Callum, give Daisy her chips back please.'

He reluctantly drops them back onto her plate.

'Anyway,' Jess says, momentarily thrown. 'Could you give me a call back if you get this?'

She stabs the red icon on her phone's screen to end the call, sits back in her chair and raises her plastic cup of Prosecco.

'Looks like I won our little bet, so I think I'll put my feet up.' She gives me a triumphant grin. 'Cheers.'

'Double or quits?'

'No chance. Anyway,' she says, 'back to your secret room – we should get someone in to give us an estimate on the work. Not yet, but when we're properly settled in.'

'What work?'

'Taking that wall out. Opening up the space will add another four feet in width so it will fit a double bed with ease.'

The thought of incurring more expense at the moment gives me a cold feeling of dread in the pit of my stomach.

'You think we should just get rid of it?'

'Of course.' She shrugs as if the answer is obvious. 'Why wouldn't we?'

'I don't know,' I say. 'It might be historical or something. It's quirky. A bit different.'

She frowns. 'A turret is quirky, Adam. A sauna cabin in the garden is quirky. A windowless top-floor room you can barely stand up in is just a waste of space.'

'Aren't you even a little curious about the bits and pieces up there?'

'This house is full of bits and pieces – they're everywhere you look. There's a toilet brush left behind in the little bathroom that would have to be carbon dated to figure out how old it is. And some of the junk in the garage is older than all of us put together. Are you suggesting we keep all of it for curiosity's sake? All this random stuff?'

'Of course not,' I say. 'Some bits are more interesting than others, that's all.'

Leah gestures at me with a long chip on the end of her wooden fork. 'Just because it's old, Dad, it doesn't make it interesting.'

'Sometimes it does.'

It was an exchange we'd had many times on holiday, when I'd insist on at least one day trip to the nearest castle as a historical interlude to the beach and the swimming pool. Or as Leah tended to call it, 'dragging us all around a pile of boring old stones'. They were not always the most popular days of the holiday but I hoped that maybe, *maybe*, a little bit of the history bug might rub off on my children. Although there wasn't much evidence of that yet.

'Or it just means no one's got around to getting rid of it.' Leah puts her red-and-white Converse up on a cardboard box, leaning back. 'Uh-oh. He's got that look, Mum.'

'I know,' Jess says, offering one last piece of fish to the cat. 'Don't encourage him.'

I hold my hands out, palms up. 'What look?'

'You know.' Leah dips another chip in brown sauce. 'That look you always get when you're taking things apart, or fixing them.'

'Feels like you two are ganging up on me.'

'You quite like it though, don't you, Dad?'

'What?'

'The annexe, the secret room, whatever you call it. You've always wanted a man cave, haven't you?'

'I'm not sure it *is* a man cave.'

'What is it then?'

'Don't know yet,' I say, reaching for one last chip. 'But I'm going to find out.'

6

Crying.

I jerk awake, heart thudding painfully in my chest, and for a moment I have absolutely no idea what time it is or where I am. A hotel? I pull the duvet off and swing my legs out of bed, cursing silently as I collide with something in the dark, hard wooden furniture that's not where it should be. Blinking in the blackness, raising my hands to the left and right, my brain still stuck in neutral.

Then I remember: not our old bedroom. A *new* bedroom, in our new house.

The crying comes again, a single word getting louder and more urgent with every repetition. 'Daddee! Dad*dee!*'

Still disorientated in the dark, I feel my way around the king-sized bed and out onto the landing. It is *pitch* black.

Along the landing, I blink for a minute, trying to get my bearings, waiting for my eyes to adjust. This house – in the dark, in the dead of night – is a strange new landscape I've never had to navigate before.

The cries come again, dissolving into sobs.

In the little box room, I stub my toe on a cardboard box full of soft toys. By the pale blue glow of the mushroom night light, I can see the small single bed pushed against the far wall. My youngest daughter is sitting up, covers bunched around her waist, her blonde hair a bird's-nest tangle around her head.

She reaches her arms up to me and clamps on like a limpet, her cheek damp with tears against my shoulder.

She clings to me, crying, shaking, and I know what's happened even before the sharp smell of urine reaches my nostrils. The sheet is wet beneath her. She's always been a good sleeper and hasn't wet the bed for at least a couple of years. But I guess the disruption of a new bedroom in a new house must have triggered something. It might even be the novelty of not sharing with her brother anymore, the sense of being alone in an unfamiliar place.

Now I'm here, she's repeating something over and over again in between her sobs. It takes a moment before I can make out her words and I shush her gently.

'It's all right,' I say. 'There's no one else. Just me. It was just a bad dream, that's all. You're OK. Let's get you some dry jim-jams and get you sorted out.'

I carry her into the bathroom, clicking the landing night light on with my toe as we pass.

'Cover your eyes for a minute, Daisy.'

She does as she's told, burying her face in her muslin cloth, and I snap on the bathroom light. Squinting against the glare from the bare bulb, I put her down carefully, wet a flannel and clean her up a little, wrapping a towel around her waist to dry her before fetching fresh pyjamas from the wardrobe in her bedroom. While I'm there, I strip the duvet cover off, ball up the sheet and the mattress protector and bring it all back to dump into the shower cubicle. It can wait until the morning.

She's still crying softly to herself, face still buried in the soft cotton of her muslin against the brightness of the bathroom light. In the middle of the high-ceilinged room she looks tiny, like a baby bird that has fallen from the nest, and I kneel down to help her with the new pyjamas. Groggily, she puts them on, her little shoulders still hitching with each sob.

'It's OK,' I say, shushing her. 'It doesn't matter. It's all OK now, I'm here.'

'Don't like the new house,' she mumbles as she pulls the T-shirt top over her head. 'Want to go back to the old house.'

'Do you want to sleep in the big bed with me and Mummy?'

She nods enthusiastically, eyes peeking out from behind her cloth. I pick her up and she clings on like a monkey, skinny arms and legs wrapping around me, head on my shoulder as I make my way carefully across the dimly lit landing.

'Want to go in the middle,' she mumbles into my neck.

Back in the master bedroom, I lift the duvet and let her climb in. Wordlessly, my wife lifts a sleepy arm and Daisy curls into her like a kitten, thumb in her mouth and cloth still gripped in her little fist.

Within minutes, my youngest is fast asleep, the soft purr of her breathing slow and regular again.

But despite the hour, I can't drift off. The strange noises of a new house, the soft creaking of old wood, the cadence of air moving through unfamiliar rooms. The question I'd been asking myself for the last two weeks: whether we had bitten off more than we could chew. The biggest mortgage we've ever had. The biggest debt, biggest commitment, biggest step we'd ever taken. And the other thing – the piece of bad news – that I still hadn't shared with my wife. Hadn't shared with anyone.

Don't think about it. Everything always seems twice as bad in the dark, in the silence, in the middle of the night.

Daisy's words are still catching in my thoughts too, snagging, like wool pulling on barbed wire. The words she'd been repeating over and over when I first went into her room.

'Don't let him get me, Daddy.' Her voice had been a trembling whisper. 'Don't let him get me.'

Don't let him get me.

7

MONDAY

For a not-quite-five-year-old, Daisy has an amazing ability to occupy space while she sleeps. Somehow she manages to take up a large proportion of our bed, her arms flung wide in the way she used to when she was a baby. Jess and I have rolled away in our sleep and now cling onto the edges of the bed like two bookends, the duvet half pulled off me and a draught cooling the skin on my back. There is also a warm weight pinning my left foot in place – the cat curled into a slumbering ball at the end of the bed, purring softly in his sleep.

I study Daisy's peaceful features for a moment in the pale morning light, strands of blonde hair falling over her face, the nightmare that had woken her in the small hours seemingly long gone. Of our three children, she had been the one who objected most strongly to the house move – which was strange because she had spent the least amount of time in our last place. Sixteen-year-old Leah had been glad to get a bedroom twice the size of her old one, more room for her overflowing collection of clothes, bags, books, shoes and everything else. Callum, who was nearly nine, had objected at first but came around to the idea when he realised he wouldn't be too far from his friends, his school, and would still be able to play for his football and tag rugby teams.

But Daisy had been at first confused, then defiant and finally tearful at the prospect of leaving the cramped shared bedroom where she'd had her first proper bed, her first toy box, her first Christmas stocking from Santa. Perhaps the bed-wetting was just another manifestation of that.

Half an hour later, we're both eating toast spread thickly with strawberry jam while Callum spoons Rice Krispies into his mouth as if he has not eaten for days. Jess is grabbing a quick shower and Leah has yet to surface, but she tends to cut it as fine as possible when it comes to school.

The kitchen is still a chaos of moving boxes, of appliances on the floor, tins and packets and bottles crowding the work-tops. It needs to wait until we have the chance to give all the dusty old shelves and cupboards a thorough going over with bleach spray and disinfectant – one of the many jobs on our to-do list.

Chewing on her toast at the kitchen counter, Daisy seems untroubled by last night's bad dream. With any luck, she will have forgotten all about it.

Callum takes a slurp of his orange juice. Like his sister, he's dressed in the grey and dark green of their school uniform.

'Why was Daisy crying?' he says. 'Last night?'

'It doesn't matter, Cal.'

'I heard her,' he persists. 'She woke me up.'

'She had a bad dream, that's all. It doesn't matter.'

Daisy frowns, gives a single shake of her head. 'Not a dream.'

'You said there was a man,' her brother says. 'I heard you. Who was the man?'

'Not a dream.'

I cover her small hand with mine. 'You know nothing in the dream can hurt you, don't you, Daisy? It's not real, it can't ever get you.'

'Wasn't though.'

'OK, so what made you—'

'Was a ghost,' she says firmly. 'In my room. Behind my door.'

I put my cup of coffee down slowly, a strange chill travelling over my skin as I remember her words from last night. *Don't let the man get me.* She's never said anything like this before. *A ghost.* She occasionally has bad dreams about monsters and went through a phase of being terrified of statues – after Callum goaded her into watching a particularly scary old episode of *Dr Who* with him – but she's never been so specific before.

'A ghost,' I repeat, keeping my voice light. 'Gosh. But you know that ghosts can't hurt you, Daze.'

Callum has stopped shovelling cereal into his mouth, his large brown eyes flicking between me and his younger sibling.

'I heard some funny noises too,' he says. 'In the night.'

'It's just the house, Callum. Every house makes different noises at night, it might take a little while to get used to.'

'Sounded like someone walking around in the night,' he says quietly.

'There wasn't anyone walking around apart from me, matey. I promise you. This is our house now – no one else here. Just us.'

'And the ghost,' Daisy mutters through a mouthful of toast.

Leah emerges into the kitchen, navy school uniform on, both hands cradled to her chest. A small pair of dark beady eyes peeps out above her fingers, pink nose twitching at the smells of breakfast.

'Look who *I* found,' she says.

Callum drops the spoon into his bowl in a splash of milk.

'Mr Stay Puft!' He stands up, holding his hands out. 'Where was he?'

Leah passes the small brown hamster – named for the character in the original *Ghostbusters* movie – carefully to her brother.

'Found him halfway down the stairs, just now. Heading for the front door like he was trying to make a break for freedom.' She goes to the sink to wash her hands. 'You shouldn't leave his cage open, Cal, you need to keep an eye on him.'

'Didn't leave it open though,' Callum says in a high voice. 'I swear.'

I lean back against the kitchen counter. 'Perhaps that's what you heard last night, Callum.'

But he's not listening to me anymore. His breakfast forgotten, he heads for the stairs, cradling the hamster and talking to it in soft tones. Daisy slides off the stool and scampers after her brother, insisting that she wants to help, to see the cage, to hold Mr Stay Puft as well. To be *involved*.

Jess sweeps in, refilling her mug from the coffee pot. She's dressed in her decorating clothes, faded jeans and an old grey sweatshirt, her short dark hair still wet from the shower. Over the last few years she's come to dislike her job – she's an account manager for a large insurance company – to the extent that she relishes every single day of leave, even if she spends it unpacking and assembling furniture.

'What was all that about?' she says.

I give her a brief recap on Daisy's dream and the hamster's escape.

My wife sips her coffee. 'We knew the move was going to be unsettling for her – new room, new house. New everything. And she's got a very vivid imagination.'

'I know.' I reach for another piece of toast from the rack.

She gives me a quizzical look. 'But?'

'But . . . the way she described it in such a vivid way, a guy in her room.' I shake my head. 'It was so *specific*. She was shaking when I went to her last night. Goodness knows where she got that from.'

'Poor baby. She just needs to get used to everything, that's all, get all of her toys unpacked and everything in its place.'

'It's your turn tonight, if it happens again.'

She grins, leaning over to give me a peck on the cheek. 'But she always shouts for you when she's scared. Always for Daddy.'

'Only because you trained her to.'

'And you do *such* a good job.' She unplugs her mobile from where it's been charging on the counter, glancing distractedly at the screen.

'Don't suppose you got a reply, did you?' I indicate her phone. 'After you left the message?'

She's scrolling something on the screen.

'What message?'

'Last night,' I say. 'The number you found in the little flip phone?'

'No. Nothing.' She slides the mobile into a pocket, picks up her cup of coffee again. 'So, what have you got on at work today? Any chance you can get away early?'

I start clearing the breakfast things. 'Just got a couple of meetings later, a report to finish.' A twinge of guilt at how easily the lie comes. 'I'll get off as early as I can, get some more jobs done around the house this evening.'

'And would those jobs, by any chance, involve you disappearing into your secret hideaway on the top floor again?'

'No.'

'You sure?' She raises an eyebrow. 'Because I know what you're like, Adam Wylie.'

'What *am* I like?'

'A dog with a bone.'

I shrug, glad to steer the conversation away from the topic of my job. 'Don't you think it's interesting though? No one's been in there for years, it's like a little time capsule, perfectly preserved.'

'Interesting to the last owners, maybe. I'd rather have the extra space in that bedroom.'

'But it's a weird thing to leave behind. And the way those things are all in individual drawers, like it might have been a kid's playroom or something. It's our own little mystery.'

I've always liked to know how things work, to get inside them and understand *what* each part did, *why* it was there. As a boy, I'd driven my parents mad by taking things apart, trying to figure them out, had raided my dad's toolbox more times than I could remember.

'Just *stuff* though, isn't it?' Jess flashes me her smile, the one that still makes me feel like the luckiest man in the world. 'And we have more than enough stuff already. Unless you've actually found a mysterious wardrobe that leads to Narnia up there?'

'Sadly not.'

'Or an original manuscript of Shakespeare's lost play?'

'Nope.'

'Maybe an old skeleton bricked up in the wall?'

I return her smile. 'Just a chair and table and an old Welsh dresser with a few bits and pieces inside.'

'Well then, I'd say we both need to crack on with unpacking and getting the house straight.'

I knew she was right – there were a million other things we needed to do, to get the house in liveable condition before we even started on the decorating.

'And anyway,' she says, 'we need to make space for the new furniture.'

'What?'

'All the new stuff I've ordered.' She takes a bite of toast. 'It's arriving next Wednesday.'

The smile freezes on my face, a cold wash of unease spreading out from the centre of my chest. I couldn't remember exactly how much we had talked about putting on the joint credit card to kit out the new house but it had been a *lot*. Thousands of pounds, that we would use my bonus from work to start paying off. Dining table, chairs, sofas, wardrobes, mirrors, desks, furniture for the kids' bedrooms.

I feel sick, a bubble of nausea rising up my throat.

'You . . . ordered it already?' I try hard to keep my tone neutral. 'I thought we were going to talk about it first?'

'We did, remember?'

'That was ages ago. *Months.*'

'But we're here now, aren't we? And John Lewis had an offer on, it was going to run out so I had to get on with ordering it all.'

'Right.'

'Are you feeling OK, Adam? You've gone a bit pale.'

'Fine.' I make a show of checking my watch. 'I'm fine. You know what? I should probably get going. Don't want to be late for work.'

Edward

He'd never told anyone. Certainly not his dad.

Not even his mum, not yet anyway. Although he suspected she might already know, deep down – she knew him better than anyone else. Not that he'd gone out of his way to hide it, not exactly, but it just never seemed to be the right time. It was always easier to put it off. And there was something about being an only child that seemed to make it harder.

He'd been meaning to do it for so long, just to get it over with. Craig's stag do had been the final straw: a whole weekend of lads' banter, of drinking and piss-taking and the rest of them trying to chat up random women in every pub, every bar. That horrific lap-dancing club on the seafront, blank-eyed girls gyrating in front of them. First the groom, then the best man and then they were all doing it, handing over twenty-pound notes for more of the same until someone – he still didn't know who – paying for him to have a dance and then this girl right up in his face and Edward trying his best to look as if he was enjoying it. Trying to pretend he was into it, like the rest of them. Cheeks burning, the rest of them seeing how awkward he looked and laughing even louder.

It was getting harder to pretend at home, too.

All that expectation. Awkward questions about girlfriends, about settling down. Listening to yet another of his dad's outbursts about George Michael or Elton John or Freddie Mercury, the comments so automatic, so routine, that he didn't even seem to realise he was making them. The weight of his grandma's expectation, that he would be the one to carry on the family name, as the only son of an only son.

But now, finally, Edward had made up his mind.

Finally, he had met someone.

Someone who understood what it was like to live half your life in secret, how exhausting it was to conceal who you really were, to hide your true self. Who knew it was important to fly under the radar but had promised to be there when he was ready. Had promised to be his wingman, his backup, or maybe more. Someone he could turn to if it all went wrong.

Tonight, they would talk things through again.

And tomorrow, he would tell his parents.

Edward checked his watch: it was nearly time. The watch had been a twenty-first birthday present, and he knew it was expensive, something to take good care of, to wear only on special days. Days like today.

Because, finally, it seemed that things were going to change.

8

Sometimes the universe does you a favour.

When that happens, I've always thought you should just go with it, accept it, without asking too many questions. Once in a while a piece of good luck falls in your lap, the cosmic dice fall the right way and you end up with double sixes. That was my first thought when I heard our offer on the house had been accepted – it had only been an opening bid, a borderline-cheeky offer that was supposed to be the starting point for negotiation. It was still near the very top of our price range, but I expected a bit of haggling at least. It didn't occur to me that first offer would be accepted without a quibble.

As I said: for whatever reason, or no reason at all, sometimes the universe just does you a favour.

Which is also what I'm thinking after ten minutes in the jeweller's shop.

It was a flash of inspiration, really, a sudden thought as I'd been about to leave the house. Work bag over my shoulder, jacket on, car keys in hand, that sick feeling of dread still rolling in my stomach as I tried to work out how we'd pay for the new furniture.

And then it came to me: *the watch*.

A few hours later, I'm standing at the counter in a small jeweller's shop in town, a little backstreet place with two reinforced window displays filled with rings, necklaces, bracelets, earrings – and watches. There's an outer door and inner door to the shop, a cramped 'airlock' of sorts between the two with cameras scrutinising your arrival. More cameras, contained within half-spheres of clear plastic, are discreetly mounted in each corner behind me; another behind the main counter that points its lens directly at the front door out onto the street. There was no way of entering this shop without being caught on at least two of them.

I've been here once before to get Jess a gift after Daisy was born, a platinum eternity ring set with three small rubies. The owner, then and now, still seems to run the place almost single-handed. Finally, she takes out the eyepiece and lays the Rolex watch back down on a cloth pad on the counter.

'Four,' she says finally. She's a slight, fiftyish woman with a cloud of wiry greying hair and half-moon spectacles on a gold chain around her neck.

I wait for her to elaborate but she doesn't say anything more.

'Four . . . what?'

'Thousand,' she says tersely. 'I can give you four thousand for it.'

For a moment, I'm thrown. A quick look on eBay in a Starbucks this morning had suggested it might be worth a bit, but I hadn't really *believed* it, hadn't really believed this was the same type, same model. Because four thousand pounds seemed like a ridiculous amount. And why would anyone leave something so valuable behind, why would they leave it in a drawer like so much junk?

'Right,' I say. 'OK.'

Four. Thousand. Pounds.

A flare of shame accompanies the next thought: perhaps I won't try *too* hard to track down the previous owner after all. It was mine, in any case. It was in my house – so legally it belonged to me, right? At least I'd been honest with the little phone, I'd done the right thing to try getting in touch with the previous owner. I had tried and that was that.

My original plan had been to give the watch back too.

Or at least mention it, when – or if – we ever got a call back from the mystery number. Although it can't have meant *that* much to the previous owner if they left it unworn, unwound, unloved in a forgotten drawer for God knows how many years. I'm reminded of something else the estate agent said to me: *People are as honest as they can afford to be.* What was it about moving house that brought out the worst in people? Money, I supposed. More money than they would ever spend on anything else.

The jeweller takes my hesitation for reticence, fixing me with a weary stare over the top of her glasses.

'You might see more for a piece like this online and if you think you can get more for it elsewhere, take your chances on eBay or wherever, be my guest.'

'I actually didn't realise—'

'The inscription on the back.' She flips it over, indicates the engraving *EJS 29–11–75* in the gold casing. 'Any kind of per-sonalisation, as a rule will tend to decrease an item's value to a general buyer.'

'Of course,' I say. 'I understand.'

'So: four thousand,' she says again. 'Cash now. Yes?'

'Yes,' I say. 'That would be great, thanks.'

'Family heirloom, is it?'

I nod. 'Something like that.'

She slides the watch off the counter and disappears into a back room. In her place a blonde teenager appears, presumably to keep an eye on me while her boss is busy. She's wearing black jeans and a white blouse, a chain around her neck with the letters *Holly* in swirling silver script. We exchange tight smiles and I let my eyes wander over the displays beneath the glass countertop. Prices range from ninety-five pounds to three thousand five hundred for a gold bracelet inlaid with pale blue stones.

The manager reappears with a thick square book of carbon-copy forms, pink copy on top, yellow and blue copies beneath. She hands me a biro to fill in the blanks. Name, address, phone number – landline and mobile – email, date of birth, date of sale, date of acquisition, agreed sale price, and so on and so on. A tick box that reads: 'I declare this is my property to sell'.

I hesitate, pen hovering over the thin carbon paper. 'Didn't realise there would be so much paperwork.'

'Provenance,' she grunts, writing out a separate receipt longhand on another sheet of paper. She has gold rings on every finger, a gold bracelet on one wrist and a gold watch on the other. 'In case any queries arise in the future over the origin of the item.'

'In case it's stolen, you mean?'

She shrugs as if the answer is obvious. 'These are the rules.'

'Are they strictly necessary, all the details requested on this form?'

She stops what she's doing, peering at me over her half-moon glasses with unblinking eyes.

'Have you changed your mind about wishing to sell the watch?'

'No.'

'Then the answer is yes, they're necessary.'

She goes back to her own paperwork, black ballpoint scoring hard into the old-fashioned receipt. 'Unless you want to sell for two-and-a-half, then we can perhaps dispense with the form-filling.' She doesn't miss a beat as she says it, doesn't look up at me, her pen still moving across the form with rapid strokes. Almost as if she hasn't spoken at all.

'That's OK,' I say. 'Four thousand is fine.'

When I've finished filling in the form, she disappears into the back room again, returning to count the money out in front of me, all red fifties, before smoothing the notes into a hefty quarter-inch stack and putting them into an envelope. I slide it into my jacket pocket, the money a solid mass resting against my heart during the nervous five-minute walk down to Lower Parliament Street where I pay it into my bank. I haven't made a cash deposit for years and the rigmarole of it – find a counter with a pen that works, fill in the deposit slip, stand in the queue for a cashier – feels like an echo from a different century.

I start to relax as the cashier stamps the slip and hands me the stub.

Maybe it was karma, I told myself. A little balancing of the cosmic books after my trouble at work. I had told Jess that my boss is fine with me working flexibly while we settle into the new house, as long as team targets are hit.

The truth is slightly more complicated than that.

The truth is that I don't have targets any more. Or a boss.

It was a fortnight before we were due to move that the redundancy notice came around, the email landing like a bomb in my inbox. A confidential invitation to the human resources department at 9 a.m. the next day to receive a white envelope with my name on it and a meaningless ten-minute chat full of HR doublespeak. It was a *restructuring*, a *downsizing*, a *reallocation of staff and resources in light of changes in project requirements*. *And regrettably some difficult choices had to be made.* All the usual corporate weasel words for when the accountants get nervous and a certain number of employees get singled out to walk the plank. This time, it had been my turn, along with half a dozen other software developers in my team. Pretty awful timing, to be honest, and a statutory minimum payout, which meant I needed to get another job lined up as soon as possible.

The second time it's happened, too.

Maybe it's me. Maybe I ask too many questions; I don't like being fobbed off. That was certainly the case first time around. And this time? Who knows.

Maybe it wasn't just bad luck that got me singled out.

It's ironic because for most of the time Jess and I have been together, she has earned more than me. It was only last year, when I'd got this job, that I finally overtook her and we started to think about moving out of our cramped semi-detached house so we could give the children a bedroom each.

I didn't tell her. I still haven't.

I'll tell her when I get a new job, but until then, there's no point in freaking her out with the news that we're one salary down when she has enough on her plate with her own job, with the kids, the new house and everything else. When she's spent so long looking forward to this move and creating the dream home we have always talked about. At least her job seems pretty secure. People will always need insurance.

It's not as if we could have pulled out at that stage anyway. We had already signed on the dotted line – we were going to move whatever happened. Just bad timing, that's all. It'll be fine. *We'll* be fine. The money I made in the jeweller's shop will help us make the first credit card payment for the furniture Jess has ordered; it will help me keep my side of the mortgage payments going for at least another month, enough to bridge the gap between my old job and the next one.

The house, the watch – the little hidden room on the top floor – would help me keep my secret until then.

9

I get lunch at a café in Sneinton Market with good Wi-Fi. It's on the eastern edge of Nottingham city centre, far enough away from my old office to minimise the risk of bumping into any former colleagues. Over a cheese sandwich and a cup of strong tea, I spend an hour on my laptop looking for jobs, firing off my CV to a handful of companies and following up with a couple of IT recruitment agencies that already have me on their books. Over a second cup, I open a new browser window and search for anything to do with the history of our new house or its previous owners, anything that might hint at the strange layout of the top floor room, whether it was a peculiarity of Victorian houses built at that time. There's plenty of general stuff about The Park – the exclusive neighbourhood we had just joined – but nothing specific on the history of 91 Regency Place.

On the Land Registry website, I click through to find out how to access information about a property but the cheapest option – a title register – has a price tag of £19.95. Surely there's a cheaper way? I send a text to the estate agent who handled the sale instead and open a new browser window to register with another couple of recruitment agencies. There are a handful of job alerts in my inbox and I go through each one, firing off my CV to a couple of places looking for immediate starters.

It's mid-afternoon when my mobile rings, Jess's number appearing on the screen. I've decamped to another café, a little place tucked away behind the ice-skating arena; the ringtone is very loud in the enclosed space.

'Hey,' Jess says. 'Can you talk? Are you on your way home soon, or can you be?'

'Should be able to.' I don't bother checking my watch. 'Why, is everything OK?'

'We've got a bit of a . . . situation,' she says, an edge of tension in her voice. 'In the garden.'

'What kind of situation?' I say, standing up from the table.

'You'll see when you get here. Are you in the office?'

I ignore her question.

'You sure everything's all right? Are the kids OK?'

'They're fine.'

'I'm on my way, leaving now.'

* * *

Everyone is in the front garden when I pull into the drive. Leah has Daisy on her back, both of them in their school uniforms and both looking up at the wide-spreading oak tree that over-hangs the front wall. Their brother is straddling a branch about twelve feet from the ground, legs swinging happily, grinning down at the four of us below him. Jess stands beneath him, hands on her hips. Our son has always been a daredevil and likes climbing, running, jumping off things. He learned to walk early, at nine months, and it wasn't long before he was swing-ing from the curtains or jumping down the stairs into cushions piled at the bottom.

Today, he seems to have discovered that the oak tree in our new front garden has great potential as a climbing frame.

'Callum?' I say, walking across the gravel. 'Are you stuck?'

He raises his fists to the sky. 'I'm the king! Woo-hoo!'

'It's a bit high, matey. How about I get the ladder and help you get down?'

'It's fine, Daddy! Don't need the ladder.'

'Not him,' Jess says, pointing higher up the tree. '*Him*.'

I follow her finger: ten feet above Callum's head is our cat, spreadeagled on an almost vertical branch, his considerable bulk clinging to the bark, ears flat to his head, tail fluffed out in alarm.

'I was trying to reach Steve,' Callum shouts. 'He's the one who's stuck.'

Steve lets out a low, plaintive *riaoooow*, his tail flicking nervously from side to side.

'Daft creature,' I say under my breath. 'How long has he been up there?'

Jess whistles to the cat but he doesn't respond.

'About an hour,' she says. 'God knows how he escaped. Callum thought he was trying to reach the bird box. I tried to get him down myself but you know I don't do heights.'

'It's OK,' I say. 'I'll go.'

I look higher into the spreading branches, shielding my eyes against the afternoon sun, and can just about see an old wooden bird box attached to the trunk above him.

Next to me, Leah bounces her little sister on her back. 'We should have called him Tigger, shouldn't we, Daze? Good at climbing up trees but rubbish at getting down again.'

'He *is* orange like Tigger,' Daisy agrees.

'We could just wait until he gets hungry?' I say. 'Or until it gets dark.'

'Don't be mean, Dad,' Leah says.

I hand my jacket to Jess, fetch the ladder from the garage and lean it up against the branch next to Callum.

'Fire brigade game,' I say, putting a hand under his arm and helping him onto the rungs. 'I'm the fireman and you're being rescued.'

When he's safely back on the front lawn, I move the ladder across and extend it, leaning it up against the branch where Steve lies flattened against the bark. He lets out another long, sad *miaow* as if he can't believe someone has stranded him in the tree. Leah offers to get his cat carrier but I learned long ago that when rescuing him from high places, trying to put him in the box was like trying to put an octopus into a string bag. He disliked being confined at the best of times, let alone when he was suffering the indignity of being rescued.

Instead, I climb up to him and give him a minute to edge nervously down towards me. The earthy, rich smell of the oak is stronger up here. The bird box is just above us but it looks old and unused, the wood darkened and split with age. *Nothing for you there, Steve.* When the cat is close enough, I pick him up with both hands and bring him to my chest. His claws, having been embedded in the tree bark, now go straight through my polo shirt like needles as he climbs up and around my neck, draping himself across my shoulders like an angry ginger shawl.

By the time we're back on solid ground, the skin on my back is stinging and raw where it's been punctured by his claws. He leaps off and runs around the side of the house without a backward glance.

'Ouch,' Jess says, looking at the back of my neck. 'Shall I get the Savlon?'

'It's fine,' I say. 'Think I might take that bird box down though. It's falling apart anyway, and he's only going to go up after it again.'

'Be careful.'

I go inside to change into clothes more appropriate for tree climbing. I'm lacing up my trainers in the bedroom when the sound of a vacuum cleaner starting up reaches me from across the landing. Which is curious, to say the least – because Jess and the kids are all still outside.

A woman in blue jeans and a pale pink housecoat is hoovering in Callum's bedroom.

She has her back to me as she slides the machine across the carpet in short, vigorous strokes. She's small and slight, mousey brown hair gathered into a short ponytail. As I stand in the doorway, she reaches behind her, without looking, to hit the light switch with a practised familiarity as if she's done it dozens, hundreds, of times before. As if she knows this house better than I do.

I have to say hello twice before she hears me over the noise, finally switching off the Dyson and turning to face me.

'So sorry,' she says. 'In a world of my own there.'

'Hi, I'm Adam. Sorry . . . who are you?'

She's somewhere in her mid- to late forties, with fine features in her prematurely lined face. She holds up a hand encased in a yellow Marigold glove.

'Helena,' she says. 'The cleaner.'

I frown. 'Right, OK.'

'I talked to your wife? I used to come in for Mr Hopkins.' There is a very slight cadence to her accent, a heaviness to the vowel sounds. 'Such a gentleman. More than ten years I worked for him. Although no one's been in while the house was empty so there's *lots* of work to do.'

'Of course. I'll let you get on.'

She nods and hits the power button on the Dyson again, filling the small room with noise.

Back outside in the garden, I jerk a thumb towards the house.

'What's with the cleaner?' I say to Jess. 'Where did you find her?'

'They both worked for the last owner *and* they were recommended on the neighbourhood WhatsApp group. Thought we could use them for a couple of hours on Mondays and Fridays at least while we were settling in. Everything needs a deep clean.'

'What do you mean *them*? There's two of them?'

'Her and her cousin, Tobias. He's in the back garden now, making a start on the hedges.'

I cringe inwardly at the extra expense of having help around the house when I had no job, no money coming in. The weekly expense would add up soon enough.

'We're not a family that has a cleaner,' I say quietly. 'Are we? We've never had one before. Let alone a gardener too.'

'We've never had a house this size before either,' she says. 'It's twice the size of our old place and has twice as many rooms.'

'Could we have talked about it first?'

'We did, remember? When we first offered on the house.'

'Did we? That was *months* ago.'

'We definitely did,' she says, with certainty in her tone. 'Now, are you sure you need to go up that tree?'

'Got the ladder out now,' I say with a shrug. 'May as well.'

I bring a selection of screwdrivers from the garage and extend the aluminium ladder as high as it will go, climbing back up so

I'm almost level with the bird box. Close up, the angle is awkward but I can see the small circular opening – just big enough for a nesting sparrow or wren – is partly blocked by a piece of eggshell. If it's in use, I should probably leave it until later in the year rather than risk disturbing a nest.

I lean closer, shifting my weight on the ladder to lift the top of the box so I can check inside, the cotton of my shirt sticking to my back with sweat. The lid won't budge. I lean further across, one palm braced against the rough bark of the tree and try to lever the lid up. With my fingertips, I can feel the smooth metal heads of a couple of screws securing the lid tightly in place. But the angle is too awkward to get any purchase with a screwdriver.

Callum's high voice reaches me from below. 'Are there any eggs or birds, Daddy?'

'Not sure yet, Cal.'

Jess's voice is louder. 'It's not safe, Adam, leaning across like that.'

'Just can't quite reach it.'

I lift one foot off the rung of the ladder, bracing it against the rising branch to my left to get a closer look at the box, blinking away a bead of sweat that runs into my eye. With the muscles of my arm starting to burn where I'm holding onto the tree, I shift my weight further across so I'm almost directly in front of the small circular aperture in the wood. Close enough to see what's blocking the hole.

A cold, liquid sensation in my stomach as I see what it is.

Because it's not an egg, or a piece of shell.

It's the lens of a camera.

PART II

You learn to blend in, to hide in the crowd like a regular person. To satisfy your craving in other ways: to go where you want, to see someone's true nature behind the artifice. To see how they live, knowing that you hold their life in the palm of your hand. But you never forget who you are.

You know that when the day comes, you can do what needs to be done.

10

'It was pointing directly at the house,' I say quietly. 'Right at the drive and the front door.'

We're sitting at the kitchen table nursing cups of tea, Jess opposite me. The bird box is opened up on the table between us, the equipment inside removed. It's a grey rectangle about the size of a packet of cigarettes, the clear plastic hemisphere of a small camera connected to it by red-and-blue coiled wire. Another wire, dark brown – presumably to camouflage it against the bark – had led up and out of the box to the next branch above, where a palm-sized solar panel was attached in a position that made it invisible from the ground. It had taken me three-quarters of an hour to remove all of it from the oak tree, which made me wonder how long it had taken to put up in the first place.

Jess crosses her arms. 'Makes my skin crawl just thinking about it. How long do you think it's been there?'

'Hard to say.' I gesture with a screwdriver. 'Although . . . you see these? The screws that were holding the bracket to the tree are still shiny, not corroded or discoloured by the weather. So I don't think it could have been there very long.'

Jess leans away as if the device might come to life and bite her. 'You're sure you've disabled it?'

'I've isolated the battery. There's no power going to it.'

The children are in the back garden, their excited voices reaching us through the open window as they play frisbee with the dog. We've told Daisy and Callum that the camera was for studying nesting birds inside the box – Leah silently agreeing to play along with the fiction so as not to alarm her younger siblings too much.

'I don't understand,' Jess says. 'What the hell is it even there for?'

I pick up the device and peer into the smooth glass eye of the camera lens as if it might hold the answers.

'I guess the last owner could have installed it,' I say. 'Keep an eye on his house when he was away?'

'But ... twenty-five feet up a tree?' She doesn't look convinced. 'In a nesting box? I thought half the point of having cameras was to make them obvious, so a burglar would know he was being filmed?'

This was new territory for us – we had never owned a house big enough to merit this kind of security.

'Maybe some are visible,' I say, 'and some hidden. This was one they forgot to take down, or something?'

'But you just said it looked quite new.'

'I'm thinking aloud.'

'We should call the police anyway,' she says firmly. 'Just in case.'

I shrug. 'To say what? We found a camera left by the previous owner?'

She fixes me with one of her serious stares, the little line deepening between her eyebrows.

'And what if it was someone else?'

'Like who?'

'We should report it, at the very least. Get someone round to look at this thing.'

She picks up her phone and dials 101, bouncing through a series of call handlers and waiting to be connected to someone who can take the details.

While she's stuck on hold, I go into the hall and call Jeremy Swann, the estate agent who handled the sale of this house, to ask whether he knows about any kind of CCTV system installed at the house or cameras in the garden.

'I believe there was a really old burglar alarm,' Jeremy says after a moment's thought. It sounds like he's driving. 'But to the best of my knowledge it's not worked for years. My recollection is that Mr Hopkins let it lapse a long way back and it was never renewed. I'm not even sure the security company still exists. I'll double-check for you, but I don't recall any external cameras being on the fixtures and fittings list.'

Jeremy had been there for all three of our viewings at 91 Regency Place, quietly professional with a knowledgeable calm which inspired confidence. A contrast to the estate agency we'd used to sell our own house in Woodthorpe, particularly the junior staff sent to handle viewings – who were perfectly nice but often had no more idea on the selling points of the house than the average stranger off the street. Whereas Jeremy always seemed very well informed; he was a specialist who handled higher-end properties, most of them in The Park.

'Listen,' he says. 'I'm actually in the area, just finished a viewing around the corner, I could pop in if you like? There's some paperwork I was going to drop off anyway.'

His gleaming white Tesla rolls carefully onto the drive a couple of minutes later. He climbs from the driver's seat and greets me with a wave and a smile, striding across the gravel in a dark navy three-piece suit. He's a small, neat man, his dark hair cut short but not *too* short, always punctual and impeccably dressed.

He hands me a thick cream A4 envelope with 'Welcome To Your New Home' in embossed gold lettering on the front, his estate agency's discreet branding on the back. In his other hand, he proffers a bottle of Moët & Chandon champagne in a gift box. He really *was* keen for us to use his agency in the future.

'To celebrate your arrival,' he says. 'So how's it all going, Adam?'

'Pretty hectic,' I say. 'But we're settling in. Actually, since you're here, I wonder if I could ask you something else? When you draw up the floorplans for a new property you're putting onto the market, who does that?'

'Typically that would be me.'

'And you calculate the square footage of each room?'

'With a laser measure.' He gestures vaguely at the house. 'To be honest, I just hold it up and point, and it does all the rest. Calculates it automatically. I pass it on to Fliss in the office and she uploads it.'

'But those measurements wouldn't include voids and storage spaces, rooms like that?'

'Not as a rule, only if they are potentially liveable spaces accessible without a ladder. Although we'll usually add the dimensions of cellars, outbuildings and garages for completeness. It all has to be accurate for the Energy Performance Certificate.' He hesitates. 'Is there a problem, Adam?'

'No, not at all. I've just discovered an extra bit of space next to one of the bedrooms. It's not much, maybe an extra fifty square feet, but it definitely wasn't on the plans on Rightmove.'

'Some of these older properties have all sorts of nooks and crannies,' he says, a wistful tone to his voice. 'They can get overlooked, particularly when you have a place that's been extended or remodelled multiple times, things can sometimes get closed off and forgotten about. There are stories about old houses in the West Country that used to have secret chambers behind the fireplace so that when the Royal Navy came to press-gang the men into service on board warships, they'd have somewhere to hide.'

'A fair way from the sea here though, aren't we?'

'But it wouldn't be unheard of for some older parts of a property to be forgotten about. Particularly when a vendor is, shall we say, more elderly? Then other factors can come into play, of course.'

'Other factors?'

'A vendor's . . . recollection,' he says carefully. 'If you're talking about a vendor who's lived in a property for twenty, thirty, forty years, and that person is in their eighties or nineties when they move, you can see how it might happen.'

'Of course.'

'Things can get missed, forgotten about, or information not passed on to relatives. I had a client once who found six cases of wine hidden behind a false panel in a walk-in wardrobe, a few weeks after he moved in. Good stuff it was, too. The story was that the previous owner hadn't wanted to declare them in his divorce settlement, but then he'd forgotten all about them.'

'And legally, that wine belonged to the new owner?'

He makes a non-committal sound in his throat. 'Hmmm. It's a grey area. To be honest, most of the time the things that get left behind, *nobody* wants. It's old mattresses and broken garden furniture, or an old sofa the vendors can't be bothered to dismantle. Then it becomes about whose responsibility it is, and you can get into legal wrangling and all sorts.'

'How about if something hadn't been touched in twenty-plus years?'

'I suppose . . . if you're going back to the owner before, then yes, it would probably default to the current owner due to passage of time.'

'The house remembers, even if the owner forgets?'

He's silent for a moment. 'That's one way of looking at it, I suppose.'

'The last owner, do you think he might know about this extra bedroom space?'

'Mr Hopkins?' Jeremy sounds doubtful. 'His son told me he found the stairs very difficult, hence the ground floor study at the back being converted into a little bedroom. He had a cleaner who came in once a week, but between you and me, I don't think he'd been upstairs for years.'

'Would it be possible to speak to him?'

'He's not a well man. He's moved into a care home nearby. Was rattling around in this big old house for years, all on his own. Rather sad, really.'

'Another family member, then? Whoever handled the sale.'

'I could pass on your number to the son if you like, ask him to give you a ring?'

'Thanks, I appreciate it.'

'Kevin's . . . a busy chap though,' Jeremy says, his tone neutral. 'A bit of an unusual character. So I wouldn't hold your breath.'

We say our goodbyes and I thank him for the champagne as he returns to his Tesla. When I walk back into the kitchen, Jess is taking pictures of the bird-box camera from different angles and sending them to her brother on WhatsApp. Dom works as a security supervisor at the University of Nottingham and is a guy who might know about this sort of thing.

I gesture at her phone. 'What did the police say?'

She waves a hand dismissively. 'Nothing much. Took my details, told me to call back if we notice any suspicious behaviour. The lad I spoke to – who sounded about twelve years old – said it had probably been left there by the previous owner.' She points a finger at me. 'And *don't* say I told you so.'

I relay a brief version of my conversation with Jeremy.

'Whatever it's doing here, I don't want it in the house,' she says, pushing the camera away from her. 'Can't bear the thought of it being in here, even if it is switched off. I don't like it. Don't like it at all.'

I gather up the box and its contents. 'I'll put it in the garage for now.'

'We should keep it for the time being though,' she says. 'For evidence.'

'Evidence of what?'

'There must be some sort of law against violating another person's privacy.' She stands, blowing out a heavy breath. 'I'm going to make the kids' tea. How was work, anyway?'

'Same as ever.' I turn away so I don't have to meet her gaze. 'You know. Same stuff, different day.'

I stash the box on a high shelf in the garage.

11

I'm about to go back outside to check for more cameras when the doorbell rings.

I'm greeted by a tall woman in her sixties, pencil thin, dressed in a grey cardigan and skirt. My son stands sheepishly beside her, rather reluctantly holding her hand, a scuffed orange football tucked under his other arm.

'Good afternoon,' she says briskly. 'One of yours, I believe?'

'Hi.' I point at my son. 'Sorry, has Callum—'

'I found this young gentleman in my back garden,' the woman says. 'Foraging among my geraniums. So I thought perhaps best to return him to you. I'm next door at number ninety-three.'

'Thanks,' I say. 'I'm Adam, by the way.'

'Eileen,' she says, her face expressionless. 'Nice to meet you.'

We shake hands awkwardly. Her palm is cold, the grip surprisingly firm, and I'm aware my own hand is still grubby with tree bark.

I gesture to my son, who looks as if he's desperate to get away.

'What were you doing, Callum?' I say. 'What happened?'

'Kicked my best football over.' He stares at the floor. 'There was a hole in the fence so I just wanted to see if I could get through and then I was trying to find my ball but I couldn't find it and then the lady came and I—'

'It doesn't matter now,' she says, cutting him off. 'Does it, young man?'

'Sorry,' Callum says. 'Can I go back to Daisy and Leah?'

She releases his hand, and he scampers off towards the kitchen without looking back.

'Settling in all right?'

'Yes, thank you. Lots to do.'

'I'm sure.'

Her voice has the slow, languorous tone of a teacher or a barrister, someone who is used to addressing others and being listened to. But she's standing slightly too close after our awkward handshake, the faintest smell of lavender rising from her cardigan. I step back into the hall and she seems to take this as an invitation, following me in, her eyes sweeping over the staircase, the tiled floor, the kitchen doorway.

'It's been such a long time since I last saw inside this old house,' she says. '*Such* a long time.'

'Did you . . . know Mr Hopkins well?'

'Oh I wouldn't say *well*. Eric was the kind of person who liked to keep himself to himself, if you know what I mean?' She continues to look around the hallway, full of curiosity, before her eyes finally come back to me. 'His son was cut from very much the same cloth. Rather an antisocial type, from what little I saw of him.'

'They liked their privacy, did they?'

'Put it this way,' she says. 'I've lived at number ninety-three for seven years now, ever since I inherited it from my mother, and this is only the second time I've set foot in this house.'

In the late afternoon light streaming through the stained glass above the front door, she looks younger. Mid-fifties rather than sixties. I gesture towards the kitchen and she follows me in, declining my offer of a drink. There is an awkward silence as her eyes take in the cardboard boxes, the tired units, a pan of peas simmering on the old gas hob, the worktops dull and chipped with age. Her gaze returns to me and I have the uncomfortable sense that she's sizing me up too, making a swift judgement of this new neighbour in torn jeans and an old paint-spattered Pearl Jam T-shirt.

I lean back against the counter. 'We're discovering new things about the house every day.'

'I'm sure you are.'

'This might sound like a weird question,' I say. 'But I don't suppose you know if Mr Hopkins ever had CCTV installed?'

A strange expression flits across her face, a tightening of her lips, a pulse in her jaw. But then it's gone, her features settling back into neutral.

'How do you mean?'

'Cameras,' I say. 'For security. We found one today in the garden and I'm trying to work out who put it there.'

'I honestly have no idea about anything like that,' she says, with quick shake of her head. 'As I said, he kept himself to himself.'

Through the window, I can see Jess playing catch with Daisy in the garden. Callum sprints past them, across the lawn and out through the side gate. He seems to be running laps around the house with the orange football under his arm and Coco in hot pursuit, barking happily. He was delighted to discover that having a detached house meant he could run an entire circuit around it on a continuous loop.

Eileen gazes after them with a slight pursing of her lips.

'It's so nice to see some children in the house again. It's been too long since there were youngsters living here, a big family home like this.' Her pinched expression, the hard frown line between her eyebrows, seems at odds with her words. 'Far too long.'

'So you didn't know Mr Hopkins well?'

Her gaze lingers on Daisy, trying to catch a sponge ball and giggling as she drops it.

'Not as well as I would have liked.'

'I would have loved to talk to him about the house,' I say. 'The history of it, you know? The work he had done to the inside, remodelling and—'

She turns her sharp eyes on me. 'You're not planning any ghastly extension work, are you?' She pronounces the words slowly, as if they leave a bad taste in her mouth. 'Tearing out all the original features and replacing them? Builders vans parked on the street, skips on the drive and noise at all times of day, dust and rubbish and goodness knows what else for months on end?'

'No, no,' I say, shaking my head. 'Nothing like that. I love all the old features, we both do, that's one of the reasons we fell in love with the house in the first place. The stonework, the hallway tiles, the stained glass. And there's no way we could afford to have major work done anyway.'

She makes a noise in her throat, either of agreement or disdain, I can't tell.

'Such a shame,' she says. 'That it's not been looked after properly.'

I try to remember what Jeremy had told us – months ago – when we'd viewed the house for the second time. When both Jess and I had already fallen in love with it, had already been talking about which bedrooms the kids could have, how we might remodel the kitchen and put in French windows out onto the back garden. When Jeremy already knew he had us on the hook. From what I can remember, the son had moved abroad years ago – to France or Spain? – and the owner had lived here mostly alone in the years that followed until the house became too much for him to manage. His son had acted on his behalf in the sale and in dealings with Jeremy from their end.

'Had Mr Hopkins lived here for a long time?'

'Twenty years or so,' Eileen says. 'But he never really recovered from the stroke, poor chap. And that was years ago, long before I moved in next door.'

'Can't have been easy, looking after such a big house on his own.'

'Oh, he had help with the day-to-day things. A gardener in the summer and a cleaner all year round. Although goodness knows she was more interested in sitting around and chatting on the phone from what I ever saw of her. Still, she was better than nothing, I suppose, especially after his health deteriorated. And that boy of his was never here.' She shakes her head. 'Always gallivanting off overseas, back for a flying visit once in a blue moon, never really seemed to want much to do with the place. Such a pity. It all got too much for Eric in the end, after the dementia took hold.'

I check there's water in the kettle, switching it on. 'Are you sure you won't have a cup of tea, or coffee?'

Her eyes flick to the unopened boxes on the floor, dirty breakfast dishes and cups stacked around the sink, before they come to rest on me again.

'I dare say I should leave you to it,' she says with a tight smile. 'You seem to have your hands full.'

I see her out through the front door and watch as she marches back up the drive, her black slip-ons crunching on the gravel. She walks quickly, shoulders back, spine straight, as if she's on parade.

When I return to the kitchen, Jess is shepherding the two younger children through the back door and telling them to wash their hands before tea.

To me, she says: 'Guess what?'

'You found another camera?'

She shakes her head, switching off the gas hob where the peas have been simmering. 'I've just had a reply.'

I take two plates from the cupboard and lay them on the kitchen table, adding cutlery and ketchup.

'A reply from who?'

'That mystery number in the ancient flip phone you found upstairs.' She lowers her voice. 'They've texted me back.'

12

My wife waits until Callum and Daisy are tucking into their tea – rice and peas with chopped fish fingers mixed in – before holding out her phone to me, the screen unlocked. There are two text messages from the same number.

Thx for message. Pls return phone and all other personal items found in house asap.

Below it, a second text gives the details of a PO box address in Nottingham.

'That's the number I called last night,' Jess says. 'The number in the memory of that old phone. Weird, isn't it? And presumptuous, sort of half-polite but rude at the same time.'

The message has no name or sign off, not even a first name. Had it been sent by Kevin Hopkins? There is a twinge of unease in my gut as I think of the watch, the only thing of any real value I'd found in the house, already sold and out of my reach.

'You're right,' I say. 'It is rude.'

'Classic passive-aggressive.'

I hand the phone back to her. 'Can't understand why they didn't just return your call, rather than sending a weird text message.'

'I don't like it.' Her face is pinched with worry. 'And what does it even mean anyway, "all other personal items"? It's like we've been dishonest, trying to get one over on them when actually we were trying to do the right thing.'

'It's not as if they didn't have plenty of time to clear the house before we moved in.'

'I thought it was just junk, what you found with the phone in that top room?'

I swallow. 'Yeah. Nothing really worth anything.'

'Who even *is* this person? Could we call Jeremy to find out?'

'Already done it. He's going to pass on my details.'

'Really wish they didn't have my number now, wish I hadn't made that stupid call. The last thing I need is some random angry stranger messaging me.' She stares at the screen. 'What shall I say?'

The twinge of guilt in my stomach pulses again.

'Listen,' I say. 'You don't need to reply. I'll deal with it. You can just block this number so he can't message you again, OK? Leave it to me.'

She gives a nod of relief. 'What are you going to say?'

'Let me worry about that,' I say. 'I'll think of something.'

* * *

It's gone eight o'clock by the time the two younger kids have had their baths and been put to bed with a story. Leah is on the sofa on her phone, while Jess swipes through a home furnishings website on her iPad looking at beds and coffee tables and picture frames. Some reality show is on the TV but neither of them are really watching.

I've sent a reply a couple of hours ago to the unknown number.

Please clarify re: personal items left at 91 Regency Place mentioned in your last text.

So far, there's been no reply.

I head upstairs to unpack a few more boxes and eventually find myself drawn back to the annexe room on the top floor, with its creaking armchair and bare bulb swinging gently above me. Perhaps it *had* been some kind of hideaway, just like Jess said. There were times when Jess or I would have paid good money for just fifteen quiet, uninterrupted minutes away from the daily chaos of family life with three children, a dog, a cat, assorted fish and a rotating cast of hamsters, gerbils and guinea pigs that occupied cages in the various kids' bedrooms and made periodic bids for freedom. .

But why had the room never been cleared out? And why was someone so keen to recover a few old odds and ends that had been left behind?

The level of secrecy, the effort that must have gone into creating this little space and making it so hard to find, suggested it was more than just a study, a den, a retreat. There was something much more deliberate about it, much more long term. Not just plasterboard, but bricks with that master-crafted wooden panelling on top, so the wall would feel as solid as an external wall to the casual observer. So well hidden, in fact, that someone had subsequently put fitted wardrobes in front of the door and forgotten all about it.

Perhaps it was a panic room, a place of last resort in case your house was broken into and you had to flee upstairs rather than down. It would certainly do that job pretty well if you could lock it from the inside.

I pull the door shut until I hear the soft *click* of the latch. Then reach up and pull the light cord, the darkness instant and absolute.

Even after my eyes have adjusted, it's a perfect blackness of a kind that's almost impossible to find in everyday life. Elsewhere in the house – even in the middle of the night – there's always a whisper of light reaching you through the edge of a curtain, the red glow of numbers on a digital clock, the muted pulse of a device plugged in to charge overnight. Outside we try to keep the dark at bay with street lights, with security lights and head-lights and permanently lit shopfronts, with our incessant need to have illumination at all times. Even when you close your eyes, you can still see the light leaking through your eyelids. We've evolved that way, to wake with the sunrise.

But the hidden room at the top of my house is perfectly dark.

Totally, fully black, like being at the bottom of the ocean. Nothing leaks through, not even the slightest grey hint of any-thing outside.

To complement the darkness, the hidden room is also silent in a way that is so rare I'd almost forgotten what it's like. A still-ness that is complete and undisturbed, all sounds from outside deadened by the bricks surrounding me, the thick rugs fixed to the walls and floor. I can't hear traffic noise, or dogs barking, or the music Leah has left on in her room, or anything. This small space is like a separate, silent world that exists in parallel to the daylight world outside. Whatever else it may be, it's very well constructed.

The darkness is so thick I can almost feel it pressing against my skin, so complete that I can't even see the fingers in front of my face when they are only inches away. No light penetrates the ceiling either.

It feels like being blind.

Being buried.

13

It's barely thirty-six hours since we moved in, since I pulled the old fitted wardrobes from the wall in the smallest of the top bedrooms and discovered this strange cobwebbed space, with its dusty dresser and motley collection of forgotten things. A day and a half in which I had looked for answers to satisfy the hunger of my own curiosity, but found only more questions.

The mystery of the little annexe had become more tantalising and frustrating with every new question. Even as I suppressed a niggling sense that I had awakened something which I didn't understand – and perhaps should have been better left alone. A threat or a warning, like a whisper on the wind that hints of a coming storm.

I take a small, tentative step, leaning down until my fingertips graze the moth-eaten fabric of the old armchair. Turning, I ease myself down into it until the old springs creak beneath my weight. Sitting there in the perfect darkness, I let my mind wander. Might this actually have been a place where someone had been kept against their will. Could that be it? No, it didn't make sense. There was a brick dividing wall but anyone shouting at the top of their lungs might still be heard in other parts of the house. Maybe not all the way down to the ground floor but on the first and second floors, almost certainly. Anyone able to shout, to scream, would be able to make themselves heard in the nearest rooms.

Unless . . . the whole house was empty? There was no window to shout through and this side of the house faced out onto the back garden, so the sound would be muffled, deadened by the bricks and timber of the rest of the house.

Someone in here would need to sit fairly still and quiet to ensure they weren't heard in any of the top floor rooms, or the landing that connected them.

Still and quiet.

I click the light back on, blinking against the sudden brightness. Jess was right. This was ridiculous. Eric Hopkins had barely been able to climb the stairs in his last years in this house, according to the estate agent; it was one of the reasons why the first and second floors were so neglected. Why the three rooms up here felt so removed from everything else, from a human touch, as if they'd been all but abandoned.

A plastic bag is in my pocket to gather up the remaining items in the dresser and leave them downstairs in the hall for getting rid of – one way or another.

Perhaps I should parcel up the items and send them to the PO box address, forget all about it and move on. Jess was right, of course. We should just dispose of it all, knock down the wall, redecorate the whole bedroom and forget this little cubbyhole ever existed.

But the plastic bag is still empty, still folded up in my back pocket. The collection of items laid out on top of the dresser.

The problem is Jess's instinct to make a clean break, to expunge all traces of this hidden room from our house.

My instinct is the exact opposite.

And the text message she'd received just made the mystery deeper and the puzzle more intriguing. An itch that I had to scratch.

This stuff *meant* something to someone.

The watch, of course, because it was valuable. Hard cash that was now sitting in my bank account. But what possible interest could they have in the rest of it? In a few old rings, a pair of glasses, a scarf?

The answer to that question wouldn't only solve a mystery – it might also get the mystery texter off our backs. Because he hadn't specified what he was *actually* looking for. And if he didn't know a particular watch was included among the 'personal items', then I could just give him the rest of the stuff and he'd be none the wiser. He'd leave us alone.

I pick up the old leather wallet, turning it over in my hands. The worn silver initials *DF* on the front bottom corner, a smaller stamp on the inside that is so faded as to be illegible. It has two compartments for notes, six slots for cards as you open it up, a small button-down pouch for coins. More slots on one side for more cards. I check each of them again, holding it under the light bulb, the worn brown leather soft against my palm. Reaching my index finger all the way into each slot, sliding it along to feel for anything, a picture, a note, something that might have a name on it. Something I might have missed first time around.

All empty. Except . . .

It's *not* empty. Not quite.

In the credit-card-sized slot behind the coin pouch, my finger brushes against something pushed right up against the lining where a casual search might not reveal it. I reach in further and pull it out with a flare of excitement: a small piece of paper, folded several times into a tiny, white square. Maybe a name? An address? I unfold it carefully, letting out a sigh of disappointment when I see what it is – and why it has probably never been missed.

It's a cashpoint receipt. Numbers and letters printed in faded black ink, an amount – £60 – and the name of a high street branch in Market Harborough. Date and time in hours, minutes, seconds. Twenty-first May, 2000, just before 9 p.m. I had been fifteen back then, studying for my GCSEs – a lifetime ago. The account number on the slip is obscured with asterisks apart from the last two digits, a three and a nine. The hard folded grooves have marked the paper slip with a criss-cross pattern in the intervening twenty-four years.

I hadn't requested one of these from the hole in the wall for years – they'd always ended up crowding my wallet or coat pockets. I fold it up into the small square again and slide it back into the wallet, running my thumb over the printed initials on the front, frustration mingling with the disappointment. *Who are you, DF? Who were you? What did you spend this sixty pounds on?*

Next to it, the tag on the dog collar is dulled with age but the engraving is still legible when I hold it nearer to the bulb over my head.

Woody. And on the other side of the disc, *167 Sumner Street.* The phone number inscribed below it is just seven digits, with no area code. I guessed that if Woody had ever run off at the park, his owner wouldn't have needed an area code because he wouldn't be that far away. The new tags I'd had cut for Coco and Steve last week have my mobile number on them, rather than a landline. Did anyone use a landline for this kind of thing anymore? I take out my phone and type the number in, prefixed by the local area code. There is a short silence before an electronic female voice comes back.

'I'm sorry, that number isn't recognised.'

I google the address. Maybe Woody's former owners still lived there, might know why or how this tag had ended up tucked away in my house. Maybe they'd lived here at some point – a lodger or a guest or a relative – and couldn't bear to part with this last memento of a much-loved pet. Perhaps Mr Hopkins himself had lived there before he moved here.

The closest Sumner Street I can find is about three miles away from here in the small town of Kimberley; there also seem to be dozens of others in towns and suburbs around the country. But Kimberley was as good a place as any to start.

I can get there and back tomorrow before anyone knows I'm gone.

14

TUESDAY

I flinch awake, tangled in the sheets. My dreams had been full of strangers, of people in the house whose faces I couldn't see, of doors and windows open to the elements. It's not long past dawn, a narrow slice of daylight working its way through the blankets we have rigged up as temporary curtains until I have time to fit the blinds.

There is a noise, too.

Something man-made, something beyond the creaks and sighs of this old Victorian house. A thin, specific noise.

Tap-tap.

A pause. Then it comes again, from somewhere downstairs.

Tap-tap.

With a shiver of unease, I swing my legs out of bed and pull on jeans and yesterday's T-shirt. Rubbing my eyes, I walk barefoot onto the landing, pausing first outside Daisy's room and then Callum's, pushing each door gently open to check they are still sleeping soundly in their beds. Perhaps Mr Stay Puft had gone walkabout again, got stuck somewhere. But whatever the noise was, it seemed a bit loud for that. Squinting into the shadows in Callum's bedroom, it looks as if the door of the hamster's cage is shut. Coco is curled at the end of his bed, also fast asleep.

Tap-tap.

I make my way slowly downstairs, the thin grey light of morning coming half-heartedly through the windows by the front door. There is no one on the drive. I pat the pocket of my jeans absently before realising I've left my phone upstairs on the bedside table. I listen for the noise again, but there is nothing. Even Steve, our cat – who would normally be appealing noisily for an early breakfast at this hour – is nowhere to be seen. Standing on the cold tiled floor of the kitchen, I strain my ears, trying to locate the source of the tapping. Probably Steve somewhere with a mouse, or an overhanging tree branch slapping against a window: there is a ton of foliage in the front and back gardens that I need to cut back. My pulse steadies, slowing down to something near normal.

I fill the kettle and set it to boil, fetching two mugs down from the cupboard. I'm awake now and know I won't be able to get back to sleep before the children stir. I find my slippers and heft the big four-pinter of milk out of the fridge-freezer, nudging the door shut with my elbow—

A dark figure looms beyond the frosted glass of the back door.

'Jesus!'

My own voice is loud in the silence of my kitchen and I almost drop the milk, heart leaping into my throat.

The figure raises a hand. A word of greeting muffled behind the glass.

It takes me a few seconds to register who it is, standing at my back door at six fifteen in the morning. Fumbling for the handle, I open up to a rush of cool morning air and gesture for him to come into the kitchen.

'Dom,' I say. 'Hi.'

My brother-in-law is a big man, thick through the chest and waist, with close-cropped dark hair and a bushy beard.

In old family album pictures of him and Jess as small children, there was a faint facial resemblance, but since then, they've grown into the chalk-and-cheese kind of siblings you wouldn't put together even when stood side by side. Now, Dom cuts an imposing figure in the dark navy uniform he wears for work, where he's a security supervisor overseeing a couple of thousand students on the university's three-hundred acre parkland campus. His battered green Skoda estate hadn't been parked on the front drive just now; presumably he's left it on the street.

'Morning, Adam,' he says cheerily. 'Just come off a night shift, didn't want to ring the doorbell and disturb the kiddies. Didn't wake you, did I?'

'No,' I say. 'I was up and about anyway. Lots to be getting on with.'

'So, this is the new pad, is it?' He lets out a low whistle. 'Very posh, very fancy. Do I need to start calling you the lord of the manor now?'

As always with Jess's older brother, I can never quite tell whether he's taking the mickey, or whether that's just the way he talks to his team members at work – and everyone else.

I shake my head. 'We got a key cut for you, by the way. It's around here somewhere.'

He leans back against the counter, arms folded over his big chest, and takes in the high ceiling, the pantry, the door to the cellar. The general *size* of everything, the grand scale of Victorian architecture, the elaborate cornices, the expanse of the garden outside.

'Jess asked me to pop by and have a look at a camera you found?'

'Thanks – it's in the garage. But first I need some caffeine.' I reach down a third mug from the cupboard. 'Tea or coffee?'

* * *

Dom and I make small talk while the coffee brews and then take our mugs into the garage, where most of the pitted concrete floor is still taken up with empty boxes and odd bits of furniture I've still not found a home for after the move. The garden shears, saws and anything else with a blade that I want to keep out of Callum's reach – as well as the bird box – are on the highest shelf against the far wall.

'Jess didn't want the camera in the house,' I say to my brother-in-law. 'So I put it up here instead.'

I stretch up, feeling next to the bowsaw, but my fingers can't quite reach high enough. Must have pushed it right to the back of the shelf. Pulling out a plastic packing crate, I step up onto it and reach up with both hands.

But the shelf is empty.

The camera, and the bird box, are gone.

15

'I don't understand,' I say, shaking my head. 'I put it up here yesterday afternoon. *Right here*, the box as well.'

'You're sure?'

'Positive.'

'I noticed that the padlock on that side door was unlocked when we came in just now,' Dom says, gesturing over his shoulder with a thumb. 'Did you secure it last night?'

'I . . . think so? I mean, probably.' Thinking back to last night, the day had been so full, my mind racing with so much that was new, that I couldn't actually remember doing it. 'Ninety per cent sure I locked it.'

He raises an eyebrow at that, but lets it go without comment. As a single man with no family of his own, he's always been very protective of his little sister and of the kids in particular. He often seems to give the impression – either deliberately or otherwise – that he's not sure I'd be up to the job of looking after them on my own, if push ever came to shove.

'Anyone else got a key?' he says, studying the door.

'Just us. I think.'

'Looks like someone paid you a visit overnight.'

The thought was already settling on me like the throb of a headache: a *stranger* had been in here, on my property, while we slept upstairs. They had come up the drive, gone around on the path and found their way into the garage. It might not be attached to the house but it was only a few metres from the kitchen – with only the back door between them and my family. The coffee turns bitter in my mouth.

'This is crazy,' I say. 'We've only been here two days.'

'Anything else stolen?'

I look around at the unsorted mess of garden furniture, bikes, tents, tools and boxes piled up by the removals team two days ago.

'Don't know. It's hard to say. Can't see anything else missing.'

'Either way,' he says, grim-faced, 'probably best to lock it now. And look at getting a new padlock to replace this one.'

Five minutes later, with Dom's coffee mug refilled, I sit with him at the kitchen table as he swipes through the pictures of the bird-box camera that Jess had sent to him on WhatsApp.

'It's a nice piece of kit,' he says, zooming in on the screen of his phone. 'Decent build quality, infrared for low light conditions. Probably either piggybacking on poorly secured Wi-Fi or uploading to a particular phone every time it's within Bluetooth range – like, that person parks up on the street outside, the camera connects to his phone and uploads all the latest footage. It would only take a few seconds.'

'Any idea how long it might have been up there?' I say. 'We never even noticed the bird box until the cat went up there.'

My brother-in-law gives a shrug of his big shoulders, studying the unit like an entomologist examining the carcass of some rare tropical insect. It's not too dissimilar, he tells me, from the cameras incorporated into the newer labs and lecture theatres on campus. Except for the fact that it was obviously meant to stay undetected.

'Solar-powered with a battery backup,' he adds, 'this sort of thing could capture content for weeks. Months, depending on the weather conditions and ambient light.'

'*Content,*' I say, a pulse of nausea low down in my stomach. 'You mean us, me and Jess, the kids, our comings and goings? On our own little *Truman Show*?'

He nods slowly. 'Assuming it had a full view of the frontage. Twenty-four-seven surveillance on your movements, who's in the house, who's not. What time you left, how long you were out. Potentially capturing your daily routines, patterns, visitors. Everything.'

'There was an old security system, the keypad's by the front door. Maybe the camera was part of that, CCTV for the property?'

My brother-in-law goes out to the hall to check it out, returns with a shake of his head.

'That system is ancient,' he says. 'Twenty years plus – and it doesn't seem to be connected to anything. The camera, on the other hand, is a much more recent piece of tech. Latest generation.'

'Maybe it was part of a general upgrading of the security?'

He gives me a sceptical frown. 'Wasn't the previous owner like ninety years old?'

'Eighty-seven,' I say. 'But he has a son, perhaps he installed it to keep an eye on his dad. I've sent him a text.'

'Is there anything you're not telling me, Adam?' He lowers his voice. 'About this place?'

'What do you mean?'

'That camera is not part of a standard home CCTV system. It's high-end surveillance kit, presumably put in by the previous owner. Unless you think someone would want to spy on my sister, my nieces and nephew? On you?'

For a second I wonder if I should lay it all out for him, the hidden room, the watch, the old flip phone and the text message. But pride pinches at me, stopping the words in my throat. I don't want him thinking I can't look after my family; I would tell him when I had worked it out for myself.

'I can't imagine it would be to do with us,' I say. 'But I'm going to find out, either way.'

'You're going all cryptic on me, Adam.'

'I'm sure there's a reasonable explanation.'

'Hmm.' He drains the last of his coffee in one large gulp. 'So, you going to give me the grand tour then? Ground floor at least.'

I give him a quick tour of the lounge, the other reception room still full of boxes, the snug, the playroom and the utility room. In the dining room, he stops.

'You see those?' He points up into the corner, where the wall meets the ceiling. Mounted just below the coving is a small off-white cube of plastic, a red light flashing on its front edge as he waves a hand towards it. 'You've still got all these old motion detectors in your downstairs rooms. Looks like a legacy system, but still wired into the mains.'

'Linked to the old alarm,' I say. 'Like you said, none of it works properly anymore.'

'I know.' He narrows his eyes. 'Maybe I'm just being paranoid.'

'But?'

He goes to stand directly underneath the detector, its red light flashing obligingly at him.

'I was just thinking . . . You found one camera. What if there are more?'

16

We find another hidden camera in the hall and a third in the kitchen.

Each of them is concealed inside one of the old motion detectors in the corners of the rooms, the bulky off-white plastic cubes fixed high off the ground. In each unit, the clunky old circuit boards and wires inside have been replaced by a small self-contained digital camera peering through the smoked glass – an ultra-modern parasite living inside the shell of its last-century host.

Dom and I end up taking *all* of the old motion detectors off the walls, dismantling each of them to check for anything hidden inside, anything that might have been added to spy on my family. A couple have been painted in place so I end up levering them off the wall with a long screwdriver, snapping them open in the process. The dangling plastic devices are not pretty but I prefer to have them out of action completely rather than seeing the red lights winking at me every time I walk across a room, certain that no one is observing every move we make.

'This is weird,' Dom says quietly as he studies the tiny digital innards of the disconnected cameras. '*Seriously* weird.'

'Jess called the police about the one outside, but they didn't seem interested. I'll try them again today.'

Dom looks sceptical. 'Good luck with that.'

'You don't think it's worth it?'

'It's worth reporting, sure. But the cops are stretched tighter now than I've ever known before. We deal with them on a weekly basis, or daily on a weekend, and they've never been as short-staffed as they are now.' He looks up from the camera. 'In fact, why don't you let me have a word with a sergeant I know in Beeston? See what he makes of it.'

'Thanks, Dom.'

He returns his attention to the camera unit, turning it on its back.

'These two are the same make and type as the camera outside, by the looks of it. Hard to say how long they've been there, could be months – or years. And forgive me for stating the obvious, but all three of them are covert. All disguised, hidden. Which is . . .' he pauses, choosing his words more carefully '. . . out of the ordinary.'

'Do you think they can pick up audio as well?'

'Doesn't look like it. But it might explain why your night-time visitor knew to look in the garage.'

'The camera in the kitchen saw me take it out of the back door yesterday.'

Dom nods. 'Suggesting you were either taking it to the wheelie bin, or the garage. If they know you at all, they'll know you're a hoarder, that you wouldn't be able to just throw it out with the rubbish.'

I look up in surprise.

'You think they *know* me?'

He shrugs. 'They know you a bit better now than they did two days ago, that's for sure.'

The thought of someone spying on my family lodges like jagged glass under my skin. Someone might have been silently watching us, observing us, ever since we moved in. Our first night meal on Sunday. The kids coming home from school and playing in the front garden.

Even though I still can't believe the cameras are anything to do with us.

The house begins to wake up around us as we discuss it further. Steve and Coco both appear, looking expectantly at me for breakfast. The big ginger cat, as ever, demands to be fed first. Then Jess emerges with a sleepy Callum in his pyjamas, his younger sister following close behind and hugging a purple-haired doll to her chest.

They all greet Dom with great surprise and enthusiasm, Callum climbing up onto his uncle's back and Daisy insisting that he sits next to her while she eats her Rice Krispies. I make Jess toast and tea as she busies herself with the kids' breakfasts, waiting until she has a spare moment to take her to one side.

Quietly, so the kids won't hear, I tell her about the other cameras we've found. Her eyes widen in alarm as I indicate the top of the freezer, where I've put them for the time being.

'What the hell?' She puts her half-eaten slice of toast onto her plate. 'This is absolutely mad, I'm calling the police again.'

'Dom's doing it,' I say. 'A sergeant he knows through work. Listen, are you around to meet in town for lunch today? I can get out for an hour, and we could go to that place near your office, talk about all this properly.'

I hate lying to her. I hate that I've got better at it over the last two weeks, that it's started to become almost routine. We've always tried to be honest with each other, no matter what. But maintaining the fiction of stability and security seems more important than ever this morning.

She shakes her head. 'I can't. Morning meeting plus lunch with some colleagues from the Zurich office and then I'm straight into back-to-back catch-ups with my team leads this afternoon.'

'Then we'll talk about this tonight, OK?' I bring her into a quick hug. 'It'll be all right. I reckon the cameras were just left over by the previous owner's son, wanting to keep an eye on his dad. But we've found them, we've switched them off, it's dealt with.'

'Have you heard anything back from the person who texted me?'

'Nothing yet.' I kiss her on the forehead. 'We'll probably never hear from them again.'

I herd Daisy and Callum upstairs to get them dressed, shoes on and faces washed, while Jess showers and gets ready in the en suite. While the kids are brushing their teeth, I put on a clean shirt and grab my work bag from the bedroom.

As I'm gathering shoes and bookbags in the hall, Leah finally thunders downstairs, grabs a banana from the fruit bowl and throws us a wave before dashing out of the front door, saying she's late for her bus.

Dom emerges through the back door.

'I've had a quick scan of your back garden but it's a needle in a haystack out there, mate. Big plot, overgrown the way it is – there are a million places you could hide another camera if you really wanted to.'

Pointing upwards with an index finger, he says to me: 'Priority next is to check the upstairs. The bathrooms. And the bedrooms.'

I nod. 'When they've gone to school.'

He gives me a quizzical look. 'Aren't you going to be late for work?'

I make a show of looking at my watch. Deceiving Dom feels almost as bad as lying to my wife, but for a different reason: because he is very good at sniffing out lies. He deals with people lying to him on a daily basis – mostly students who are drunk, drugged or otherwise misbehaving – and it has turned his bullshit detector into a finely tuned instrument.

'Yeah,' I say. 'Should probably head into the office, actually. I'll give the upstairs rooms a thorough check later.'

He pulls his car keys from a pocket. 'I can give you a lift to work, if you like?'

'You've done enough for one day, Dom.' I grab my own car keys from the hook by the door. 'You should get home and get your head down for a few hours. I'll drive myself.'

I lock up the house behind us, making sure I wait until he's walked out to his Skoda and driven off before I start the engine of my own car.

I wait another minute, idling on the drive, to make sure he's gone.

Two minutes later, I pull up to the junction with Derby Road. A right turn here will take me uphill towards the city, towards the job I no longer have, the place where I no longer work.

I swing the car left instead and accelerate away down the hill.

17

It feels good to be out of the house.

Which is crazy, because we've just mortgaged ourselves to the hilt to buy it, sunk all our savings into it too. We spent six months searching for a dream home, and another six waiting for the chain to complete, for the paperwork to go through – but it still feels like someone else's property. Like it is still full of old ghosts waiting to be exorcised. Full of old questions that don't yet have answers.

Perhaps I could answer one of those questions today.

I head north-west out of the city, beyond the snaking grey artery of the M1 motorway until I see signs for Kimberley, a small town just beyond Nottingham's western suburbs. After pulling off the dual carriageway, I pass warehouses and industrial units, allotments and football pitches, bypassing the main shopping street as the maps app on my phone guides me to the address on the old dog tag. Sumner Street is on the edge of the town, a long row of unremarkable post-war semis with small front gardens and short drives of pockmarked block paving. Kimberley is a former pit village and has seen its share of hard times over the years – full of good people, for sure, but it feels a *long* way away from an upscale neighbourhood like The Park.

Number 167 is two-thirds of the way down. I pull the car to a stop across the street and study the house for a moment. The curtains are open and there is no car outside, no other signs of life visible through the downstairs window. I've put the dog collar into a plastic shopping bag – it feels too weird just carrying it around in my hand as if I'm looking for a lost pet – and I grab it from the passenger seat before locking the car and walking up the drive. The bell is an old-fashioned two-tone chime, a *ding-dong* that clangs mournfully through the dappled glass of the front door.

There is no answer.

I wait before trying the doorbell again, then tap the metal letterbox, flapping it noisily for good measure. But still no one comes to the door. It is the middle of the morning – I guess the owners are out at work. I stand there for another hopeful minute before returning to my car, hunting around in the glove compartment for a pen and paper.

I'm just scribbling my mobile number at the bottom of the note when a small red Peugeot slows next to me and turns carefully into the drive of number 167, suspension squeaking audibly as it bumps up the kerb. A woman gets out of the driver's side and goes around to the boot, lifting out two bulging bags of shopping. She's around fifty, in dungarees and trainers, with flushed cheeks and brown hair tied back in an unfussy ponytail. Leaving the boot open, she takes the shopping and walks to the house next door where the door has already been opened by an elderly man in slippers, leaning on a walking stick. She disappears inside.

A few minutes later, she emerges empty-handed and takes the remaining two bags of shopping from the Peugeot, going into number 167 and nudging the front door shut with her foot. I give her a minute then follow, ringing the doorbell for the third time in ten minutes. This time I can see the shape of movement through the frosted glass as she approaches, already talking as she pulls open the door.

'I've told you, Bill, I was doing a shop anyway and I'm not taking any extra money for—'

She sees me, and stops.

'Hi,' I say, holding a hand up in greeting. 'Sorry to drop in on you like this.'

'Oh,' she says. 'Thought you were the neighbour.'

'Have you got a minute?'

The smile fades from her face. 'I was just unpacking the shopping, then I've got some other things to be getting on with before I pick my son up.'

'It really won't take—'

'And I don't buy on the doorstep, but you can leave a leaflet if you want.'

'I'm not selling anything,' I say. 'I just wanted to talk to you about your dog.'

She starts to push the door shut. 'Sorry, I think you've got the wrong house, love. I don't have a dog.'

'I found his collar.' I raise the plastic bag. 'Was passing by today and I thought I'd drop it around to you.'

'Like I said,' she repeats, 'I don't have a dog. Haven't had one for years.'

I feel a little tug of disappointment at her certainty, the bubble of hope deflating.

'Do you mind if I ask how long you've lived at this address?'

She leans around to see if there's anyone else on the drive behind me.

'Is this some sort of prank?'

'It might be that the dog belonged to a previous—'

'Not sure it's any of your business how long I've been here.' She moves to push the door all the way shut. 'Sorry, but I can't help you.'

'His name was Woody.' I take the collar out of the plastic bag and hold out the tag to show her. 'The dog. I found the collar at my house and I was curious to know how it ended up there.'

For a second, I think she's going to slam the door in my face but instead she stops, her mouth slightly open, eyes settling on the worn black leather collar. A trio of frown lines deepen on her forehead as she reaches out a tentative hand to touch the dull silver disc of the name tag. She turns it this way and that, reading the handful of letters and numbers, her thumb rubbing the rough lines of engraving etched into the metal.

All the colour has drained from her cheeks.

'Where?' she says finally, taking the collar in both hands now. 'Where did you find this?'

I repeat what I said about finding it at my house, giving her the street name without going into too many other details. She looks up from the collar and finds my eyes, and then she pulls open the front door, showing me into a short hallway with stairs on the right and a small, neat kitchen at the end. Gesturing towards another open door on the left, she ushers me into a lounge, sparsely furnished in shades of beige and dark brown. She gestures for me to take a seat on a sofa by the window. I'm half expecting a dog to trot into the room and give me a good checking over. But the house is silent and still; it feels empty apart from the two of us.

She hovers by the door, as if still not quite sure whether to trust me, the collar clutched in both hands.

'Would you like a drink?' she says. 'Tea?'

'No, thank you.'

'I'm Maxine, by the way. Most people call me Max.'

'Adam,' I say. 'Nice to meet you.'

She moves a little further into the room, seeming to come to a decision.

'Woody was my husband's dog,' she says at last. 'At least, at first. Adrian was the one who got him from the rescue place, who brought him out of his shell, trained him.' She stops, shaking her head. 'I'm sorry, this is all a bit of a shock coming so out of the blue.'

She lays the collar carefully on the sofa and takes a black-framed picture from the mantelpiece, handing it to me. It's a countryside shot of a slight, bespectacled man in a green ano-rak, with a kind, open face. His hand is laid affectionately on the head of a scrappy, caramel-coloured cross-breed with its tongue hanging out; the dog looks as if it is smiling.

'We got Woody from a rescue kennel when he was already two or three, they didn't quite know how old he was but they knew he'd been horribly mistreated. Took him a week to come out from behind the sofa, a month before he'd let anyone stroke him. He was just frightened of everyone, and everything. But not nasty with it, just petrified. Adrian brought him round. We both loved him. But I never thought . . .' She sits down on the armchair. I notice for the first time that she wears a gold band on the fourth finger of her right hand, not her left. The only other jewellery she wears is a plain silver necklace, one hand now sliding a locket along the chain. 'Never thought I'd end up looking after that dog on my own.'

'I'm sorry.'

'Just brings it all back, you know?'

'Your husband . . .?' I let the question hang in the air, trying to think of a delicate way of phrasing it. 'You're not . . . together anymore?'

'No.' She looks at the other pictures lined up on the mantel-piece. 'No, we're not together. I've not seen Adrian in more than twenty years.'

Adrian

Woody didn't care about the rain.

In fact, he seemed to enjoy it, racing through puddles with his coarse yellow fur plastered to his back, splashing and skidding along the path by the woods. Running for the old green ball again and again, returning each time with a delighted wag of his tail. It was hard to believe he was the same dog as a year ago, back when he'd been a skinny little thing frightened of his own shadow.

Adrian checked his watch, drops of rain spattering the digital display. Almost time to head back, to get both of them dry and warm, to put the fire on for Woody. Time to sit down with Max and ask about her day. Tea would be almost ready.

He was winding up to throw the ball one last time when he heard the cries. The same name, over and over again, a single word that he couldn't quite identify over the steady patter of rain on the hood of his anorak.

The calls grew louder as a figure came into view, splashing unsteadily along the path and still shouting that single word into the woods, thick with dark dripping trees. A slight figure in a long yellow coat, face hidden beneath the soaking spines of a purple umbrella. Young, perhaps twenty, a brown leather leash doubled uselessly in their other hand.

Adrian called to his own dog, who came obediently to heel to have his black collar clipped to the lead. He looked into the trees as the figure approached, but the light was fading and his rain-spattered glasses made it difficult to make out any movement.

'Are you OK?' he called out. 'Have you lost someone?'

The figure turned towards him, tentative, but moving a little nearer.

'My dog, she's still a puppy really and we're still training her, my dad said I shouldn't let her off the lead yet but I thought if I kept her close it would be OK.' The words came out in a rush, tumbling over each other. 'Then she saw a rabbit and just went flying off into the woods and I couldn't keep up with her. Dad's going to kill me.'

'She can't have gone far,' Adrian said calmly. 'What's her name?'

'Bella.' The voice was high and tight, almost hitching with a sob. 'I'm just worried that if she gets through to the other side of the woods there's a road there and she's not really the best with roads, she doesn't understand the danger. She's lovely but she's silly, you know? She loves everyone she meets but when she gets excited she just runs and runs, oblivious to everything else. God I'm so stupid for unclipping her. She's a Dalmatian, as mad as they come.' Woody allowed his head to be stroked, tail wagging slowly. 'What breed is yours?'

'Oh, this little guy is a Heinz beans breed – fifty-seven different varieties.' He took his glasses off, wiped them on his jeans. 'Look, do you have any dog treats on you, that Bella likes?'

'No, they're at home.'

'She's probably close by,' Adrian said. 'Don't run when you see her because she might think that's part of a game and run away even further, or else she'll get scared. And when she does come back to you, don't be cross with her, OK? Just be calm, and positive.'

The stranger stared into the trees.

'Could you . . . help me look?' Another sob. 'Just for a few minutes?'

Adrian checked his watch again. He didn't like leaving Max at home on her own too long. She'd been so low recently, always blaming herself – especially after the last time, getting to fourteen weeks before things went wrong. He'd been thinking maybe it was time they asked for help: there was a lot they could do now on the NHS. They would find a way. And maybe one day it would be his own son or daughter out by these woods, walking a dog, asking a stranger for help.

He would help a fellow animal-lover today.

Then he would go home.

'Of course,' he said. 'Come on, let's find Bella.'

18

'He just . . . vanished.' Maxine grips a white china mug of tea in both hands. 'Went out one evening and never came back.'

She's made us both a cup and now sits opposite me on the small sofa in her living room. The opposite wall is decorated with pictures of Adrian, a wedding day picture together with Maxine and a few framed holiday snaps, the colours blanching with age. There are also pictures of a baby, of a bespectacled boy in a smart school uniform on the doorstep of this house, then pictures of a teenager and finally of a young man in a graduation gown.

The house is eerily quiet, the only sound the occasional car on the street outside and Maxine's soft Nottinghamshire vowels as she tells me about the husband she's not seen for more than two decades.

'He came back from work and took the dog out before tea,' she says. 'Just like he always did. Same time, same place, up the park at the end of the road. He seemed normal and he was never more than about half an hour, and it was throwing it down with rain that night, so I thought he'd be keen to get back. At first I thought he'd probably just met one of the lads from the Royal Oak darts team and was having a natter. But after an hour I started to get worried – he would never have missed his tea like that. When he'd been gone an hour and a half I walked up there myself even though it was pretty much dark by then and there were no lights on the park. And that was when I found Woody, soaked to the skin and shivering, just wandering around on his own, no collar, no lead. No Adrian. That night was the last time anyone ever saw or heard from him. It didn't make any sense . . . it still doesn't.'

'I'm so sorry,' I say, feeling the inadequacy of the words. 'Can't begin to imagine how awful that must have been.'

'I knocked on some neighbours' doors, asked if they'd seen him but no one had. Then I started ringing round friends, all the time expecting him to walk through the door, wet through and with a smile on his face and a story to tell about something or other. I didn't care where he'd been by that point, I just wanted him to come home. An hour after that I called the police.'

'And he'd never talked about . . .'

She's already shaking her head.

'Leaving? No. Never. We were happy, he would never have done that to me.' She gives a rueful smile, but it's full of pain even all these years later. 'More to the point, he wouldn't have left Woody roaming around off the lead near a road. He loved that dog. He wouldn't have abandoned him like that. Woody had been dumped by his first owners when he was young, that's why we got him from the shelter.'

'What did the police make of it?'

'Not much. They never really seemed to get going, even after a week when his bank account hadn't been touched, there were no eyewitness sightings of him, no suggestion that he'd gone abroad. I mean, he didn't even own a passport. They never seemed to put much effort into finding him, said he wasn't a child or a vulnerable adult, not at risk of exploitation or harm, to himself or anyone else, blah blah blah. When I told them I was pregnant with

Charlie, it made it worse, like it was the oldest story in the world: *sketchy bloke gets his missus pregnant, decides he doesn't want to be tied down, goes out for a packet of fags one night and never comes back. That sort of thing.*

'But that would have been out of character for Adrian?'

'*God* yes. He'd be the last man on earth to do something like that.'

It occurs to me that a million women before her have probably said something similar, but her tone is unwavering even all these years later.

'So the police decided he'd cut and run?'

'More or less.' She bites her lip. 'Then when his debit card was found a few weeks later up near Flamborough Head, in a car park near the cliffs, they just assumed there was only one reason he would have gone there. But Adrian wouldn't have done that either. *Never.*'

'Were there any phone records?'

'He didn't have one.'

I finish my tea and put the mug down on a side table, trying to imagine myself in her situation. To be the one left behind if Jess ever went missing, if she simply vanished one day and never came back, knowing that I had to carry on for the sake of the children. The idea of life without her – without knowing what had happened to her – is almost unthinkable, impossible. Inconceivable.

'I'm sorry to just turn up on your doorstep and stir everything up again. I realise it must be very difficult for you.'

'No,' she says, shaking her head. 'Don't apologise. I like talking about Adrian but no one ever asks anymore, you know? You're the first person to even bring him up in . . . God, I don't know how many years. I like talking about him, but people think you should *move on*. What if you don't want to move on?'

'What was your husband like?'

Her eyes fill with tears.

'Kind. That's what I remember most. And he was funny too, in his own way. He could come across as shy, reserved. You know that thing they say about how opposites attract? That was never the case with us. We were happy in our own little world, our little team of just the two of us. Soulmates. Then Woody came along, and the baby was going to make it complete.' She pulls a tissue from the pocket of her dungarees and dabs at her eyes with it. 'I've never had any answers, never been able to grieve properly. We've never had a funeral, there's no gravestone, nothing to remember him by. Nowhere I can take Charlie. It's like Adrian didn't even exist. Everyone just seemed to forget, except me and Woody: that dog used to wait for him, for years after. He'd always go to the front door at quarter to six in the evening, that was when Adrian would get in from work. That little dog would sit there, and wait, almost to the end.'

She talks more about Adrian, his job as a warehouseman, his hobbies, how they met. Her efforts over the years to keep his disappearance on the radar of local police and residents of the area.

'I've tried to get the media interested over the years,' she says. 'There's been a few stories in the local papers here and there, not that it ever led to anything. They always say there's nothing *new*, no new *angle* or whatever to write about. Even tried to get one of those missing persons podcasts interested on the twenty-year anniversary but they never even got back to me. Not interesting or unusual enough for them, I s'pose.'

I wait a beat, before posing the question I came here to ask.

'Why do you think that collar ended up in my house?'

'Honestly?' She shakes her head. 'I have no idea. I've never even been to The Park, and I'm pretty sure Adrian wouldn't have had a reason to go there either. No reason to be there unless you live in one of those big houses, is there?'

'Not really.' It was true enough. There were no businesses, no bars or cafés in The Park. No office blocks, no shops. No obvious link that I could see between a small semi-detached house in a small town on the western side of the county, and a house in the heart of the city.

She looks up, as if struck by a new idea, a tiny flicker of hope.

'Perhaps he was a lodger, a house guest, perhaps he stayed there for a while on his way somewhere else? Perhaps . . . I don't know.'

I give her a sympathetic smile. 'It's possible, I suppose.'

We lapse into silence. She picks up the collar again and holds it carefully, almost reverently, as if it's a precious artefact that might crumble to dust at any moment.

'Can I . . . can I keep it? Just for a few days at least?'

'To show to the police?'

She shakes her head. 'The police are long past caring what happened to my husband. Not that they ever really did in the first place. No, I'd like to show it to my son.'

'Of course.'

'He never met his dad, you see. Not even once. And it's just uncanny how alike they are, I see my Adrian in him every day in his mannerisms, the way he smiles.'

She takes her phone from the pocket of her dungarees and taps it, holds it out to me. The screen is filled with a picture of a skinny young guy in his early twenties, with a wide, toothy grin and dark-rimmed glasses. He's wearing a black leather jacket over a black T-shirt; his hair is long and wild and he's leaning on a metal cane.

I smile and hand the phone back. 'He looks like you.'

'All I can see is Adrian.' She glances at the collar again. 'Did you find anything else? Anything that might have belonged to Adrian? It would mean a lot to me, to have something else of his from back then.'

I give a brief description of what else I found in the hidden room – except for the Rolex – and she listens intently as I describe each item. Each one perhaps a link back to the past.

'But I didn't bring them with me,' I say. 'Just the collar. I'm sorry.'

'I've got to be at work soon but I'll be in Nottingham later in the week, maybe I could meet you somewhere?'

We swap phone numbers and she says she'll let me know, then I leave Maxine in peace, in her empty house, with her memories.

I drive down the road to the park she had mentioned, the last place anyone had seen Adrian. It's a fairly unremarkable bit of green space, long and thin, looping away from the road with a thick ribbon of trees on the north side. I walk around for ten minutes but see only a single solitary dog walker. Even now, it seemed, it was a good place to find some peace and quiet.

Where did you go, Adrian?

Who did you meet?

What happened that day?

On the little town's main shopping street, I find a café and buy a ham salad sandwich, eating it while googling the name Adrian Parish. There are only a handful of results, the most recent a local newspaper piece on the fifteenth anniversary of his disappearance. A brief mention of a Detective Constable Phil Goode asking for information from the public but no indication of any progress in finding out what happened to the missing man. Scanning through the few other online mentions, I'm struck by how small the digital footprint is, how limited the effort seems to have been to find him, or to find out what happened to him. As if Adrian Parish had left few ripples on the world – both when he was here and after he was gone.

There is a heaviness, a sadness, to the story that sits like a weight on my chest.

One thing seems very clear: no one really seemed to care about Adrian Parish anymore. He was all but forgotten, a missing person who had never returned. No one had given him a second thought for years.

Except for Maxine.

19

Jess texts me as I'm about to leave the café.

Where are you? x

I sit up, suppressing a twinge of guilt as I type a reply.

In town, getting a sandwich for lunch.

Which was technically true, just not the town she might assume.

What's up? x

Callum's year are doing futuristic day at school tomorrow so can you get a load of tinfoil and silver spray paint or something? Will bodge something up later. x

I text back a thumbs up. The school seemed to do one of these days every few months and it was always a mad rush to get something made for one or other of the kids to wear. I grab the things for Callum's school fancy dress from a Tesco Express – tinfoil, glue, silver gaffer tape and magic markers – and head back to the car.

The drive back into the city goes quickly as I mull over everything Max told me about her missing husband, trying to tease out the connection between Adrian and my house. His friends, and what little family he had at the time, had been in Kimberley. He'd gone to school in Eastwood, the neighbouring town. He had worked in Nottingham, but on a big industrial estate in Beeston Rylands – nowhere near The Park.

I had driven out this morning in search of answers, but found more questions instead.

The curiosity is like a drug, an intoxicating itch that I can't *quite* scratch.

Back in the city, I crawl along Castle Boulevard in stop-start traffic until I can finally turn left onto Peveril Drive and join a short queue of cars at the access gate, each driver waiting for the green light to show the barrier has dropped. A large STOP sign painted on the road is echoed by another at eye level, alongside more capital letter instructions:

RESIDENTS ONLY

ANPR IN USE FOR ACCESS

NO TAILGATING

I inch the car forward, waiting while the automatic number plate recognition system scans the front of the car, before the steel bollard depresses flat and the light turns green. I'm still new enough to the neighbourhood for there to be a little novelty to it, at being able to use a road I've only ever driven past before. Although the entrances to the estate on the north side and to the east – by the castle – always seem to be open, so I'm still not really sure why they limit access here on the south side. To stop people cutting through, I suppose, and reduce traffic in general.

I pull away over the twenty miles per hour speed limit sign painted on the road, ease over the speed bump and head up the gentle gradient of Peveril Drive into the heart of The Park estate.

Mature trees line a wide road of handsome Victorian houses, each in its own generous plot of space, and I'm struck again by a sense of unreality that we've ended up here. This strange enclave in the middle of the city, with its access gates and RESIDENTS ONLY signs, all of it overlooked by the pale stone of the castle further up the hill.

I make the turn onto Regency Place and I'm about to call Dom on the hands-free, to see if he's heard anything from his police contact yet. But the words die in my throat as I turn into the driveway of my house.

A man is staring into the lounge window, hands cupped against the glass.

He turns as I pull up, raising a large hand in my direction.

He's easily six foot three, a few inches taller than me, shoulders straining against a navy bomber jacket and a grey V-neck that accentuates the swell of his chest. One hand clasps the strap of a backpack over his shoulder.

'Can I help you?' I grab the Tesco shopping bag from the passenger seat and lock the car. 'Are you looking for someone?'

'Hi,' he says, his stubble-thick face breaking into a smile. 'Sorry to bother you, is this a bad time?'

'That depends.'

He smiles. 'Of course.'

There's no lanyard around his thick neck, no indication that he's selling anything or collecting sign-ups for a charity. I keep the keys in my right hand as I walk across the drive.

'Sorry,' I say, remembering the way I had surprised Max on her doorstep just a few hours ago. 'I don't really buy on the doorstep, as a rule, but if you've got a leaflet or something you can leave . . .'

'It's OK, I'm not selling anything.' He hitches the strap of the backpack a little higher up his large shoulder. 'But I wonder if you have a couple of minutes? I think you can help me with something and I'd really appreciate it. My name's Shaun, by the way.'

He's good-looking in a rugby-player kind of way, with his square jaw and uncomplicated face. His voice is heavy and deep, a local accent but not strong.

'Help you with what?' I say. 'We're a bit busy at the moment, we've just moved in and still trying to get the house straight.'

'I know, that's kind of why I'm here.'

'Really?'

'I spoke to the estate agent and he said it would be OK to drop round.'

I frown. 'You spoke to Jeremy?'

'Yeah.'

'Is there a problem? He normally rings me if there's anything we need to talk about, but I thought all the legal stuff was done and dusted.'

'No, no problem.' He musters another smile full of unnaturally white teeth. 'More of a favour, really. My family, we've been sorting through all the stuff from the house move, going through it all, and obviously a lot of it isn't worth keeping. I mean, a lot of it will just end up at the tip because it's so old.'

'Oh,' I say, finally making the connection. 'Right. Mr Hopkins is your . . . grandad?'

'Yeah.' He nods emphatically. 'Sorry. This was his house. You know, before.'

'I see.'

'You're Adam, right?' He takes a half-step nearer. 'So, we've been going through all the stuff cleared out of the house, and most of it's junk, like I said, but there's a few things that we can't find. Family things with sentimental value, mementos and such like. Things that belonged to my grandpa.' He glances over my shoulder, at the house behind me. 'And the thing is . . . if it's not too much trouble, we'd like them back.'

20

Shaun stands his ground, one thumb looped beneath the strap of his rucksack.

'Would that be OK?' he says. 'To get my grandpa's stuff back?'

I reach for my front door key. 'Is this about the text message?'

'What message?'

'My wife had a text asking if we could send anything we found to a PO box address.'

He shakes his head slowly, his mouth turning down briefly at the corners.

'No, that's . . . I don't know anything about that.'

I stare at him for a moment, watching for any signs of deceit. Any flicker of nerves in his deep-set eyes. But either he's a very good actor or he genuinely doesn't know what I'm talking about.

'Strange,' I say. 'Assumed that was why you were here.'

'No one's sent any texts, that I'm aware of.'

He continues to stand there, not fazed by my questions, apparently willing to keep on chatting until I let him in. There is no offer to *come back at another time*, or *let me ask my dad about that text*. He stands quite still, feet planted shoulder-width apart, neither advancing nor retreating. My first instinct – as soon as I'd seen him staring in the front window – had been to send him on his way. With the discovery of the cameras, the weird message

Jess had received, the strange story I'd heard today from Maxine Parish, I wasn't about to trust the word of a total stranger.

And yet . . .

I didn't want him to leave either – not until I knew who he really was. And for all I knew, he could be telling the truth. Maybe he *was* Mr Hopkins senior's grandson. Which would mean whoever sent the text message was someone else entirely – and they had no right to anything in our house.

'So,' I say, 'you came by because your dad's abroad, is that it?'

'Yeah,' he says. 'That's right.'

'Sorry, I didn't catch your surname.'

'Hopkins,' he says. 'Nice to meet you, by the way.'

I give him a tight smile as an idea forms in my head.

'Listen,' I say, 'can you just give me a second? Need to make sure the kitchen door's shut otherwise the dog will make a run for it.'

He nods, without taking his eyes off me. 'Sure.'

I unlock the front door and step into the hall. With my back to the visitor, I pull out my phone and fire off a text to Jeremy, the vendor's estate agent, who had sold the house on Mr Hopkins's behalf.

Hi did you speak to Mr H son/grandson today about him coming to the house?

The two ticks next to the message appear to show it's been delivered. I stare at the screen a moment longer willing them to turn blue to show it's been read. But they stay stubbornly grey. I shove the phone back into my pocket.

Coco is curled, asleep, in her basket in the corner of the kitchen.

I return to the hall and gesture for Shaun to come in, showing him through to the kitchen where he accepts the offer of a cup of tea. Dumping the Tesco bag on the side, I fill the kettle and flick it on, fetching two mugs down from the cupboard.

'Excuse the mess,' I say. 'Only been a few days since we moved in.'

We exchange small talk about the house move while he settles his bulk on one of the high black stools against the counter. There is a whiff of aftershave surrounding him, something unsubtle and citrus-sharp that seems to fill the air between us. Close up, he looks a little older, mid- to late twenties, a faint scar curving beneath his eye.

'Obviously there's tons of stuff that got cleared out in the house move, so many of the old boy's things.' His eyes rove around the kitchen, over the boxes and bags and crates of food, crockery, glasses and appliances. 'Most of it's crap, you know? Too old to use or sell on. But we were thinking there were a few things in particular that got missed by the removal men, maybe left behind or stashed away somewhere.'

'You could have just called me.'

He shrugs. 'Dad thought it would be easier to do in person.'

'And did your grandad tell you exactly what sort of family heirlooms you're looking for, or where they might be? It's a big house, lots of rooms, plus the cellar, two attic spaces, the garage, the shed, the summer house.'

He gives a small shake of his head. 'Grandpa's not really . . . with it any more. Most of the time, anyway. Dementia. He has good days and bad days, you know? Sometimes you can sort of have a conversation with him but most of the time he doesn't even know who you are. Let alone where he might have put the old family heirlooms for safekeeping. It's tragic, really.'

'Is that why your dad put the cameras up?' I hand him a mug of tea. 'To keep an eye on him?'

He frowns. 'What cameras?'

'Two inside.' I point up to the coving where the kitchen camera had been mounted. 'And one outside, on a tree looking down at the drive.'

Again, he looks genuinely nonplussed at the question.

And again, I can't tell whether he's a very skilled actor or honestly doesn't know what I'm talking about.

'Dad never . . . mentioned that.' He shrugs. 'But he's the type that just gets on with stuff.'

'Oh,' I say. 'Curious.'

There is suddenly a strange, charged atmosphere between us and I'm very aware that we're alone in the house. As if to break the spell, Coco rouses herself from her basket in the corner of the kitchen. She stretches out her front legs, shakes lazily and wanders over to park herself next to Shaun. Tongue hanging out, she stares up adoringly at him, her tail swishing a slow back-and-forth on the lino as he strokes the top of her head.

'Lovely girl,' he says, scratching under her chin. 'We've always had retrievers too. Best dogs in the world.'

'*We*, as in . . .'

'Me and my dad. Family.' He smiles down at Coco, making a clicking noise with his tongue. 'Retrievers are the best, aren't they, girl?'

He starts telling me about his own dog, Mabel, about the litter of six puppies she'd had recently and the smallest one – Bonnie – they'd decided to keep even though the plan had been to sell all the pups. I check my phone quickly while he talks. The message to Jeremy is shown as delivered but still unread, the two ticks still grey.

'So,' I say, trying to get him back on track. 'These family heirlooms you're looking for, can you give me any clues? Big? Small? Expensive? There was quite a lot of stuff left here.'

'Dad just said they'd probably be all together in one place.' He thinks for a moment. 'And most of it might look like junk, to someone who didn't know.'

I take a sip of my tea. 'Right.'

'Like I said, it's mostly just sentimental value. Family stuff, not really valuable to anyone else.' He reaches for his tea on the counter, the sleeve of his bomber jacket riding up to reveal a large tattoo wrapping around his wrist, a cobra with its fangs bared. 'Except for one thing. An old watch.'

21

There is an unpleasant tightening in my stomach, as if I've been caught doing something I shouldn't. Caught out in a lie. Which is ridiculous, because I've broken no laws, done nothing illegal. Everything in this house belongs to me, and if I decide to sell it on that's nobody's business but mine.

Nevertheless, my pulse kicks up a notch.

He knows.

I nod slowly, as if hearing this news for the first time.

'A watch?'

'Yeah.' His gaze holds mine. 'Good make, wind-up one, bit of an antique maybe. Like I said, it's not really worth anything but it means a lot to my dad.'

Shaun's visit starts to make more sense: his dad knows the Rolex is worth a few thousand, and yet he can't find it. So he's sent his son on this errand to retrieve it.

It's not really worth anything. His lie, to match mine.

'Belonged to your grandad, did it?'

'Yeah.' He takes another slurp of tea. 'So . . . have you come across anything like that?'

Coco ambles back to her basket and lies back down with a *huff* of contentment.

I could just go upstairs and retrieve the rest of the stuff from the annexe, the rings, the old key, the old phone and everything else – hand it all over to him. Simply lie about the wristwatch, pretend I'd never seen it. But then I'd never know what it all meant; I'd never solve the mystery of the little room.

More importantly, there's still something about this stranger – about his story – that doesn't feel quite right. I just can't figure out what it is yet.

'Doesn't ring any bells,' I say, shaking my head. 'Sorry.'

His face falls. 'That's a shame. You're sure?'

'Pretty sure. Leave me a number, I'll get in touch if anything turns up.'

I take my phone out and type in the digits he recites. Casually, as if I'm still typing in his name, I switch the phone to silent and select the camera, taking a surreptitious picture of the man sitting opposite me. If he notices me doing it, he doesn't give anything away.

I'm about to give him my number in return when the doorbell rings.

Eileen Evans greets me on the doorstep. She's dressed in a dark-green belted raincoat and matching bucket hat, despite the sunny weather, a long purple skirt, and thick-soled black pumps. A circular white cake tin with an orange lid is clasped carefully under one arm.

After a brief greeting, she says: 'I hope you like Victoria sponge? A little moving-in present for you and your lovely family.'

'That's very kind,' I say. 'Thank you. The kids will love that.'

She holds out the cake tin in both hands.

'No allergies, intolerances, vegans or other food-related nonsense in the household, I hope?'

I shake my head. 'No, they're definitely cake fans. Especially Callum, he could eat—'

'Good,' she says. 'Glad to hear it. Far too much of that kind of guff around today, in my opinion.'

'Thanks again, Eileen, it really is a lovely gift.' I gesture behind me towards the kitchen. 'Listen, I'm really sorry but I've actually got someone here at the moment? I should probably . . .'

'I see,' she says curtly. 'In that case I'll let you get back to your guest. I do hope you enjoy the sponge cake.'

When I come back Shaun is standing near the back door, his empty mug on the kitchen counter.

'Thanks for the cuppa.' He glances back towards the hall. 'Actually, could I just quickly use your toilet before I head off?'

'Sure.'

He walks back into the entrance hall, slowly, eyeing first the closed door to the snug, then the cupboard under the stairs.

'Top of the stairs,' I say. 'Then turn right.'

He gives me a sheepish thumbs up and disappears up the staircase.

I take my phone out and check the messages, but there is still no response from Jeremy. Next, I check the photo of Shaun and see that it's satisfyingly sharp despite being taken sneakily. With his picture and his phone number, there must be a way of figuring out if he is who he says he is.

But something is still nagging at me and before I've even put the phone back in my jeans pocket, I realise what it is. I check the back door is locked and climb the stairs two at a time. The door to the bathroom is open, the room empty. The little toilet down the corridor too.

I find Shaun in the master bedroom, his back to me as he pushes the drawer of my bedside table quickly shut.

22

I push the door all the way open, an electric pulse of alarm racing up my spine.

'What are you doing?'

Shaun turns around, straightening up to his full height, hoisting the backpack onto his shoulder.

'Sorry, I just used the en suite instead, I couldn't find the—'

'I mean what were you doing, looking in my bedside drawer?'

'It's not what it looks like,' he says. 'An honest mistake.'

'This is your grandfather's house, right?'

'Yeah.' He nods, once. 'Or it used to be, at least.'

'Visit him often, did you?'

'From time to time, when he was—'

'But you didn't know there was no downstairs toilet.' I cross my arms over my chest. 'You had to ask me where it was.'

The beginnings of a red flush are creeping up from the base of his broad neck. 'It's been a while since I was last here.'

'Why are you lying?'

'Don't know what you're talking about, Adam.'

'You've never been here before, have you?' I feel the tingle of adrenaline in my stomach. 'Who are you? How about you show me some ID?'

The friendly smile slides off his face. 'Told you who I am.'

'Why are you here?'

'Told you that as well.' He hitches the strap of the rucksack higher on his shoulder. 'Collecting some stuff for my grandad.'

'You mean your grandpa?'

His eyes narrow. 'What?'

'A few minutes ago you called him your grandpa,' I say. 'Now you're calling grandad. Which one is it?'

'Both,' he says with an annoyed shrug. 'Either. What does it matter? The point is, you've got his stuff, and I'm here to get it back.'

I shake my head. 'Everything in this house belongs to me now. That's how it works.'

'That's bullshit.'

'No,' I say. 'It's the law.'

'Better for you if you just hand it over, all of it.' He takes a step towards me. 'Trust me on that one.'

I drop my hands to my sides. 'Are you *threatening* me?'

'Better for you, your wife, your kids.'

A ball of hot rage flares in my chest.

'You need to leave,' I say. 'Right *now*.'

He comes closer, tension crackling between us like static electricity, the rapid sluice of adrenaline tingling all the way to my fingertips.

'I don't know who you are,' I say. 'But I want you out of my house.'

He pauses when he's only a foot from my face, his eyes as flat and hard as black pebbles. Close enough for me to see the darkness behind them.

'Whatever,' he says. 'You don't have to be an arsehole about it.'

And then he's brushing past me, the sharp smell of his sweat curdling into the hard citrus of his aftershave, kicking a cardboard box out of his way as he goes. As he turns at the top of the staircase, I notice the knuckles of the hand gripping his backpack strap are white.

'Your bag,' I say, clamping down on my fear now he's walking away. 'Show it to me.'

'What?'

'Show me what's in your bag.'

He starts to descend the stairs. 'Are you having a laugh?'

I grab the blue backpack from behind and wrench it from his shoulder. He tries to keep hold of the strap but he's already on the third step down, off balance, and I have the height advantage now. He turns on the staircase and for a moment he's pulling back against me, pivoting, before he lets go of the strap and grabs the bannister instead.

'What the hell!' He spreads his hands, palms up, but doesn't move back up the stairs towards me. 'You want me to bang you out, mate?'

I unzip the top of the backpack, pulling it fully open and rooting through the contents. Inside is a half-full bottle of Sprite, a phone charging cable, a black baseball cap, an empty plastic Asda bag, a battered pair of sunglasses, a small can of orange spray paint, two screwdrivers and a torch.

In among these contents is the little Motorola flip phone.

I take it out and hold it up to him.

'This just fell into your bag, did it?'

'Screw you.'

Pocketing the phone, I throw the rucksack back to him and he catches it against his chest.

'If I see you again,' I say, 'I'm calling the police.'

'Doubt that,' he says, zipping the bag and swinging it back onto his shoulder. 'Because next time you won't see us coming.'

Jeremy's reply to my text drops in as I'm watching Shaun walk away down the drive.

No, not heard back from Kevin Hopkins yet. Can I help with something?

23

'So who the hell was he?' Jess studies the image on my phone, the surreptitious picture I'd taken of the man who'd called himself Shaun Hopkins. 'And how did he know where we lived?'

I tell her about the afternoon's strange visit as I slice onions for a spaghetti Bolognese supper.

'Said he was the grandson of the previous owner. Seemed quite genuine, at first.'

'And Jeremy had never heard of him?'

'No.'

She hands the phone back to me and crosses her arms tightly over her chest, seeming to fold in on herself.

'But you just let him in anyway?'

'Didn't get Jeremy's text until after he'd left.'

I don't believe Shaun Hopkins is his real name and a Google search throws up five million hits, none of which seem relevant anyway. It was possible that he just didn't have much of an online footprint, I supposed, but it seemed much more likely to be an alias. A fake name to match the previous owner, a bogus story to get him through the door. Or perhaps there *was* some kind of family connection, some distant relative who guessed that old Mr Hopkins would overlook a few expensive trinkets in the house move.

The mobile number Shaun had given me is not recognised.

'He was a fairly young guy,' I say, 'Just standing there at the front door when I pulled up. I was curious to know what he wanted.'

'Sometimes I wish you were a little *less* curious, Adam.'

I let that go without comment. Instead, I take two wine glasses down from the cupboard.

'Glass of red?'

She looks as if she's about to say no, then sighs instead. 'Go on then, just a small one. Do you think we should try the police again?'

I reach for a half-full bottle of Pinot Noir next to the hob, pouring each of us half a glass. 'And tell them what?'

'That this weirdo conned his way into the house and was going through stuff in our bedroom?'

'What would be the actual crime, though?'

'I don't know, Adam. What do they call it, a distraction burglary?' She eyes the wine glass but doesn't touch it. 'And what if he comes back when I'm on my own with the kids? Or if Leah answers the door? What then?'

'We'll just ... be careful, OK? I can work some days from home, I'll be on the lookout. We'll keep the chain on the door.'

She goes to the back door, tries the handle to check that it's locked.

'Was there something in particular he was looking for?'

I open my mouth to reply, to tell her about the watch. But telling her about the Rolex would mean telling her about the jeweller's and the fat envelope of cash I'd sold it for. And going into that would mean explaining *why* I had sold it.

'He didn't really specify,' I say instead, taking carrots from the fridge for dinner. 'Just said there were some family heirlooms with sentimental value.'

I list the things I found in the secret room, leaving out the watch. A sharp prickle of guilt at how easily the half-truth comes to me.

'Oh God,' she says. 'I've just had a thought: what if they're stolen goods, or something? What if they're not even his?'

'You think old Mr Hopkins was some eighty-seven-year-old cat burglar?'

'He wasn't always eighty-seven, was he?'

I put a hand on her arm. 'Listen, if he gets in touch again, we can just tell him we chucked it all out, right? Tell him it's all gone to the tip, everything we've found.'

She says nothing, and won't look at me.

'Jess?' I say. 'It'll be OK. I don't think he's going to come back.'

'I don't like this.' She takes a small sip of her wine, putting the glass back on the counter with a shaky hand. 'Any of it. First the cameras, then the messages, now this stranger turning up. This house was supposed to be a fresh start, a clean slate to make into whatever we wanted, but it's starting to feel like it doesn't even fully belong to us.'

Her voice has gone very soft and I know it's partly to stop the children overhearing our conversation. But it's also because she's unnerved, unsettled by what I've told her about today's visitor. I pull her into a hug, holding her close, the smell of her apple shampoo mingling with the faintest remainder of the smoky perfume she put on this morning.

'It's going to be OK,' I say again. 'We'll figure it out. We've only been here a few days, things will start to settle down soon. I promise. In the meantime we probably need to be careful around strangers.'

'I don't like it,' she says, her head flat against my chest. 'Don't like some weird guy *being* here, in our house, with all our things.'

'He won't come back.' I say it with rather more confidence than I feel. 'And if he does, we just call the police and let them handle it.'

We stand like that for a moment longer, the tension between us softening as the warmth of her body presses against mine. It feels like the first time we've been close in days, with all the rush and bustle of the move, of settling the children into a new house, all the planning and organising and uprooting of our old life to come here. We've had almost no time for each other, just the two of us, and I've missed that. Missed *her*.

When my wife speaks again, her voice is almost a whisper. 'Do you think he was dangerous?'

I think back to the confrontation on the stairs, the look in his eyes when I'd grabbed his rucksack. The threat. *You want me to bang you out, mate?*

'He was . . . hostile,' I say. 'Rather than dangerous.'

'What's the difference?'

'Well, he wasn't happy, but I didn't feel like he was going to take a swing at me.' I stroke her back. 'He was pretty pissed off by the time I got rid of him, but I didn't really think he'd do anything stupid. Felt like it was more for show than anything else, like he was just putting it on to make a point.'

She hugs me a little tighter, her small palms flat against my shoulder blades.

'Maybe you could bag up those things he wanted,' she says, her head still on my chest, 'and put them somewhere, ready to hand over if he turns up at the house again? So we can get rid of him?'

I rub her back. 'Good idea. I'm not going to let anything happen to you or the kids. I'll look after our family. It'll be OK, I promise.'

She looks up, right into my eyes.

'And who's going to look after you?'

24

The house is silent by the time I take my laptop into the lounge. Jess has gone upstairs, most of the lights are off, the animals are fed, front and back doors locked, children in bed. Callum's outfit for Futuristic Day at school tomorrow – a silver-foil-wrapped jacket and bike helmet, plus an old pair of trainers spray-painted metallic grey – is laid out in the dining room after two hours of my wife's painstaking labour.

I pull up Google and type the name 'Shaun Hopkins' into the search bar for the second time today, going through the results more carefully this time. But there is nothing that looks like it might relate to the man who'd turned up at my door this afternoon. Just a lengthy collection of LinkedIn pages, Facebook accounts, businesses and a Wikipedia entry for a nineteenth-century American railroad executive. What was the connection between this stranger and a twenty-three-year-old missing persons case? Shaun Hopkins – or whatever his real name might be – was only mid-twenties himself, maybe a few years older. So he couldn't have been involved in the disappearance of Adrian Parish.

A search using the four words 'Shaun Hopkins Adrian Parish' yields nothing that might point to a connection. Nothing that ties them together. The next hour is lost going down various internet rabbit holes, trying without success to link Sumner

Street in Kimberley to an antique watch engraved with initials, to our address or to any of the other finds in the little hidden room. It was even possible, I supposed, that Adrian had sent the text message: that he was the one who wanted his things returned to him.

I lean back into the sofa, staring at a patch of yellowing Artex that is peeling off the ceiling above the TV. It's already half past eleven but I no longer feel tired.

Kevin Hopkins still hasn't called me back even though Jeremy assures me he's passed on my number. According to Mrs Evans, Kevin had left the UK to work abroad, first to Dubai and then various other places around the world until he had ended up in Spain. She wasn't sure where he was now or exactly what he did – something to do with computers, she thought.

'His overseas jobs were only supposed to be for a few months,' Eileen Evans had told me in hushed tones. 'But the stays kept getting longer and longer until he hardly ever used to come back to visit. So poor Eric was all on his own in this big house for years.' The Google findings on Kevin Hopkins yield similarly slim pickings.

My thoughts return to Shaun. It seemed clear that I didn't have his real name but I *did* have his picture: the quick snap I'd taken earlier. I pull it up on my phone and study the hard planes of his face, dark hair shaved short at the sides, the cobra tattoo emerging from his sleeve. The only problem was, I had no idea what to do with the picture.

I send it to Maxine in case she recognises him – even though it seems like the longest of long shots – and asking if she still wants to meet tomorrow. Then to Jeremy in case he's ever seen the guy hanging around the house while he was doing a viewing, or perhaps he'd even shown him around when it was still on the market, months ago before our offer had even been—

There is a creak from the stairs.

I freeze, thumbs hovering over the phone, staring at the door.

Silence.

I listen, barely breathing.

Quietly, carefully, I move the laptop onto the sofa beside me and stand up, moving to the door as noiselessly as I can.

I stand for a moment longer, ears straining in the silence, heart thudding in my chest. There are only a handful of lights still on and the big high-ceilinged room is deep in shadow.

The creak comes again.

Just the sound of an old wooden staircase, that's all. The sigh of an old house as it cools down for the night.

The hall is empty and there is no one in the dining room. I double-check the French doors are locked anyway. Coco is in the kitchen, curled in her basket by the radiator, snoring quietly in her sleep.

When I flick the landing light on, a figure is illuminated on the stairs.

My son, in his pyjamas, throws a hand up to his face to shield against the sudden brightness.

'Cal?' I say. 'Mate, what are you doing up so late?'

His thick brown hair is sticking up in all directions.

'Can't find him.'

'Who?'

'Mr Stay Puft.'

'He's got out again?'

He nods, still blinking against the light.

'The noises woke me up. Got up to check on him and couldn't see him.'

I move up the stairs and take his small hand in mine. 'Come on, let's find him together.'

From experience of dealing with my kids' 'lost' clothes and 'lost' toys, I look in the most obvious place first. I flick the light on in Callum's room and sure enough, the hamster is still right there in his cage, safe and sound, nestled at the bottom of a large pile of shredded newspaper.

Callum's voice is thick with confusion.

'But I couldn't see him. Thought he'd run off again.'

'He's fine,' I say. 'He's just sleeping. Like you should be.'

I tuck him back into bed, pull his door closed and stand on the landing, listening to the house again.

Everything's OK.

I go back to the lounge to collect my laptop. But instead of shutting it down, I perch on the sofa again and check my phone. I've called the mystery number three more times since Shaun's visit but it went to voicemail every time.

It's well past midnight when Steve appears in the doorway with a small *miaow*, amber eyes blinking sleepily. He stretches his front legs, flexing his claws into the rug, then pads over to me and jumps up, flopping half on me and half onto the keyboard. Any time could be food time on Steve's schedule, if someone was still awake – and now was as good a time as any. I yawn again and rub his tummy idly as he purrs his deep bass purr before I'm interrupted by the electronic *ping* of a message arriving on my phone.

Maxine wants to meet again.

And this time she wants to see everything I found in the hidden room.

25

WEDNESDAY

Daisy wets the bed again that night.

She doesn't scream this time and doesn't mention a ghost when I go to her room to put her in new pyjamas, strip the little single bed and – inevitably – bring her into our bed for the rest of the night. In the morning, when Jess has already left to drop Leah at school and Callum is skidding noisily up and down the hall in his silver-foil astronaut's outfit, I pour milk on her Rice Krispies and ask gently if she had the bad dream again. But she simply frowns and shakes her head, digging into her cereal with an orange plastic spoon.

Hopefully, she's forgotten about the man behind the door.

Back at the house after dropping the two of them at school, I put a pot of coffee on and take a quick shower, digging my best suit out of the wardrobe and printing out a couple of fresh copies of my CV. The job interview is only for a six-month contract but it will keep me going until I find something more permanent. I still have half an hour to kill before I need to head into the city, so I sit at the kitchen table with a fresh cup of coffee and dial 101. Maxine Parish may have given up on the police, but I could give them a try.

Fifteen minutes later, I'm still sitting with the phone pressed to my ear, on-hold music looping round and around as I peer out of the kitchen window at the gap low down in the side fence. I really needed to fix that.

My heart sinks slightly when I eventually establish that the police officer mentioned in the most recent news story about Adrian Parish's disappearance has retired. But no one seems to know who has inherited DC Phil Goode's cases – or what to do with my call. Finally, there is a click and an older female voice comes on the line, introducing herself as DC Tanya Rubin and asking – for the fourth time – about the nature of my enquiry. When I'm finished going through the same spiel about Adrian Parish, the dog collar and where I'd found it, there is a short silence filled only with the faint hubbub of other conversations happening at her end of the line.

'So,' DC Rubin says finally, 'you're calling to report that you've found stolen property?'

'No,' I say. 'It's not stolen, as such, I mean it might be. I found it at my house and I was googling the address and I found out there might be a link to this missing guy.'

'And is the gentleman a relative of yours or a member of your extended family?'

'No, I never met him. Just found him on the internet. But I did go to meet his wife, or ex-wife, or widow or whatever she is.'

There is a moment of silence on the line and I imagine the officer sighing and shaking her head.

'Are you calling to report a criminal offence, sir?'

No,' I say. 'Not exactly. I mean, there may have been. Mr Parish disappeared a while ago.'

'But you're not next of kin?'

'No.'

'Not actually a relative of this individual?'

'No, I'm not but—'

'Sir?' The detective's voice is on the edge of impatience. 'Just to clarify, does this relate to a current or recent incident, to the best of your knowledge?'

'It was a while back, I mean it happened twenty-plus years ago but—'

'Twenty *years*?' she says. 'Sorry I thought you said just now that it was twenty *days* ago.'

'No, it's from . . . a while back.'

In the background at her end, a male voice is calling a name. *Tanya? Where's Tanya?* There is a pause for a minute, the sound muffled as if she's put a hand over the receiver, before she comes back.

A note of exasperation is creeping into her voice. 'So you think this item belonged to Mr Parsons, do you?'

'Parish,' I say. 'Adrian Parish. He lived in Kimberley, he had a dog called Woody and he's a missing person. He's been missing for a while, as I said. I just thought it was curious that this thing turned up in my house and thought I should let the police know, that's all.'

'Do you have any proof that the collar belonged to his dog, or in fact, that this gentleman is still actually missing and unaccounted for?'

'Well, no, not cast-iron proof but I just thought it was something that the police should know about in case it might help to show where he went, what happened to him.'

'Don't take this the wrong way, sir, but are you a person who watches a lot of true crime on Netflix? Would you consider yourself a bit of an expert, something of an amateur investigator, perhaps?'

'No, not really.'

'And do you have any idea how many calls I get from people who think they are? From folks who think they know the job better than we do?'

'I really think there's something more to this,' I say. 'Something that's never been uncovered.'

The sound at her end is muffled again.

'Right,' she says, her tone indicating the conversation is at an end. 'Listen, we're up to our necks in it here and I have to go. But, thanks for getting in touch, someone will look into it.'

She takes my name and number and says someone will call me back, cutting off the call before I can even say goodbye.

26

The interview doesn't go well.

It's one of those where you get a bad vibe right from the moment you walk in, from their body language, their faces as you answer the first question. Where they don't like you as a candidate and you don't really like them either, but both of you have to string it out for at least another half an hour, to do the dance, go through the motions before it can be brought to a merciful end. Even though I know, deep down, that I would snap their hand off if they offered me the role just to be able to sleep at night when the first of those huge mortgage payments slides out of the joint account.

I find a café to drown my sorrows, drinking a strong black coffee as I fire off my CV to another recruitment agency. I have a hefty mortgage and no job, but until something comes along I still have a purpose – a chance to do something meaningful. A chance to help Maxine and her son.

*   *   *

Market Square is a wide open expanse of grey granite bounded by the old Council House to the east and a water feature – its fountains out of action – to the west. All the way around the main square are handsome late nineteenth-century buildings mixed in with ugly grey 1960s blocks that were home to dozens of shops, pubs, bars and restaurants.

I'm a few minutes early, so I take up position in front of the large statue of a reclining lion that flanks the left side of the steps. The left lion is the traditional meeting place for anyone who knows the city even a little, one of a pair of statues that guards the entrance to the council building.

The square is busy, as usual. Office workers eating sandwiches on their lunch break, shoppers laden with bags, a group of teenage skateboarders lounge on the steps next to me, laughing and joking, phones pointed at one of their mates as he tries to flip his board and land on it right side up.

There is a faint but lingering smell of weed on the breeze. A silver-and-green tram winds its way slowly down the hill and around the edge of the square, stopping in front of the Wetherspoons to disgorge passengers onto South Parade.

Just as I'm starting to think Maxine has stood me up, I turn back to find a young man in a black leather jacket making his way towards me. He's in his early twenties, with wild black hair and dark-framed glasses, making steady but careful progress with the aid of a metallic walking stick. He stops in front of me as if sizing me up.

'Adam?' His voice is calm and quite soft.

In person, the resemblance to his mother is even more striking. Perhaps a few inches taller but the same slight build, the same cheekbones, the same dimple in his chin.

'Yes,' I say. 'Hi, you must be . . . Charlie?'

'Yeah.' He extends a hand and we shake. 'Mum says sorry we're late, it was a nightmare finding parking so she dropped me a bit closer.'

'No problem.'

He points across the square. 'There's a little place just off Friar Lane that she likes. She's going to meet us there.'

We make our way down to the café – an old-fashioned place called Stapley's Tea Room – Charlie walking steadily beside me accompanied by the *tap-tap-tap* of his stick on the pavement.

'Cerebral palsy,' he says. 'In case you're wondering. Most people stare but don't want to ask, or they just assume the stick is a fashion accessory.'

'Sorry.'

'For what?' His tone is even, as if this is a conversation he's had many times. 'Mum had me by emergency C-section, cord was wrapped around my neck when I was born.'

Maxine is already at the counter when we arrive, greeting me with a hesitant wave and asking what I'd like to drink before following her son to a table tucked away in the far corner. Only two other tables are occupied, a pair of elderly ladies sipping tea and a couple with a teenage son in the seat by the window. The air is filled with the smells of freshly ground coffee beans and the sharp sweetness of thickly iced cakes on the counter.

I take off my backpack and pull out a chair. Charlie sits down stiffly opposite me, propping his walking stick against the wall and appraising me with careful, intelligent eyes.

'Mum's not stopped talking about you,' he says quietly. 'You're not a wind-up merchant, are you?'

'Absolutely not.'

'You don't look the type.' He pushes his glasses up his nose. 'But then again, it can be hard to tell.'

I start to explain what had led me to his mother's house yesterday when Maxine arrives with the coffees on a tray, setting a cappuccino down on the table in front of me.

'Thanks for coming,' she says. 'Charlie wanted to meet you too, I hope that's OK.'

'Of course.'

She's wearing white jeans and trainers, with a lightweight beige jacket that she makes no move to take off, despite the warmth of the café.

'This is so weird,' she says abruptly, shaking her head. 'Still can't get my head around it.'

'I can't begin to imagine how hard it's been for you.'

'Sorry.' She holds both hands up. 'It's just been so long since we heard anything, like *anything* at all, about Adrian's disappearance. So long since anyone even mentioned him apart from us. I've just got used to having zero expectations, got used to the idea that we're never going to know what happened, where he went or where . . . where he is now.'

'I hope I can help.'

'Sorry,' she says again. 'Had to get that off my chest. I was awake half the night thinking about it.'

Charlie puts a hand on her arm. 'Stop apologising, Mum. It's OK.'

I open my backpack and lay out the other contents of the dresser on the table between us, one by one. The scarf. The wallet. The glasses. The old mobile phone. The single key, two rings looped through the key ring. The dusty little collection looks incongruous in this homely café with its net curtains and doilies on the tables. Maxine doesn't say it, but I know she's hoping to recognise some of these things, hoping the dog collar wasn't a one-off. Because if there is more here that belonged to her husband, more clues, then perhaps she will be one step closer to finding out what happened to him.

One step closer to the truth.

'I don't know if we'll find an answer,' I say, putting the backpack down on the floor. 'But maybe it means we can ask the police questions about your husband again.'

I try to imagine the thread that might connect the Hopkins family to Adrian Parish. They had lived in different parts of the county and presumably moved in different circles. Could the two men have worked together, or had something else in common? Adrian Parish would be in his fifties now, decades younger than Eric Hopkins. Maybe there had been a professional connection through work. Combining their names in a Google search last night hadn't generated anything useful – but it was more than twenty years ago, when the internet was nothing like it was today.

Maxine's eyes flick from one object to the next and back again, a hand covering her mouth as if she's frightened of crying out. After a long moment she reaches out tentatively and begins to pick up each item in turn, starting with the wallet. Holding it gingerly, almost reverently, as if concerned that it might fall to pieces. Studying it from all angles, lifting her glasses to her forehead so she can peer close up.

None of us speak. Charlie rests a protective hand on her back while she goes from one item to the next. He catches my eye for a moment and the message is the same as when we first sat down: *This better not be a wind-up*. I give him a tight smile and turn back to Maxine as she lays the wallet down on the table and picks up the glasses with their cracked lens. The only other sounds in the café are the low background hum of a radio some-where in the kitchen, the occasional *chink* of crockery, the soft murmur of conversation at another table.

Finally, Maxine lays the last item back on the table with a trembling hand.

There are tears streaming down her face. Charlie hands her a napkin.

'What is it, Mum?' he says. 'Did some of this stuff belong to Dad as well? Do you recognise it?'

She tries to speak but at first it comes out in a choking sob.

Instead, she shakes her head.

'I hoped I would,' she says through her tears. 'I prayed that I would. But I don't remember any of this. Not a single thing.'

27

Charlie puts an arm around his mother's shoulders.

'It's OK, Mum. It's all right. It was worth a try.'

Maxine is still shaking her head. She picks up the key again, turns it over, puts it back down. A heavy tear falls from her chin onto the grooved wooden table.

'I thought . . .' She sniffs. 'If all this stuff, all these things were his, it might *mean* something, you know? That he'd gone somewhere, or lived somewhere else after he left me – he'd got tired of me and wanted a clean break, a fresh start or whatever. We had something special, the two of us, but there was always a tiny part of me that hoped he *had* left, that he'd got bored of me and wanted to start a new life. Because it was easier to imagine than the alternative.'

My sympathy for her is tempered by a powerful sense of anti-climax, of discovering more questions without answers. The slumping sensation of another dead end, that all my efforts so far have been for nothing. But I've never liked to admit defeat and it makes me even more determined to help her – and her son.

Charlie pats her arm and gently suggests she drink some of her coffee. She gives him a watery smile and takes a sip of the latte, the cup clasped tightly in both hands.

To me, he says: 'The collar you found, that belonged to Woody? What if the police could, like, analyse it for forensic evidence or something? Might be a clue to finding my dad.'

'That's what I thought, too,' I say. 'Tried speaking to a detect-ive this morning, but she wasn't very interested.'

I describe my call with DC Rubin, an overworked detective with too many cases and not enough time.

Maxine snorts, puts her coffee cup down with a clatter.

'You want to know the police theory at the time, about why Woody was found without a collar?' She cuffs another tear angrily away. 'Their brilliant theory was that Adrian had deliber-ately taken it off because he wanted someone else to take Woody in – that they'd see him wandering without a collar, without an owner, and assume he was a stray in need of a new home. Which is an absolute load of crap. It was then and it still is now.'

It's the most animated she's been since she arrived, a hint of the fire that still smouldered even though she had lost her husband all those years ago. I study her for a moment over my coffee cup, only the low chatter of other customers and the whirr of the coffee machine to fill the silence.

'So there was never a criminal investigation?'

'Adrian was only ever classified as a missing person, which made a massive difference in terms of how much attention he got. The police never elevated it to anything higher, more urgent – and this was before Facebook and all the rest so I didn't have many options to get the word out.' She glances at her son with a sad smile. 'And I was pregnant, of course, then looking after a little one, which made it all the more difficult to keep badgering the police.'

'I'm sure you did all you could,' I say. 'Just sorry I couldn't be more help.'

Charlie has been studying the old Motorola while we've been talking, turning it over in his hand. He holds it up to me now, as if to ask my permission.

'Go ahead,' I say. 'I charged it up. Think it's probably older than you are, though.'

He flicks it open, his face a picture of concentration.

'Wow.' He holds down the power button, a small smile as the screen lights up. 'This thing is *ancient.*'

'Not much on it, unfortunately.'

'What about the people who lived there before you?' He says it without looking up at me, still pressing buttons on the old mobile. 'They couldn't tell you anything about this stuff?'

'The dad's in a care home and the son lives abroad. The estate agent's passed on my number to the son but he's being a bit elusive.'

I pull up the picture of Shaun on my phone but neither of them recognise him. Charlie glances up from the Motorola only long enough to shake his head, before he resumes clicking through the phone's menus.

'So if he wasn't the grandson, who was he?'

'No idea.'

'Nothing flagged on a reverse image search?'

'A reverse what?'

He raises an eyebrow.

'You have *done* that, right?'

'Not . . . sure I know what one of those is.'

He looks at me the way my eldest daughter sometimes does – a mixture of disbelief, pity and amusement. He's a few years older than Leah, but the generational gap still feels like a chasm.

'Really?' he says.

'Really.'

'Well, basically you just upload an image,' he says matter-of-factly, 'and it looks for matches. You can do it on Google or there are a ton of different apps that do the same thing. Works better with specific images of things and places but it's still worth a go with a head-and-shoulders shot. The comparison algorithms are getting better and better all the time with AI.'

Before I can ask him to explain further, he holds the little flip phone out to me.

'Speaking of pictures, what's this?'

The tiny screen shows the picture that Jess had found on the flip phone on Sunday night, the image so blurry and indistinct it might have been a hand, or a thumb, or a face or nothing at all – probably the photo equivalent of a pocket dial.

'Your guess is as good as mine,' I say. 'Impossible to tell on a screen so tiny.'

'There might be *something* there though, if you have a play with the contrast, the saturation, the colours.'

'Yes, but I assumed there was no way of extracting it.' I point at the phone's rudimentary connection ports. 'The phone's not on a network anymore so you can't send it, and there's no USB, no modern connector for a cable, no Bluetooth.'

He gives me that look again.

'There's always a way, Adam, if you know how.' He snaps the phone shut. 'Do you mind if I borrow this for a few days?'

'Sure,' I say. 'Let me know what you find.'

While we've been talking, Maxine has been snapping pictures of all the items laid out on the table in front of us.

'I've got old photo albums at home,' she says. 'From back in the day. Thought I'd go through them and double-check, in case any of these things appear in an old picture somewhere.'

I turn back to her. 'Has anything come back to you? Something ringing a bell?'

She touches the key ring again with a small index finger, tracing the jagged ridges of the key's teeth as if she can tell just by touch whether it belongs in her house.

'I suppose . . . maybe this? I just don't remember. Looks a bit like our front door key, but I can't be sure.'

'Have you changed the locks since it happened?'

'I should have, but it seemed so final.' Her voice is still very small, very low. 'Didn't want him locked out of his own house, it was like admitting to myself that I'd never hear his key in the door again.'

I push the brass key across the table towards her.

'Then you should take it home,' I say. 'See if it fits.'

Carys

Running was pure. It was simplicity. There was no day-to-day, no juggling all of the usual crap that came with everything else. Not having ten things bouncing around inside your head at the same time. With running there was only one thing: don't stop. Keep going. Don't surrender to the burning in your lungs, the iron-heaviness of your legs, don't listen to the little voice in your head that says just take a little rest, give yourself a breather, just for a minute.

Carys knew better than to listen to the little voice.

She also knew it was bad form to stick to the same old route, week after week, however pretty the scenery might be. Even if it was the most accurate way of comparing one time with another. Overall, it was better to get used to novelty, to terrain she'd never seen before. Especially if she was going to have a chance at that ultra-marathon in Norway. The local marathon had been fine, and the Iron Man and the other events, but it was better to challenge herself, to do something different – she would be able to get more in sponsorship for the charity that way. She'd be able to achieve the target she'd set herself by the end of the year, keep the promise she'd made.

She climbed through the stile, up the track towards the big field, the familiar burn in her legs and lungs telling her to keep going, keep pushing. Rolling countryside stretching out below the ridge as she climbed.

Being out here, doing something, anything, was preferable to the helplessness she'd felt as her dad slowly faded away, a spectator to the slow cruelty of a disease as it ravaged his body. That vast bottomless feeling that nothing could be done apart from sitting and waiting for the inevitable. And, most important of all, it was peaceful. The quietest route, especially on a weekday. You might see a few ramblers, the occasional runner, but mostly it was just sheep out here. No ogling teenagers, no catcalling builders, no white van men hooting and shouting disgusting things as she ran by. No idiot ex who wasn't willing to accept that it was over between them.

Out here she was unencumbered, just the key on its key ring zipped inside her pocket, stopwatch running on her wrist, trainers pounding the path. It was pure. Simple.

She nodded to a runner coming the other way, dressed in dark orange and pale green. Something vaguely familiar about the stride, the smile. It would be good to have a pacer, Carys thought. A running buddy to give her that little bit extra motivation when the mornings were cold and dark, like this one.

Someone else who understood the beauty of it all.

28

My phone buzzes twice in my pocket as I'm unclipping Daisy from her booster seat on the drive. Callum is already out of the car and heading for the house ahead of his sister, who scrambles to catch up. His futuristic outfit is in tatters, strips of silver foil hanging from his jacket, but he seems to have had a good time at school, telling me at enthusiastic length on the ride home about a game of tag with his friends during morning break which had ended with Josh being sent to the headteacher's office.

I gather the book bags, swimming bags, coats and pieces of artwork from the back seat and hook them over one arm, digging out my phone with my free hand. The text messages are from Charlie Parish, Maxine's son, the first one letting me know that the key didn't fit any of the doors in their house. The second text has a link to a website called DiscoverImage365 that will do a reverse image search. I click on it and begin to scroll through the instructions, which all look quite straightforward, I just need to upload—

A high-pitched squeal of alarm makes my head jerk up.

Daisy.

I shove the phone into my pocket and run around to find the kids standing either side of the two wide stone steps that lead up to the front door. Daisy has a hand over her mouth, both her and her brother staring at something on the ground between them. As I approach, I get a glimpse of something small and pale on the doorstep, an animal, motionless.

My first thought is, *Steve, please don't let it be Steve, please don't let him have got out of the house, out onto the road where some idiot was driving too fast.*

But it's not Steve.

As I get closer I can make out the plump, inert shape of a large pigeon right by the front door. Lying on its side, wings furled back, claws curled tight. The bird's tiny eyes are half-closed, a darkening of blood across its beak and head.

Daisy takes my hand, her voice trembling.

'What happened to the bird, Daddy?'

She moves as if to touch the small body but I hold onto her.

'I think he just flew into the window, Daze.' I look up at the door, but there's no obvious mark anywhere on the glass. 'Sometimes birds do that. They get confused when they're flying around very fast and they bump into things.'

But even as I say it, I know it doesn't make sense. The glass in the top half of the front door is frosted and coloured in small panels, there's no reflection to confuse a bird in flight. It had happened once or twice before at our old house, but only ever against the French windows which had big panes of clear glass.

A flush of unease rises up from my stomach.

Callum is still transfixed by the sight on his doorstep, as if he's unable to look away.

'Is he . . . asleep?'

'I think he must have had a really big bang on the head, Cal.'

'So can you wake him up?' There is a doubtful note in his voice. 'Daddy? Can we take him inside?'

Daisy tugs at my hand. 'Make the birdie better.'

I bend over and take a closer look at the stricken creature. It's completely motionless, the blood on its beak starting to dry to a dark crimson crust. Even without touching it, I can tell it's beyond help.

'I don't think we should take it inside.'

'Why?' Daisy says. 'Why can't we?'

'Let's all of us go inside first, then I'll take it into the back garden and we'll have a proper look.'

Callum doesn't move.

'Is he dead?' he says simply.

All his exuberance from the car has vanished, replaced by a downward set to his mouth that I normally only see on the football pitch after he's had a bad game. My middle child is normally a cheerful, ebullient sort who doesn't let most things bother him.

'Yes,' I say reluctantly. 'I think he is.'

A tear rolls down Daisy's cheek.

'Why has he died, Daddy?' Her voice wobbles. 'Why did he die on our step?'

I finally get the two of them inside, all of us stepping carefully around the corpse on the doorstep, trying to distract them with TV which is not normally allowed before teatime. But they're still full of questions ten minutes later as I pick up the pigeon in the folds of a plastic bag and carry it around the side of the house to the back garden.

We find a shoebox for the bird, which Daisy insists on lining with tissues, and both children watch as I dig a hole in one of the few flowerbeds that is not thick with weeds, Callum stealing glances at the box as if he still expects the pigeon to rise from the

dead, bursting from its makeshift coffin. Once the box is carefully interred, I push the earth back into the hole and the two
of them gather small white pebbles from the rockery to mark
the spot and arrange them into a lopsided circle in the flattened
patch of flowerbed.

When it's all done I stand up and lean the spade against the
fence. My heart clenches when I see that Daisy is holding her
brother's hand, her little face solemn, the knees of her trousers
muddy from helping him gather stones. She sniffs, cuffing tears
away with the sleeve of her green school jumper.

'Come on, you two.' I take Callum's other hand. 'Let's go inside
and play a game of something. And there's some nice cake in the
kitchen from our lovely new neighbour, Mrs Evans. Who's going
to wash their hands so they can have a slice?'

*   *   *

I cut three slices of sponge cake and hand them each a piece on
a small plastic plate, watching as they tuck in hungrily with bare
hands. I've just taken a bite of my own slice when my phone
starts buzzing with a string of texts landing one after the other. I
take it out of my pocket, assuming it's Charlie to ask whether I've
had any luck with the reverse-image search. But it's not him. It's
from the number we found in the old flip phone.

I click on the message thread, a chill stealing over my skin as
I read each one in turn.

I asked you politely.
You didn't listen.
You know what we want, and how to get it to us.

I reply with the phone gripped tight in my hand.

Stay away from my house.

The blue ticks appear almost immediately, showing that my message has been read. The reply arrives seconds later.

This is your last chance.
Otherwise what happens next will be your fault.

29

'We should go to the police,' Jess says. 'This is harassment.'

She's still in her work clothes – a pale taupe jacket and trousers with a white blouse – as she studies the messages on my phone, index finger scrolling up and down the screen. As soon as she'd walked in the front door, Callum and Daisy had told her in solemn detail about the story of the pigeon and its burial in the back garden. Now Leah plays a game of Hungry Hippos with her two younger siblings in the lounge while Jess and I sit at the kitchen table, our heads close together, talking in low voices.

She hands the phone back to me. 'It's obviously a threat.'

'I've already left a message with the detective I spoke to before, DC Rubin.'

'Feels like we need to do more than that.'

'I know,' I say. 'It's just that . . .'

'What?'

'Whoever sent the text doesn't actually admit to leaving the pigeon, and even if they did, I don't know if that's something the police would act on. I mean, for all anyone can say, that bird might have flown into the window or been killed by a cat.'

She raises her eyebrows.

'You don't really think it was a coincidence, do you? Obviously, it was put there for a reason, hence the texts. A dead bird – it's disgusting.'

'I agree,' I say. 'Just thinking of what the police will probably say.'

'But we could get a restraining order, or something?'

'Against who?'

'There must be *something* more we can do.' She blows out a heavy breath. 'Can they trace the phone number, find out who it is? And what about the evidence, did you take a picture of it?'

'A picture?'

'Of the pigeon.'

I open my mouth to reply, close it again. In between talking to the children about the poor creature, answering their questions about death and digging a makeshift grave in the flowerbed, I have to admit it hadn't occurred to me to take a picture.

'I guess I could dig it up again,' I say. 'But like I said, whether we have a picture or not, it doesn't necessarily prove anything. Unless there is a witness who saw someone on the drive today.'

She gives me a bewildered look, her face lined with worry.

'How can you be so calm? This week is just getting more and more weird, like someone is playing with us, toying with us, and any moment they might decide to do something bad. I don't like it at all.'

'Believe me, I'm as wound up as you are,' I say. 'But I also want to figure out the best way to put all of this behind us.'

My wife traces a line on the grooved surface of the old oak kitchen table, the fingertips of her right hand going back and forth, back and forth. She's silent for a moment, and when she speaks again she won't look at me.

'What if we just . . . gave them what they wanted?'

'Hand everything over, you mean?'

'You know me,' she says. 'I hate bullies. *Hate* them. And I hate the fact that they left a dead animal at our front door when they knew our kids would probably be the first to see it coming home from school. But what if we just . . .' She gives a shrug of resignation. 'What if we let them have what they want? Then do you think they'd go away? Leave us alone?'

It's on the tip of my tongue to confess. To admit that's not an option – because the little collection from the hidden room is now in three different locations. Getting the collar and the key back from Maxine shouldn't be a problem but I can't tell her I sold the watch for cash at a jeweller's shop; can't tell her about the redundancy without piling more worries on her and opening up a whole new can of worms. I can't explain the sense of purpose I've found these last few days, the chance to right a wrong, to do something *good*.

Instead, I take the easy way out, a burn of shame at the base of my throat.

'I think if we give in now, they'll probably be back next week asking for something else.' I put my hand over hers. 'For something more.'

I hate lying to my wife. But I can't tell her the whole truth *just* yet. Instead, I tell her that I'll keep trying DC Rubin until I get through to her, that I'll look into getting a doorbell camera to capture any more visitors to the house, that I'll find out who's behind the threats and make sure the police act on that information. Above all else, I promise that I will keep our family safe. Keep our children safe.

'I'm not going to let anything happen,' I say quietly. 'I promise.'

* * *

It's not until the younger children are tucked up in bed that I get a chance to have a look at the website Charlie Parish recommended. I download the photo of Shaun to my laptop and type in the web address for DiscoverImage365 into the browser. The site advertises itself as the 'premium free search service using the latest AI technology to get the results you want'. Charlie had told me it was one of many such sites that would search the internet for images that match the one I'd taken of Shaun in my kitchen, but it occurs to me that this won't work if Shaun is the kind of person who keeps a low profile, if he's one of those rare people who's managed to keep their face off the internet, despite all the different ways it could turn up there. Still, I guessed people like that were in a small minority nowadays.

The website has a fairly simple interface with a search bar in the top left. I click on it and a prompt box opens asking me to drag an image into it. I select the image I'd snapped of Shaun in my kitchen and click 'Search'. An egg timer appears very briefly before the page fills with results, my original picture on the left side of the screen and a rack of lookalike pictures on the right, all good-looking dark-haired guys who bear a strong resemblance to the man who turned up at my house yesterday. The caption says 'DiscoverImage365 searched over 67.5 billion images in 0.8 seconds for your selected image.'

The results page shows row after row of pictures, mostly head-and-shoulders shots of generically handsome men in their late twenties to mid-forties, all of them looking as if they've emerged from the same corner of the gene pool. There are many, many pictures of Henry Cavill, the Superman actor, along with a selection of other men who share Shaun's strong jaw and short dark hair. I roll down the page quickly. There are hundreds of results.

I take it slowly, row by row and checking each picture in turn. There are other actors featured, plus lots of professional head-shots from business websites, thumbnails from LinkedIn, blogs and articles in languages I don't understand. As I scroll down the page, it keeps on refreshing: there is no end to the results. A few are very close matches, but it's not until I'm a couple of hundred images in before I recognise him.

There.

Half a dozen pictures side by side. Professional shots that look as if they've been taken in a studio. In a couple of them he's smiling with the same confident grin he'd used on the doorstep of my house and I feel a thrum of adrenaline, of success at finding this particular needle in the digital haystack. At the same time there is a quiet pulse of alarm, that feeling you get when you're in unknown waters with your toes stretched towards the bottom, unsure whether you're already out of your depth.

I click on the link and it takes me to a website called Portfo-lioPro, which describes itself as a website for actors and models of all levels looking for professional work.

Got you.

There are more images of him here, including a moody black-and-white one in a T-shirt that clearly shows off the cobra tattoo on the inside of his right wrist. His name is listed as Shaun Rutherford and he describes himself as a semi-professional model and aspiring actor, available for work on an hourly, half-day or daily rate. There is a short bio: 'I am relaxed, easy to get on with and very genuine. I have modelled on and off for 5+ years and am willing to consider all kinds of acting/photographic/advertising work.'

He wasn't related to anyone who had lived in my house. He was an actor, a fake, a cut-out so that someone else could stay in the shadows.

He had been hired to do a job. All I had to do was find out who hired him.

I move the cursor to the button marked 'Book an introductory chat' and begin to type.

30

THURSDAY

Shaun Rutherford is only too keen to meet. I create a profile under the name Anthony Smith on the website's messaging service and we exchange messages over the course of the morning while I sit in a pub by the marina. He waxes lyrical about his professional background while I tell him I have at least three days' work modelling for a clothing retailer and I think he'd be *perfect* for the job.

Dom has already agreed, without needing any persuasion, to be my wingman and joins me at the Canalboat Inn half an hour early so we can talk tactics. He's on nightshifts but has gone home to change into a hoodie, jeans, a puffer jacket that accentuates his already large frame. With his close-cropped hair and beard, the overall effect would be quite intimidating if you didn't know Dom was an absolute sweetheart. At ten minutes to one o'clock, I move across the half-empty saloon bar of the pub and sit in a separate booth. With my back to the door and wearing my old blue baseball cap, I'm hoping Shaun won't recognise me when he walks in.

He's punctual, I'll give him that. He turns up on the dot of 1 p.m. and I recognise him immediately – he's even wearing the same dark bomber jacket as he had on when he came to my house. Dom raises a hand to the visitor, gesturing to Shaun to join him in a booth at the back of the pub and introducing himself as Anthony.

I sit across from them, half hidden behind a copy of the *Racing Post*, listening in as the two men exchange pleasantries. After a minute of small talk, Dom gets up saying he'll go to the bar – our pre-arranged signal – and I stand up at the same moment. But instead of buying the younger man a drink, Dom sits down next to him, trapping him in the booth's window seat and blocking his way out. I slide into the bench seat opposite that my brother-in-law has just vacated.

'What . . .?' Shaun looks from me to Dom, and back again. 'What's going on? Who are you?'

I take off the baseball cap and look him straight in the eyes.

'Hello, Shaun,' I say. 'We met a couple of days ago, remember?'

His expression hardens in recognition, his dark eyes narrowing. He shifts his weight and for a split second I think he's going to kick off, but then Dom turns towards him in his seat, squares his shoulders, puts a large right fist on the table. He gives a single shake of his head. He's spent years working in security, years before that as a bouncer – dealing with every kind of idiot, every drunk full of bravado and every wannabe tough guy – and he knows the best outcome in any confrontation is to *not* have to fight. To convince the other bloke that throwing the first punch would be a very bad idea.

Shaun Rutherford is quick to catch on. He's a big guy but I'm guessing it's muscle built for the gym, for the selfies, for the ladies, rather than for brawling in the back room of a sticky-floored pub.

'We're just going to have a quiet chat,' Dom says softly. 'Just the three of us. No drama.'

'This is bullshit,' Shaun says, moving as if to stand up and climb out over the table. 'I didn't come here for this.'

'Sit.' Dom puts a heavy hand on his shoulder. '*Down.*'

Shaun's eyes flick towards the bar. But most of the customers – and the only member of staff – are around the front of the pub in the lounge bar.

I put my phone on the table between us.

'Who hired you?' I say. 'To come to my house?'

'I'm telling you nothing. That's confidential information.'

'Just give me a name.'

'Screw you.'

'What instructions did he give you?'

'I told you, I'm saying nothing about the client. Or any client for that matter, it's between me and them.'

'Listen, you can either have me asking.' I gesture at Dom. 'Or him. Your choice.'

'You know what?' Shaun moves a hand to his jacket pocket. 'I'm calling the—'

Dom brings his fist down hard on the table, so fast I barely even register it, a flat heavy *crack* that rattles the whole booth and makes Shaun jump visibly back in his seat.

'I say we take him out the back,' Dom says in a gravelly monotone. 'Have a little *chat* in the car park.'

Shaun holds his hand up, shrinking back into the corner of the booth. I remember how he was at my house: potentially threatening but only in a superficial way. It was bluster with nothing behind it.

'OK,' he says. 'OK. Jesus. Whatever. It was just some guy, all right?'

'Who?'

'I don't know. He messaged me on the website, just like you did, said he had a cash job that was short notice and needed sensitive handling. He wanted someone plausible, calm under pressure, good at improv, and I'm like telling him, "Yes, yes, I'm good at all those things." And so he gave me the address and said he needed it done asap. Five hundred quid up front and another five hundred quid if I got the watch and everything else.'

'And what else were you expecting to get?'

Shaun frowns in recollection. 'A . . . wallet, a phone, an old scarf or something? Can't remember the rest but he reckoned it would all be together in one place. Said he lived abroad and he couldn't get to the UK, he didn't want to go through all the formal channels, all the legal stuff, he just wanted to get his grandad's old watch and a few other bits and bobs. Return them to the old boy before the cancer finally got him. Felt like this would be the quickest way to recover his old stuff.'

'And it didn't strike you as a bit odd? A bit cloak-and-dagger?'

He shrugs. 'It was good money. Things have been a bit tight recently, been doing loads of auditions but still waiting to hear back. I've had weirder acting jobs than this, believe me. *Much* weirder. But that's why it's better than a boring nine-to-five.'

'And the client was a man?'

'I mean . . . it was all done on the messaging app on the website. I sent a couple of my showreels with some of my acting work. But I never spoke to them or met them face to face, I just—'

Dom interrupts. 'You know they're stolen goods, right?'

Shaun turns to him.

'What?'

'And by involving you he's made you an accomplice in a criminal activity. Whether you walked away with those stolen goods or not, you're already complicit under the common law doctrine of joint criminal enterprise – each individual being responsible for the crimes committed by the group.'

Dom is freestyling now, making it up as he goes along, but he sounds almost like a police officer and it seems to be working. Shaun's eyes widen in alarm.

'What?'

'He used you. Hung you out to dry.'

'Look, I didn't want to get involved in anything illegal. He said they were family heirlooms but it was never supposed to be—'

'He made you take all the risks, didn't even pay you all the money. You don't owe him any loyalty. You don't owe him anything.'

Shaun's cheeks are flushed beneath his dark beard, his nostrils flaring. But he's nodding, as if he's suddenly seen the truth of his situation.

'The name was Mason,' he says reluctantly. 'That's the name they went by on the website, anyway. Assumed it was a surname but I didn't actually ask.'

'Good,' Dom says. 'That's good. What else did Mason say? Anything unusual about the instructions they gave you?'

'There were a couple of things that struck me as a bit weird.'

I lean toward him, forearms on the table. 'Go on.'

'They said I should try to find out from you exactly where the stuff had been found. Like, *exactly*. I should find out if it was like an attic room or under the floorboards or something, exactly where and which room. They kept banging on about that. I didn't really get it, like why did it matter where they'd been as long as their grandad got them back, right?'

'And what was the other thing?'

'They said there were seven things to get back: the watch, the phone, the wallet and the other stuff I can't remember. Anyway, they were dead specific about it, said I had to get all of them to get the other five hundred quid. It was no good just getting a few. They needed all seven. All or nothing.'

31

I sit at a red traffic light on the way home, the conversation with Shaun still ringing in my head. There had been a strange, surreal intensity to the whole exchange, an undercurrent of tension beneath it all. It feels I've been handed another two pieces of a thousand-piece jigsaw – but I still had no idea where any of the pieces went, or how they might fit together.

And yet those few fragments of information had to mean *something*.

The story he'd been told by 'Mason' was obviously bogus, but as Shaun had said himself: what difference did it make *where* in the house they were found? It didn't seem relevant to anything, apart from maybe satisfying a curiosity. More to the point, why did it matter so much that *all* of the items were recovered, rather than only some of them? Why was that significant, unless Mason was a completist, an all-or-nothing kind of person? If each of them represented one part of a greater whole, then what could that possibly be? The motive for hiring Shaun can't have been financial, because the only thing of any real value was the Rolex. The rest of it would barely merit a second look at the average car-boot sale. The fact that Shaun had been tasked with recovering all seven suggested that they were all equally valuable, in some way. Equally important.

Or perhaps equally dangerous.

As the traffic light turns green, I finally let my thoughts wander in a direction I've resisted up until now – a direction that seemed too outlandish, too fantastical, to merit any serious thought.

A chill creeps over my skin and I shiver despite the warmth of the day.

The key with its distinctive key ring had not belonged to Adrian Parish. His wife – widow? – had not recognised anything apart from the collar and tag that had once, a long time ago, been worn by a beloved family pet.

So if the collar was a link to one missing person, what about the scarf, the glasses, the other odds and ends? What if each of the items I'd discovered in the room had a similar story to tell?

There was something else that Shaun let slip, without even realising it might be significant. Something Mason had said to him.

He said he lived abroad.

What was the old saying about a lie? That all the most convincing lies contained an element of the truth? Because there *was* someone with a direct link to my house, someone who lived abroad. Someone who still hadn't returned my message.

The previous owner's son: Kevin Hopkins.

I arrive at school early to pick up Callum and Daisy, a low-level buzz of worry that I need to be *there* when they emerge into the playground, to be extra-vigilant for strangers lurking around, for anything unusual. While I'm waiting, I call Jeremy and get his voicemail, so I leave a message asking him to pass on my number to Kevin Hopkins again as a matter of urgency.

Pulling up on the drive with the kids in the back, I see with relief there's no nasty surprise left on the doorstep today.

Before we head inside, I shepherd both children around to next door to deliver the thank-you card for Mrs Evans that they'd made the previous night. Normally I'd just take it around myself but I don't want to leave them home alone, even for a few minutes.

The doorbell of number ninety-three is still echoing when the door swings abruptly open. Mrs Evans stands there in a lilac pinny over her grey cashmere jumper and skirt, yellow rubber gloves and a small silver-handled paring knife in her hand.

'Hi,' I say, holding out the envelope. 'This is from the children, a thank-you for the cake.'

She takes it from me, her face expressionless.

'How sweet.' She opens the envelope with a single slash of the knife and pulls out the card, studying the thick strokes of crayon briefly without a twitch of a smile. Daisy has drawn a picture of a cake and five stick people on the front, with Callum adding a few words and both their names inside.

'Lovely,' Mrs Evans says, slotting the card into the pocket of her apron.

The hall behind her is similar to ours, doors off to the sitting room and dining room, second reception room off to the left, straight through to the kitchen at the back. Except the décor in hers looks even older than ours, fading wallpaper, yellowed skirting boards, a large picture of a sailing ship in a dark wooden frame on the wall.

'Looks like you're in the middle of something,' I say, holding a hand up. 'Or do you have a minute?'

'How's your littlest one enjoying school?' She fixes Daisy with an unblinking stare. 'Is she settling into Mrs Pett's class?'

'Yes thanks, she loves it.' I can't remember ever telling my neighbour about Daisy's teacher. 'You . . . know the school, do you?'

'Her jumper. The school crest?' She taps her chest. 'She's what – four and a half?'

'Five at the end of July.'

'But rather small for her age.'

'A little bit.'

'Bright as a button though.' She wipes the blade of the knife on her pinny. 'I know Mrs Pett teaches Reception. I know all the teachers at the school.'

'All the kids seem to love her.'

'Of course they do.'

I give her a tight smile. If she'd had children of her own – and there had been no mention of any – they would have been a long way past primary school age. But Mrs Evans did genuinely seem to be one of those people who had a nose for everyone else's business. An observer, a watcher. A collector of facts.

She has pushed open her front door a little wider and my eye is drawn to a dozen pairs of eyes, all staring at me. On a windowsill at the bottom of her staircase, a line of lifelike dolls are seated in a row, moon-faced and passive, hands folded in their laps. They are horribly real-looking, dressed like small children, glassy eyes staring into nowhere and yet all seeming to focus on me.

'I wanted to ask,' I say, 'did you by chance see anyone come by my house yesterday? Anyone who looked like they might be delivering something, or dropping something off?'

'An *Amazon* person?'

'No,' I say. 'Not a delivery company. Someone else, maybe in a car, or on foot.'

She considers for a moment before shaking her head.

'Did you have a parcel stolen off the doorstep? I've heard about that happening. Scandalous. People just wandering up bold as brass and walking off with them.'

'No, it was . . .' I glance down at Daisy but she's transfixed by the row of dolls on the windowsill. 'There was a pigeon left on the doorstep.'

'Oh.' She looks taken aback. 'That's awful. Could have been that big ginger cat of yours, I suppose?'

'We're not really letting Steve out yet,' I say. 'Until he gets his bearings in the new house. So, you didn't see anyone?'

'Afraid not.'

Callum tugs my hand, a silent message that says, *Dad, can we go now?* I squeeze gently back: *In a minute.*

'There was one other thing,' I say to my neighbour. 'And forgive me for a rather random question, but does the name Adrian Parish mean anything to you?'

She considers me for a moment, unblinking, before giving a single shake of her head.

'Can't say that it does, no. Who was he?'

'I wondered if he might have been a friend of Mr Hopkins.'

'The name doesn't ring any bells, I'm afraid.'

'Doesn't matter, it was just—'

'What makes you think they were friends?'

'Nothing,' I say. 'It's not important.'

The knife is still gripped tightly in her gloved hand, the steel tapering to a razor-sharp point. There is an odd feeling at my shirt collar and it's only after a moment that I realise the small hairs at the back of my neck are standing up. I shift position to look towards my house, through the screen of hedges. I can just make out my car on the drive, an edge of the front door. All quiet.

I take a step back, out of the glassy-eyed view of the creepy dolls.

'Anyway, thanks again for the cake. I'll leave you to it.'

It's only when I'm in back in my kitchen, putting pasta in a pan for the children's tea, that Eileen's words come back to me. *Who was he?* The way she had referred to Adrian Parish in the past tense. Or was that just one of her peculiarities? Perhaps she assumed everything was past tense if it related to my house and its previous owner. I'm mulling over the rest of our conversation when a faint sound reaches me, quickly growing louder, the crunch of gravel on our driveway. Running feet pounding up to the house, nearer and nearer until the crunching is replaced with a desperate hammering on the door – *bang bang bang* – the temporary doorbell chiming at the same time, then more impacts against the wooden frame of the door – *bang bang bang—*

I run to the front door and wrench it open to find Leah, red-faced, panting, hurling herself into the hall and slamming the big front door shut behind her. She lets out a huge sigh and doubles over, hands on her knees from the exertion of running.

The first shot of adrenaline is already thrumming in my chest, my legs, my fists, the need to protect my eldest child and deal with any threat.

'What's the matter?' I put my hands on her thin shoulders, the straps of her school backpack cinched tight. She is shaking with fear. 'Leah, are you OK? What happened?'

It takes her a moment to gather enough breath to speak and her voice, when it finally comes, is broken by a sob.

'Someone was following me.' She's still gasping, pulling in great shuddering breaths. 'Someone in a car followed me home.'

32

'Are you hurt?' I study my daughter for any signs of injury. It's rare to see her so upset and I feel a flare of rage at those responsible. 'Are you all right?'

'I'm OK,' she says. The tears are coming now, fear giving way to shock. 'I'm all right, I ran, they didn't catch me.'

I look out of the window onto the drive. 'What sort of car, Leah? Did you get a good look?'

She gasps out a few words of description. A long car, grey, dirty, old. A foreign make but she doesn't know which one.

'Stay here.' I grab my phone from the hall table. 'Lock the door behind me and don't let anyone in but me, OK? No one else.'

She nods and I wrench the door open, running down my drive towards the street. Adrenaline is racing hard through me now, obliterating rational thought and leaving only the animal desire to confront the threat, to deal with it, to meet it with as much force as was needed to make sure they never came here again. *Fight or flight*. Small stones from the drive jab painfully through my socks, but I barely register the discomfort.

I run into the middle of the street, eyes scanning left, right, left again in search of a grey car. There's little traffic on the estate at this time of day, just a few cars going through the junction further down the hill. *Think*. Access to the Park estate was controlled and only a couple of roads to the north and one to the east would be open at this time of day. I turn left and sprint up the middle of the street towards the roundabout that would take a driver north up to Derby Road, checking every car I can see.

A black Audi going too fast into the junction has to brake to avoid me, honking and swerving rather more dramatically than necessary. I ignore the driver, scanning the three roads leading away from here but there is no grey car that I can see. I run back to the top of my drive and stop, check the front door is still safely shut, then squint into the sun towards the junction at the far end.

There.

A gunmetal-grey Volvo is pulled tight to the kerb, front window down, a ghost of vapour rising from the exhaust.

'Hey!' I move towards it, breaking into a run. *See how you like being pursued, you bastard.* 'Hey you!'

When I'm still twenty metres away, the Volvo pulls away from the kerb and accelerates into the street, engine revving hard, automatic transmission climbing quickly through the gears. I run faster, my lungs starting to burn.

'Stop!' The car's back window is opaque with grime and a layer of dirt obscures half the number plate, the first four characters look like *FP55* or maybe *FP58* but the rest is buried beneath a film of crusted-on mud. The Volvo continues to accelerate and a split-second glimpse of the wing mirror reveals a flash of dark hair and sunglasses. But it's too quick to tell whether it's male or female.

I shout again, legs and arms pumping as I sprint barefoot down the street. 'Stop!'

A van brakes sharply to avoid a collision with the Volvo as it roars through the crossroads without stopping, heading right up the centre of the wide road to increase the distance between us. Finally, I remember the phone in my hand and try to unlock it and select the camera while I'm still running, stopping to snap a shaky picture as the Volvo pulls further away. It disappears around a bend in the road, and is gone.

I stop, hands on my knees, chest heaving as I pant for breath.

All three kids have their faces up against the bay window when I walk back up the drive. Leah has picked Daisy up and is holding her on her hip as she opens the front door.

I make sure the door is double-locked again before pulling my oldest child into a hug.

'You sure you're OK?'

She nods. 'Just . . . yeah. I'm all right. It was horrible.'

Jess calls straight back when I text her, and I spend a few minutes reassuring her that our eldest daughter is shaken but OK. Leah is mature for her age and has always been so good with her brother and sister that I sometimes forgot she's still only sixteen, still a child herself. I'd rather her siblings didn't hear all the details but they both refuse to leave their big sister's side, so we sit together in the kitchen while Leah explains what happened.

She had first seen the car outside school this morning, she says. Her friend Liv had made a comment because it was parked on the yellow zigzag lines near the school gates, where parents were always getting named and shamed by the headteacher for stopping to drop off or pick up. Then she saw the Volvo again at the end of the school day, when she was waiting at the bus stop on Aspley Lane. She normally got the bus home with a friend but today she'd been on her own.

The car was there again when she got off the bus in the middle of the city, she says in a shaky voice.

'It was just waiting across the road,' Leah says. 'I got off the bus on Angel Row and it was in a taxi rank, just sitting there, it looked out of place because all the rest were black cabs. I started walking my usual way home and thought it'd be OK because it's the middle of town and there were loads of people around, right? Then like, ten minutes later, I'm coming up through Castle Gate and I thought he was gone, thought I was OK because I was properly back in The Park. But I'm coming down the hill and I saw it again on a side street as I came past, just sitting there with his engine running.' She wipes a tear away. 'I just freaked, I panicked, thought I was never going to get home. I was thinking about that thing I saw on Netflix the other week about that girl who got abducted off the street and . . .' She tails off, suddenly aware of her two younger siblings staring at her, wide-eyed. 'And so I just started running, and ran all the way home from there.'

It was less than half a mile to our house from that junction, but I could imagine the terror she had felt at being stalked, pursued, with the threat of being cornered and plucked off the street at any moment. Although I didn't have to imagine it – I had seen it on her face when she burst through the door. The fact that this car had been waiting for her on a side road in The Park meant the driver knew the area well, knew there was little passing traffic because access to the estate was limited.

That was one of the upsides of living here – but it also meant the streets were rarely busy. On a quiet Thursday afternoon, there would probably be few pedestrians around.

The perfect place, in fact, to snatch someone without being seen. To bundle them into the back of a car and drive away.

The conclusion is clear, but it still hits me like a kick to the chest: whoever this was, they knew Leah's routine already. They knew her school, they knew which bus she took, they knew her route home from the bus stop to the house. But then why had they pulled over and waited on my street, when Leah had already fled into the house and shut the door behind her? Why had they still been there when I came out to look?

I already know the answer: because they wanted to send me another message.

We know where you live. We can get to your family. Unless you give us what we want.

33

Sitting there at the kitchen table the rage is still burning, a bubble of acid at the base of my throat. But overwhelming the anger there is fear as well, a parent's darkest fear about how vulnerable a sixteen-year-old girl could be, alone on the streets of the city. The raw, undiluted fear of harm coming to those I loved most in the world – and the sense that I might be indirectly responsible.

I squeeze her hand across the kitchen table. 'Are you sure you're all right?'

'Yes, Dad.' She takes a sip of orange squash. 'You can stop asking me that now.'

'What happened to your keys?' I say.

'Don't know,' she says. 'Thought they were in my bag but I couldn't look while I was running. Probably up in my room somewhere.'

'Have you still got that alarm in your schoolbag too?'

She nods. Leah had carried an attack alarm in her school backpack – the same type Jess had in her handbag – for the last few years.

The picture I took out on the street is next to useless. There had been no time to zoom in and the Volvo is a blurry grey smudge turning away on the edge of the shot. Nothing discernible of the driver or any markings on the car, let alone any part of the number plate.

Callum has sat close to his big sister the whole time, holding her hand.

'Why was there a man in his car, Leah?' His voice is uncharacteristically quiet. 'What was he doing?'

'Don't know, Cal,' she says, putting an arm around his small shoulders. 'But it's all OK now, isn't it? Dad's here, and we're all fine.'

'Was he trying to . . . get you?'

'No. Of course not.'

'But you ran.'

'I was just a bit spooked because I kept on seeing the same car, that's all. But there's nothing for you to worry about.'

'I would run,' my son says gravely. 'I would run *so* fast.'

She gives him a squeeze. 'You're a good runner, little man.'

'Will he come back?'

'No chance. Dad will put him on the naughty step if he does.' She gives me a meaningful look. 'Isn't that right, Dad?'

'Absolutely,' I say. 'And then a policeman will take him away and put him in jail.'

I call 101 and give a description of the incident, a call handler taking down the fragment of the number plate I thought I could make out and advising me to call 999 if the car returns. He says they'll try to route some more patrols through the area for the next few days.

Despite Leah's protests, I call her school's main office next to let them know what happened and give them a description of the car.

She's been absorbed in her iPhone for the last fifteen minutes and it's now pinging with new messages from concerned friends every few seconds. I make her toast with Nutella and she picks at it in between rapid two-thumb typing on her mobile, some of her customary teenage nonchalance starting to return.

It could be a one-off, of course. A coincidence that it just *happens* to have taken place within days of discovering the secret room, the hidden cameras. Of making a phone call that first brought a stranger to my door.

But I don't really believe that.

'Leah?' I say. 'How about you stay home tomorrow?'

'GCSE revision classes for maths and English. Can't miss them.'

'How about I pick you up from school?'

She doesn't look up from her phone. 'I'm not nine years old, Dad.'

'Seriously, with what's happened this afternoon, I don't like the idea of you getting the bus again tomorrow.'

'Hannah's back though, I can walk with her again. Her house is only around the corner.'

I shake my head. 'Your mum will drop you in the morning and I'll get you from school at the end of the day.'

'I don't need—'

'Just for tomorrow, then we'll see about what to do next week.' I give her a smile. 'Or I can take a day off, you can stay home and help me with the decorating.'

She blows out a breath. 'Fine.'

Jess gets back early from work and has Leah take her through the whole thing again while I make tea for Callum and Daisy. Then I get in my car and do slow circuits of the neighbourhood, cruising up and down all the nearby streets, looking for the grey Volvo as the last of the daylight fades into dusk. The lights in The Park are the original gas lights which are quaint and authentic but don't throw as much light as regular street lamps. Instead, they give off a kind of half-hearted glow that accentuates the quiet of empty pavements on wide streets, deep shadows thrown by three-storey Victorian houses.

When I get back, Jess gives me a questioning look but I just shake my head.

'I don't like this,' she says, handing me a glass of wine. 'Feels like . . . I don't know.'

'What?'

'This house.'

'What do you mean?'

'Secret cameras, a hidden room, the dead bird on our door-step, some weird guy being paid to come here and try to trick us.' She takes a sip of her own wine. 'Now Leah gets followed home from school. We've not even been here a week.'

'I know. But we'll figure it out. I won't let anything happen to you or the kids.'

'Maybe coming here was a mistake. It's like there's . . .' She is silent for a long moment. 'I don't know. I loved this house right from the first time we saw it. It was our dream home, wasn't it? I loved the character, the architecture, all the little Victorian quirks of the place. I loved the area, the sense of history. But now it feels like there's another side to it. A darker side.'

'You don't believe in haunted houses.'

'It's not that. More like, maybe a feeling that something's just a bit *off* with it.' She runs a hand through her dark hair. 'Like a picture that's slightly out of focus, and you only realise when you look at it really closely.'

'I know what you mean,' I say. 'It's been pretty hard to settle in.'

'Well I'm nowhere *near* settled in.' She shakes her head. 'If anything, quite the opposite.'

Once we've finished our wine and she's headed upstairs to the bedroom, I take out my phone and bring up the text exchange from yesterday. I type a new message, sending it before I've even thought through what I'm going to do next.

I'll talk to you, but leave my family out of this.

Once it's gone I write another, deliberating for a moment before I finally press 'send'.

By the way I gave your number plate to the police.

The replies come back almost straightaway, three messages dropping in one after the other.

Your daughter is very pretty
You know what we want. And you know how to make this
go away
Otherwise this is just the start

34

FRIDAY

Jess wants to keep Leah off school the next morning.

Daisy doesn't want to go in either.

And Callum is very much against the idea that he should be the only one to spend the day in a classroom.

In the event – after a short period of confusion, arguing and general disruption to the morning schedule – all three of them go to school as normal. Jess drops Leah, promising to watch her right to the school gate, and I do the run to St Jude's Primary.

There is a dull ache low in my chest as I watch Daisy join a line of other four- and five-year-olds filing into the Reception classroom. Mrs Pett stands smiling by the door, as she always does, greeting each child by name and giving out the unspoken message to the parents who are lingering just a little too long: *You can go. Your child will be fine. I've got it from here.*

There's no danger, I tell myself. Not while they're here. This is a good school, a safe place surrounded by a seven-foot steel fence, and the staff know what they're doing.

I walk Callum around to the junior school side, waiting and watching until he's safely through the door. On the way back, I take my time, checking the long rows of tightly parked cars for any sign of the grey Volvo, studying the individuals hurrying back to their cars on the way to the office or the motorway. Checking the knots of stay-at-home parents too, the ones in less of a hurry to get on with the rest of their day. *That's me now*, I realise with a twinge of recognition. For the first time since the week of paternity leave I'd taken after Daisy's birth, I'm a stay-at-home parent too. Even if I can't quite bring myself to admit it to my wife yet.

There's no grey Volvo and no one who looks especially out of place.

But there is a police patrol car parked outside my house when I get home.

Two uniformed officers are knocking on my front door as I pull onto the drive. There is a sick plunge of alarm in my stomach as I imagine they're here to give me bad news – that there's been an accident, a crash, that Leah and Jess are in the hospital after the threat of last night's message. *What comes next will be all your fault* . . .

'Mr Wylie?' the younger officer says.

'Is everything all right?' I say as I get out of the car. 'Has something happened?'

The older one, trim and wiry, with a strands of grey in his neat beard, holds up a calming hand.

'Everything's fine, sir. We were in the neighbourhood, hoping to have a quick chat about yesterday.'

I feel myself relax slightly as he introduces himself as Sergeant Goodridge and his younger colleague as PC James. Both of them are bulky with stab vests, radios, pouches, pockets and equipment on their belts. PC James is younger, fresh-faced, at least six foot three and built like a rugby player.

I show them into the lounge, offering tea which they both decline in favour of water.

'So,' Goodridge says, perching on the edge of the sofa. 'You reported an incident yesterday involving your daughter?'

He takes notes in a small pad as I run through the events of yesterday, from Leah initially noticing the car waiting outside her school, to its appearance three more times on her journey home and her headlong dash for the house. He frowns when I relate my own dash out into the street in an effort to track down the Volvo.

'As a rule,' he says evenly, 'we'd generally advise you to lock your doors, stay inside with your family and call us first in that kind of situation – if it should ever happen again. Rather than running out into the street seeking out a confrontation with someone who may or may not have committed a criminal offence.'

'He followed her home,' I say. 'There's no "may" about it. And I wasn't looking for a confrontation.'

'So what *were* you looking for?'

'To see who it was, see if he was still there. Get a look at him.'

'And did you?'

'No.'

'How about the number plate?'

I describe the part of the car registration plate that I thought I'd seen as he writes it in his notebook.

'I get it,' he says. 'Your daughter was upset. You wanted to scare this person off.'

'If I had to, yes.'

He takes a sip from his glass of water. 'I understand that. But if there's no immediate threat to you or your family, you're always – *always* – going to be better off dialling three nines and letting us handle it.' He scribbles something else in his notebook. 'Now, is there any reason why you think this person might have targeted your daughter in particular?'

I show him the string of text messages on my phone, the warning that *This is just the start.*

'Can you trace the number? Find out who it is, stop them harassing my family?'

Goodridge turns to his colleague. 'PC James, do you want to answer that one?'

The younger officer sits up a little straighter, clearing his throat. 'In dealing with a suspect in a serious crime,' he says, 'that is, a crime punishable by imprisonment, the police can apply under the Investigatory Powers Act 2016 to obtain information from an individual's phone. They have to apply for this authorisation from a judge or a senior police officer, demonstrating sufficient grounds to justify such a method of investigation.'

He sounds like he's reading from a manual, something recently memorised as part of his training.

Goodridge gives him a nod of approval. 'Very good, Michael.'

I look from the young PC to his sergeant.

'So, you're saying you can't actually do anything? You can't trace this number, go and talk to them?'

'Correct,' Goodridge says. 'Not unless there is a threat to life or a serious crime, or if there are genuine concerns for the safety of a missing person.'

'My sixteen-year-old daughter being followed home from school is pretty bloody serious.'

'I understand your concerns, Mr Wylie, but I'm afraid it just doesn't meet the threshold of serious criminal activity. There's also no clear evidence to link the appearance of this vehicle to the text messages you've received.'

'But *obviously* they're linked, it stands to reason that—'

'They might be, sir, but they could simply be coincidental.' He points at my phone with his pen as if to shut down any further questions. 'So you don't actually know this person, you've never met them?'

'No,' I say quietly. 'He thinks there is something in the house that belongs to him, is demanding I return it.'

Goodridge frowns wearily, as if he's seen this kind of neighbourhood dispute a million times before, a squabble that starts small and gets more and more rancorous until no one can even remember why it began in the first place.

'And that's not something you'd consider doing, just to bring this . . . dispute to an end?'

'It's not a dispute,' I say. 'It's malicious and threatening behaviour by someone who knows where I live, where my kids go to school. Have you've spoken to your colleague DC Rubin?' When he shakes his head, I start to tell him about the dog collar, about Maxine Parish and her missing husband Adrian, the cameras I'd found and the visit from Shaun Rutherford. But it's too nebulous, too difficult to form the narrative into some kind of recognisable shape, the story sounding garbled and incoherent even to my own ears. I grind to a halt before I get to the end.

Goodridge checks his watch. He's already stopped taking notes. 'You called in to report this as well, did you?'

'A couple of days ago,' I say. 'DC Rubin said someone was going to look into it and call me back, but they haven't so far.'

He exchanges a sidelong glance with his partner, slipping the notebook back into a pouch on his stab vest.

'I'll pick it up with her.' He signals to the young constable and both men stand up. 'We'll route some extra patrols through The Park in the next few days, OK? In the meantime, call us straightaway if you see that car again. Don't go running after it yourself.'

The two officers are already moving into the hall, putting their helmets back on. I pull open the front door and thank them for coming by.

'Nice house,' PC James says as he steps out onto the drive. 'Thanks for the water.'

I stand in the doorway, watching them crunch across the gravel as they hurry back to their patrol car. Heading off to the next call, the next incident, the next dispute or domestic or public disturbance. The unceasing demands of a busy city on a police force already stretched far too thin.

It was on *me* to fix this, to deal with the situation and the threat to my family, however unpalatable the solution might be.

Because I knew what I had to do.

35

I call Maxine on my way into town and leave a message to say I'm going to need the collar and the flip phone back as soon as possible. I park in the multi-storey at Trinity Square and head down to street level, stopping at the bank on the way to withdraw the cash I deposited only a few days ago. It's already depleted from the first mortgage payment and I have to supplement it from what little remains in my savings account, standing at the same counter as the clerk counts out a thick stack of fifty-pound notes.

I'm the only customer at Silverjoy. The owner buzzes me through the heavy front door into the shop, blinking up at me over the top of her glasses. I greet her with a smiling hello as she locks one of the glass display cabinets beneath the counter.

'I was here on Monday,' I say. 'You bought a wristwatch from me.'

She gives a careful nod of recognition. 'What can I do for you today, sir? I have a couple of very nice Tag watches just over there in the window, very reasonably priced and tend to hold their value very well. Or perhaps some earrings for your wife? Birthday, is it? Anniversary?'

'No, nothing like that.' I rub my chin. 'Actually it's about the same watch.'

'Ah, yes. The Rolex?'

'That's right.'

'A very nice piece.'

'The thing is,' I say, 'I'd like to buy it back.'

She cocks her head slightly to one side. 'I'm sorry?'

I take the paperwork from my pocket, unfolding the receipt and the pink carbon copy she'd handed to me four days ago, and laying them both on the counter.

'This watch.' I tap the receipt. 'I need it back. I have the money, I'll pay the same price. Cash or credit card, whatever you prefer.'

'Ah,' she says again. 'I see. I'm afraid that's not going to be possible, sir.'

'I know it's a strange request, but it's very important that I get the watch back. Can't really explain why but it has to be that one.'

'I understand, sir. It was a very nice piece.'

'Selling it was . . . a mistake, as it turns out.' I can sense her hesitation. 'How about the same price I sold it for plus five per cent on top? That's an extra two hundred pounds for your trouble.'

'It's not a matter of price. That piece is not for sale.'

'Why not?'

'Because it's no longer in stock. Another customer bought it, a few days after you came in.'

My stomach drops. *Shit.*

'But I thought . . . I didn't realise it would sell so quickly, at that price.'

'Some customers just know what they want.' She indicates a display case to her left with rows of watches inside, small paper price tags attached to each. 'I have some other pieces that are quite similar in style and design, or I could source—'

'I don't want another watch, it has to be *that* one. I have to get it back. Who bought it from you?'

Her eyes narrow. 'A customer.'

I try to remember our conversation from this time last week. Had there been a hint that an off-the-books deal could be done, that there might be a negotiation to be started here?

'Was the buyer a man or a woman?' I say. 'Old, young?'

'That's not information I can—'

'I could make them an offer for it, if you can put us in contact.'

She stiffens. 'Obviously, sir, I can't divulge personal customer information.'

I glance over my shoulder, to check no one's about to walk in behind me.

'Look, I could pay you instead.' I tap the pink carbon copy on the counter again. 'Just let me have a glance at your sales records for ten seconds, you must have a name, address or phone number, right? And I'll give you that two hundred pounds right now.'

'I can't help you.'

I take my wallet from my jeans pocket. 'Three hundred?'

She glances up at the wall-mounted camera covering this side of the shop.

'Are you trying to entrap me, sir?'

'What?' I shake my head. 'No. I just have to get that watch back. It's really, *really* important. For family reasons.' I try to judge how much I should tell her; how honest I should be. But it seems I have nothing to lose. 'The truth is, there's been a . . . misunderstanding and there's someone else who thinks it belongs to them. They've started to get nasty. Making threats unless I return it.'

Her face softens with concern.

'In that case you should go to the police.'

'I've tried that already. They said there wasn't much they could do, hence why I've come back here.'

She peers at me over the half-moon glasses, a hint of warmth in her eyes.

'Perhaps,' she says finally, 'you could leave your number with me? I'll drop a message to the buyer, pass on your details. Leave it up to him as to whether he gets in touch.'

'Thank you.' I scribble my number on the back of a receipt. 'I really appreciate it.'

'Obviously I can't make any promises,' she says. 'But you never know. Perhaps he might be willing to come to an arrangement.'

36

Leah's school day ends at 2.30 p.m. but I get there forty minutes early. Bluecoat Academy sits beside the ring road, and I pull off the dual carriageway to circle the school site a couple of times slowly looking for a grey Volvo parked up anywhere nearby. There is no sign of it.

I replay my conversation with the jeweller. Whoever had bought the watch probably wouldn't sell it back to another shop – there was more margin to be made by selling it online. I buzz the windows down and spend fifteen minutes trawling eBay, Facebook Marketplace and a few other sales sites in the hope it might already be for sale, but there is nothing even similar to the Rolex being advertised by a local seller.

If they even wanted to sell.

As per Leah's request, I wait on a side street off Aspley Lane, in sight of the school's main entrance but not too close. Also as agreed, I stay in the car and don't do anything to draw attention to myself. *No waving, Dad, no shouting and definitely no hugging.* The digital clock on the dashboard ticks past two thirty and I watch as grey-uniformed pupils start to stream out of the gates, Leah among them. She gets into the passenger side, sliding down in her seat as if she doesn't want to be seen. I start the engine and pull up to the junction. 'Hey, Leah. How was your day?'

'Terrible,' she says, yanking her seat belt down. 'The head of Year Eleven made a big thing of what happened yesterday during full-year assembly, warning everyone to "be vigilant" and "walk with a friend if possible" and "report anything suspicious". Oh my God, it was *so* embarrassing. I nearly died.'

'She mentioned your name?'

'No, of course not. But everyone knew it was me by the end of first break. *So* cringe. Like when they used to bang on about "stranger danger" all the time back in primary school.'

It's only five minutes later, after I've turned right off the ring road – away from the city, away from home – that she seems to sense even without paying attention that we've deviated from the normal route. She glances up from the screen, the smile fading from her face.

'Why are you going the wrong way, Dad?'

I mumble something about roadworks on the direct route home and not wanting to get stuck in a traffic jam. After a moment, she goes back to Snapchat, thumbs flying over the screen of her mobile as she reads, replies, responds to a string of messages.

I don't tell her about the grey car I've spotted in the rear-view mirror.

It slid into the lane behind us a couple of minutes before and has been keeping pace in the stop-start traffic ever since. Only shifting lanes when I do, keeping at least three other cars between us the whole time. Not speeding up to pass or turning off, flashes of grey just about visible in my rear-view mirror.

The grey car follows me all the way around the double round-about at Crown Island, still steady behind me as I embark on the little detour but never close enough for me to get a good look at the driver. I'll take the long way around Wollaton Park, all the way around and back to this junction – a full circle that won't make any sense except if the grey car *is* actually following me.

In fact, I can do better than that. I drop down to third gear and slow my speed to twenty miles per hour, waving an arm out of the window for the white van behind to overtake. Gripping the wheel a little tighter with my left hand as the van driver comes close, flashes his lights, honks his horn then pulls out in a roar of exhaust and comes past me to flash through an orange traffic light on Wollaton Road. If I can get the grey car close enough, I can make a note of the number plate and get a proper look at the driver. For a strange moment I wonder whether it might be Maxine or Charlie behind the wheel. But that wouldn't make any sense.

The light turns green and I slowly pull away, keeping my speed down and waving for a black SUV to pass me. I flick my hazard lights on for good measure, but he has to wait for a break in traffic before he can overtake. Only two cars now.

Leah glances up from her phone again. 'What are you doing, Dad?'

'Detour.'

'No,' she says, 'I mean, why have you got your hazards on?'

'The engine's making a funny noise.'

She listens for a moment. 'Is it?'

I don't want to freak her out. 'Thought there was a knocking noise in third gear.'

'I can't hear anything.' She looks over her shoulder at the heavy grille of the pickup truck filling the back window. 'That guy's *very* close and he's, like, shouting something.'

The pickup truck finally pulls out and overtakes in an angry burst of acceleration, but in the same moment the grey car behind him turns off to the right, cutting through a line of traffic as my mirror is obscured by the bulk of the pickup passing on my right-hand side.

By the time my mirrors are clear, the street behind me is empty. The grey car is disappearing down a side road onto a housing estate, the tail end just visible for a split second before it's gone. I'm not even sure it was a Volvo estate after all.

Leah looks at me as if I'm losing the plot. 'OK, well, that was weird.'

'You're right,' I say. 'The engine seems all right now.'

'Where even *are* we?'

'Wollaton.' I switch the hazards off and accelerate back up to the speed limit. 'Home in ten minutes.'

My daughter shakes her head and we pass the rest of the journey in silence.

At home, she heads straight up to her bedroom and I go into the lounge, peering through the front window at traffic passing on the street. But it's mid-afternoon and there are very few cars; no grey Volvos in any case.

My phone chirps with a notification on WhatsApp – two messages from Charlie Parish. The first one is a voice note.

'OK,' he says, his recorded voice is quick and precise, older sounding than when I'd met him in person. 'So, I've been playing around with that photo, the one in the memory of the old flip phone? I managed to extract it and download it to my Mac, and I've been doing some work on it to enhance the detail, sharpen it up, brighten it, remove the noise and so on. I've got some software that uses an AI algorithm for resolution upscaling, which is kind of like filling in the blanks and making it better than the original. Basically, it's the best software there is.' He pauses, a few seconds of dead air on the recording. 'Anyway, I don't . . . quite know what to make of the picture, but have a look and see what you think. Give me or Mum a call back, yeah?'

The second message is an image without a caption. I tap the display to blow it up to full-screen size. It's recognisable as the blurred picture Jess had discovered on the Motorola on Sunday evening. But whereas before it had been tiny, like looking through frosted glass at something that *might* have been a hand or a thumb or the side of someone's face, now it's bigger and sharper and much clearer, clean lines and distinct shapes.

I pinch the image to blow it up, zooming in closer.

The skin that's visible is ivory pale, the thin blue line of a vein threading through it. It's not a hand, not quite. It's the underside of a wrist – two wrists – one laid on top of the other.

Binding the wrists tightly together is a purple-checked scarf.

Sian

She couldn't sleep. She'd dropped off for maybe an hour or two after the usual shouting and screaming and door slamming had blown itself out. But in truth she hadn't really slept properly, deeply, in months – it was hard when she always listening for Colin's heavy tread as he crossed the landing, the squeak of her door swinging open, his rough hands reaching for her in the darkness. It was the reason she'd started to go to bed fully clothed, to make it just that little bit more difficult for him at one or two or three o'clock in the morning when he crept out of the main bedroom and came look-ing for her instead, the air around him thick with the cloying stink of rum and sweat and expectation.

Today, there was another reason for sleeping in her clothes.

Today was going to be different: the first good day in a long time.

Silently, she pulled off the blanket and sat up, swinging her legs out of bed. She unplugged her phone from the charger, bundled up the cable and stashed it in her backpack. The little Nokia's cracked screen said it was 4:04 a.m. Still a couple of hours of darkness left. She wouldn't make the same mistake as last time, or the time before that, she would be long gone before they realised she wasn't in bed, before the call from the college truancy officer, before either of them emerged in search of a fresh bottle.

Sian crept down the stairs, taking care to avoid the creaky third step from the bottom. She pulled on her Reeboks, the old size fours as familiar as a best friend, slid her arms into the sleeves of her denim jacket and looped her favourite purple-checked scarf once around her neck. Reached for her key on the windowsill and stopped, pulled her hand back when she remembered: she wouldn't need the key anymore. She wasn't coming back. She would walk out of this house and by the time the sun came up she'd be on her way to London. To a new life. Any life had to be better than this one.

The only thing she'd miss about this place was currently scratching at the kitchen door. She opened it and Samson blinked up at her with his yellow-gold eyes, winding his way between her legs with his tail held high. Sian knelt down and buried her face in his fluffy tabby fur, kissing the top of his head and whispering her goodbyes. Telling herself not to cry, not now. She found a half-full box of Whiskas amid the chaos of the kitchen table and poured some into his bowl, the tomcat eating and purring at the same time.

Out on the street, the air was frosty with cold and sharp enough to take her breath away. She used the cut-through down past the corner shop, hooked left and in a few minutes she was out on the footpath beside the A52. She turned right and started walking towards Radcliffe-on-Trent, the little backpack bouncing with every step, her breath steaming in the chill of a dark January morning.

It was too early for the buses to run, and besides, the little spare money she had in the pocket of her jeans was better spent on a bacon cob at the station in town. She would buy it from the kiosk and eat it when the coach left, when she was on her way. There wasn't much traffic around, but she crossed to the other side and stuck her thumb out anyway at the first sound of an approaching car. It passed her without slowing, headlights blazing on full beam.

A second car droned by a minute later, then a speeding lorry that passed so close she was buffeted by a backwash of diesel-tainted pre-dawn air. She pulled the scarf a little closer around her neck and picked up her pace. Sooner or later, someone would stop; some city-bound driver would pull over and give her a lift.

She stuck out her thumb again as more headlights approached.

Sure enough, this car began to slow as it passed her, engine tone shifting down through the gears, its indicator blazing bright amber in the darkness. The car – something dark and nondescript with a smiley face sticker in the back window – pulled to a stop ten metres in front of her.

Sian smiled as she walked quickly towards it.

Today was going to be a good day after all.

37

The scarf lies folded on top of the dresser.

I don't want to touch it. Not now.

Instead I hold my phone next to it, the image filling the screen, comparing the pattern.

Could it be the scarf in this picture? The colours were faded, the wool frayed with time, the pattern distorted in the picture because of how tightly it had been tied around the wrists . . .

I shiver.

It *looked* the same.

Jesus. Who was this person in the picture, with their hands tied behind their back? For a moment I wonder if it's Adrian Parish but the wrists look too slender, too feminine. Almost childlike. If not him, then who – and had they suffered the same fate? Of course there were probably thousands of scarves just like this one, it was mass-produced and it could just be a coincidence that it looked like the one in the photo.

But things have already gone too far to write this off as a coincidence.

My thoughts spin back to the conversation with Shaun Rutherford, and the instructions he'd been given about the items he was supposed to recover from my house. *It was no good just getting a few. They needed all seven. All or nothing.*

I send Charlie a message of thanks, adding that the scarf looks like a match.

The photo feels important and the fact that we'd nearly missed it lodges like a splinter under my skin – the knowledge that we had all but dismissed this picture, had not tried to download it or understand what it meant, and it was only through Charlie's interest and expertise that we could see it for what it was. It had almost passed us by.

Which begs the question: if we had missed this, what *else* had we missed?

I reach out a hand, find the smooth, solid wooden surface of the dresser. Let my fingertips trace the front, the small metal handles of each drawer, one below the next. Was there something else here? Something that I had overlooked on that busy first day when I'd discovered the room, had failed to notice in the days since?

The key to the drawers had been artfully hidden in the back of the dresser itself, laid in a small groove of chiselled-out wood that was invisible until I'd pulled the whole thing away from the wall. I do the same thing again now, heaving the dresser forward into the middle of the small room, so I can see behind it. Perhaps there was something else here, another secret that this place had yet to give up.

I use my phone torch to examine the back, hunting for any other flaws or inconsistencies in the frame, any panels or gaps that might hide something else. But there is only old, dark wood, musty with age. Next, I move around to the front and pull out all of the drawers individually, examining the undersides of each one and feeling for any gaps or panels that I'd not noticed before. On my knees, I shine the torch into each of the cavities in the dresser, illuminating every angle, reaching for anything else that might be secreted in the bowels of this thing.

Nothing.

I stand and look around the small space, feeling the walls, the thick felt tacked to the ceiling. But it's all secure, nailed tight, as thick and robust as the day it was put up. The fabric of the old armchair is tired but unbroken, with no holes or openings where something else might be hidden. The little side table beside it is plain and without drawers or decoration.

No. If there was anything else here, it would be in the dresser like everything else. It *had* to be.

There are still a handful of tools here from moving-in day, the chisel, the broken screwdriver and the crowbar lying abandoned under the armchair. I pick up the crowbar and heft it in my hand, a serious weight of solid steel flattening to a half-inch blade at each end like an oversized screwdriver. It would be easy enough to work the blade between the wooden joints of the dresser and wrench as hard as I could, pulling the sections apart piece by piece, rending and smashing the whole bloody thing until it surrendered any last secrets it still retained. I fit the sharp end of the crowbar into a small gap in the frame and get ready to put my weight into it.

The sight of the purple-checked scarf makes me pause. The image of bound hands is still vivid and it has changed things in a way I don't yet want to admit – and don't even understand. I heft the crowbar again, and stop. I *could* destroy the dresser, but what else might I destroy in the process? Might it be important in itself, in the same way as the items I'd found within it?

This was ridiculous. I didn't even know what I was looking for. I sit back heavily on the armchair and toss the crowbar into a corner in disgust.

It lands on the rug with a strange *thud*.

A weirdly hollow sound in this noise-deadened room.

I turn my phone torch towards it, towards the corner, where you couldn't stand up straight because of the slope of the roof. Where you wouldn't have any reason to stand because you'd be bent over to avoid banging your head.

I scoot over on my hands and knees, then move the crowbar out of the way and feel for the edge of the rug, pulling it up where it tucks into the wall. Pulling the heavy woven fabric towards me, coughing as a cloud of dust rises into my face. My phone torch illuminates the old oak floorboards beneath the rug, the wooden planks perfectly flat and straight, tight up against each other.

All except one.

Right in the corner, one six-inch section of the floorboards is not quite flush with the one next to it. I shine the light closer and the joins are more visible, the wood cut neatly through just before it met the wall. I grab the broken screwdriver and work the end gently into the join, moving it back and forth until the section of wood starts to lift free of the rest. It comes out cleanly to reveal a small cavity beneath, a few inches deep and lined with thick plastic. Inside the cavity is a rectangular tobacco tin, the old-fashioned kind with a picture of a bearded sailor on the front. *Player's Navy Cut Cigarettes*. I ease the lid up and it comes off easily, as if untouched by the passing of the years. Inside is a black Bic lighter, the stub of a pencil and a half-empty box of Swan Vesta matches. The lighter sparks but there's no flame; I guess the fuel evaporated long ago.

Beneath the tin is a bed of fine, dark ash. Something else, too.

A half-burned piece of notepaper.

38

What remains of the paper is bone dry, creases set hard with age where it's been crumpled into a ball, almost as if it will crack into pieces as I flatten it out. It may have been white once but now it's jaundiced with age like some ancient manuscript that's not seen the light of day for centuries. The bottom half is gone, the edge browned and uneven, consumed by some long-ago flame. On what remains of the paper, scribbles of black pencil are faded but still legible, a line drawn down the centre of the page with a heading written on each side, underlined.

My hopes are dashed when I scan the text: I can't understand a word of it. The heading on the left reads: *Yziild*. On the right of the line is *Kzipvi*. Below each of them, more jumbled letters, five on one side of the page but only three on the other above the scorched edge of the paper. I run my eye down the first entries in the left-hand column, trying to discern any kind of pattern or meaning.

xlmurin nvvgrmt
olxzgrlm
zxxvhh

A foreign language? The placement of vowels and conson-ants seemed too haphazard. It looks more like some kind of encryption. I take the paper downstairs and set to work at my laptop on the kitchen table.

Perhaps they're anagrams? On an A4 pad I write out both headings, playing about with the letters and putting them in a different order. But none of them look plausible, and there are too many of the letters V, Z and H for them to be real words. Putting each of the headings into Google yields a result I'm not sure I've seen before: *It looks like there aren't many great matches for your search.* The search engine throws up some random brand names and foreign words that aren't exact matches. I try some of the other words with the same result. I'm so absorbed in the search that I don't even hear anyone else in the house until I sense the movement of air behind me. I flinch and turn.

'Leah, you made me jump . . .'

It's not my daughter.

Helena, the cleaner, stands in the kitchen doorway with a mop and bucket in her Marigold-gloved hands.

'Sorry,' she says calmly. 'Did I startle you?'

'No, it's fine.' I give her a tight smile. 'Just thought you were my eldest.'

'I was upstairs,' she says. 'Doing the bathrooms. Didn't realise you were home.'

That makes two of us, I think. An idea occurs to me. 'Actually, I was wondering about something: my wife said you used to work for Mr Hopkins?'

She nods, moving past me towards the sink. A faint trace of cigarette smoke rises from her housecoat.

'Ten years or more.'

'I would have liked to talk to him about the house, it's such an amazing old place. So much history.'

'It's good to have a family here again with young children. Nice for Daisy and Callum to have some space too, I imagine.'

There is a flutter of unease in my stomach at how easily this stranger throws in the names of my two youngest children, but I try to keep my tone to one of casual interest.

'Did Mr Hopkins do much renovation work, do you know? Rebuilding or . . . remodelling?'

'He never wanted to change it, not after his wife passed.' She empties the mop bucket into the sink. 'After she died he wanted to keep it all the same. Keep it how it was when she was alive.'

'Of course.' I close my laptop. 'So he didn't make changes to the layout, as far as you know? Didn't alter the floorplan of any rooms?'

Her eyes narrow slightly. 'Which room?'

'Any of them.'

'You mean one of the bedrooms?'

I shrug. 'Bedrooms, reception rooms, dining room, kitchen. Curious about all of it, really.'

'As far as I know he didn't touch the house after Janet passed on, God rest her. Never wanted to change anything.'

'This is going to sound a bit random, but I don't suppose he ever mentioned someone called Adrian Parish? A friend, perhaps? Colleague?'

Something passes quickly across her face but it's gone before I can identify it.

'He didn't talk about his friends to me,' she says, turning away. 'He was always a very private man. I should probably be getting on with things now.'

She turns both taps on full blast over the mop bucket, filling the air between us with the noise of rushing water before I can ask anything else.

39

Jess arrives soon after with Daisy and Callum, and I fold the piece of notepaper into my pocket. My wife and I exchange the usual truncated updates about our respective working days and I move on quickly to tell her about the police visit instead. Once the kids are tucking into an early evening tea of baked potatoes with tuna, I take a couple of zero-alcohol beers out of the fridge and offer one to her.

'Helena is still working upstairs,' I say. 'She crept up on me earlier like some kind of ninja. I swear I didn't even hear her until she was right behind me.'

Jess takes the beer from me, popping it open.

'But she seems nice, don't you think? Bit of a godsend.' Seeing the sceptical look on my face, she adds: 'What?'

'I'm just . . . I don't know. Who even *is* she?' I gesture towards the ceiling with my beer, where even now I imagine she might be rifling through our cupboards. The coded note in my pocket is a new ingredient in the strange brew that has been bubbling ever since I discovered the hidden room at the top of the house. 'We don't know her. She could be anyone.'

It had only been a few days ago, I remind her, that Shaun had turned up on our doorstep completely out of the blue.

Jess takes out her phone and pulls up WhatsApp, selecting a group at the top of the list called Park West Residents.

Its membership, she tells me, is made up of homeowners on our road and half a dozen neighbouring streets. She scrolls through the latest messages, everything from missed deliveries and thoughtlessly parked cars to recommendations for a reliable painter and decorator. Most of it looks pretty banal but I ask her to add me to the group anyway.

'I just asked about a cleaner when we were getting ready to move in,' Jess says, 'and got chatting to some of our new neighbours. Helena was recommended – really good references too.'

'Can we even afford a cleaner?'

'It's only a few hours a week, but it'll really give us a head start on everything around the house. And with what's happened this week, I think we both need our wits about us to keep a proper eye on the kids – we can't do that if we're looking after this big house on our own, and both working full-time, both running around and redecorating and cutting down that jungle of a garden so the kids can enjoy it for the summer holidays.'

'Her cousin's here too?'

'Tobias,' Jess says, pointing out of the kitchen window. 'There he is.'

I follow her finger across the expanse of lawn at the back of the house. The hedges at the back are hugely overgrown, the grass shin-high and years' worth of rotting leaves piled two feet deep. Standing by the hedge is a small, unassuming man in jeans, work boots and a tattered black sweatshirt bearing a faded *JCB* logo. His dark hair is cut short all over and there is a windburned redness beneath the stubble on his cheeks.

In his gloved hands, he's wielding a pair of long loppers with a curved scissor-blade, slicing overhanging branches from Mrs Evans's horse chestnut tree. Each one falls with a single clean slice of the crescent-shaped blades. *Chop.* Another severed branch drops to the ground at his feet.

'She offered Tobias as a kind of two-for-one deal. He works cheap, does a lot of the gardens around here, apparently. He prefers to be outside. Helena says he's . . . he doesn't really like being shut in. Enclosed.'

I stare through the window at the man working in my garden.

'But is it a good idea? Bringing strangers into the house, with what's been happening this week?'

'They're not strangers,' she says. 'They were recommended. And it's only for a trial period – we'll see what they're like for a couple of weeks and take it from there. OK?'

* * *

It's only later, when the younger children are in bed, that I open up my laptop again and return to the strange piece of half-burned notepaper from the top room.

Jess finds me in the kitchen. I gesture for her to shut the door before I show her the coded note, then pull up the picture on my phone that Charlie had sent a few hours previously. I still haven't worked out a way to tell her about Maxine and her son without admitting that I suddenly have a lot of free time on my hands. Instead, I tell her it came from Dom.

She frowns as she studies the picture.

'It looks like . . .' Lines deepen on her forehead. 'That's horrible. Like it's wrapped around someone's wrists. Grim.'

'I know.'

'What if it's the same scarf as you found? It could be important, couldn't it?'

We discuss another approach to the police, even as I recount the number of times we'd been in touch with them already this week.

'They'll think we're time-wasters,' Jess says with a sigh. 'Attention-seekers.'

'I think some of them already do.'

Leah wanders in with a grin, her phone in hand, to show us a video on TikTok. It's titled 'Weird Embarrassing Dads on Holiday Vol. 3' and features a middle-aged guy and all the ways he embarrasses his teenage children.

'This is *so* you, Dad.' She leans on my shoulder, giggling as I watch, her arm warm through my shirt. In the video, a middle-aged man is making awkwardly self-conscious moves on the dance floor to 'Stayin' Alive' by the Bee Gees, watched by a pair of cringing teens. As the clip finishes and rolls onto the next one, she points at the crumpled, half-burnt notepaper next to my laptop. 'What's that?'

'I think it's some kind of coded message. Found it hidden upstairs.'

She wrinkles her nose. 'A reflecting cipher's not really much of a code though, is it?'

'A what?'

'We did them in computer science. Like, a few years ago.'

She pulls up a browser on my laptop and types *reflecting cipher* into the search bar, clicking on the first result. The page has a few lines of text about reflecting ciphers – also apparently called mirror codes, or Atbash ciphers – and a text box that says 'Enter message here' . . .

My daughter types in the first entry on the notepaper.

xlmurin nvvgrmt becomes *confirm meeting*.

She points to a graphic on the screen, the alphabet laid out A to Z from left to right. Below it, the sequence of letters is reversed so it runs from right to left.

'See?' Leah says. 'You pair each letter with its reverse in the sequence so A becomes Z, B is Y, C is X and so on. Not really much of a code. Too easy.'

I type one word after another into the text box, writing the decrypted entries in pencil next to the originals.

location
access
traffic
call log

Decoded, the heading at the top of this column is *barrow*.

'What's that?' Jess says. 'A place, a person?'

'It's a town not far from the Lake District. Cumbria, I think.'

'Or Barrow-on-Soar, near Loughborough? That's a lot closer to us here.'

Leah studies the list over my shoulder. 'Isn't a barrow a Viking burial mound, or something?'

I type in the coded heading above the right-hand column and get *parker*.

The three of us study the scribbled column of decoded words. I guess this list might have been written before Google existed. Before unscrambling it was as easy as typing letters into a web page. It wouldn't have troubled any serious investigator for more than a minute, but it would have been enough to disguise what it was from a casual viewer, from someone who just stumbled upon it.

Someone else in the house who came across it by accident, perhaps.

'I don't get it,' Jess says. 'Was there anything else in the tin?'

'A lighter, some matches. The tin was on top of a little pile of ash, like paper had been burned there before.'

'What's that phrase?' she says quietly, almost to herself. '*Burn after reading*?'

'That's what I was thinking.'

Our daughter wanders off, absorbed in her phone again. Jess points at the paper, the three coded words below the heading *parker* on the right-hand side. Three coded entries, the rest presumably burned away.

'Do the words in the other column.'

I go through the same process again, decoding each entry and writing the plain text in pencil next to it.

When I'm finished, we both sit in silence, staring at the other half of the list.

cable ties
shoe covers
spades x2

There is a sick twisting in my stomach.

It wasn't a message.

It was a to-do list.

40

I sleep badly, unable to drift off and waking repeatedly through the night to every strange noise the house makes. Awake, I lie in the dark and try to decide what we should do about the strange note and the hints of darkness carried by a few coded words. Asleep, my dreams are a troubling mix of Adrian Parish and Shaun Rutherford – both speaking a language I can't understand – of Leah and the car that had followed her home from school.

Helena and Tobias appear too.

There is something about the two of them that doesn't sit quite right, doesn't ring true. They had come to us via a recommendation on WhatsApp from someone we'd never even met, first appearing almost as soon as we moved in. Helena had told us she'd worked for the previous owner and we had taken her at face value. But what if there was more to it than that? What if there was something else going on with them?

My restless thoughts keep returning to the last item on the coded list, like a compass pointing to true north.

Spades x2

Not a single spade. Two.

Partners. Each with a different half of that to-do list. *Parker* with a simple note of things to buy from the local DIY shop; *Barrow* with more cerebral tasks to do with watching, waiting, monitoring. There is something about the names that is familiar but I can't remember where I've heard them before.

I make a strong brew in the cafetière to get my brain going but both younger children are up early and there's no time to sit down and really think, in between getting them both fed and dressed, making sure Daisy has everything she needs for her swimming lesson and the birthday party for her little friend, Olive, which will follow straight after. I wrap the present while she eats her Cheerios. Callum has no football match this morning, so he settles down in the lounge to play Minecraft on the Xbox instead. Leah will sleep in until at least midday.

As soon as Jess has taken Daisy to her swimming lesson, I take my coffee into the lounge to sit with Callum, pulling up WhatsApp on my phone and diving into the Park West Residents group. The thread is a huge repository of messages ranging from the half useful to the mind-bogglingly trivial, everything from requests to recommend reliable tradesmen to queries about the local water pressure and passive-aggressive messages about inconsiderate parking, pleas for missing wheelie bins and offers of unwanted second-hand clothes, books, wooden hangers, plant pots, children's fancy dress items and anything else that people are trying to get rid of.

I find the 'Search' option in the menu and enter 'Parker'. The results appear as highlighted mentions of the nearby Wollaton *Park*, *Park* Drive and requests for people to move cars that have been *parked* badly. No matches on the actual word itself. 'Barrow' produces a single solitary search result about a resident asking if anyone in the neighbourhood has a wheelbarrow they could borrow.

I click out of the search function.

The group members use a mixture of usernames, all with first names, some with surnames too, many with a house number and street initials to signify their membership of one of the most exclusive WhatsApp groups in the city. I had muted notifications on the thread within a day of Jess getting me added to the group because of the constant pinging as each new message landed; there are dozens from the last few days alone.

But eventually, among the morass, I find what I'm looking for: a request from Jess, posted the day before we moved in, to ask if any of our new neighbours could recommend a cleaner and/or gardener. Within half an hour, there is a response from someone calling herself Sarah@84GT suggesting Helena and Tobias as 'a very reliable pair, excellent work, good rates'.

A useful recommendation from a helpful neighbour. Unless it was something else.

Because I had no idea who Sarah@84GT *actually* was. Neither of us did. But she was the reason Helena and Tobias were at my house, claiming to have worked for the previous owner. 'Sarah' was a blank, a mystery. An unknown quantity.

Or was I just being paranoid?

I text Jess at the pool to ask whether she'd had any private messages from 'Sarah', or actually spoken to her on the phone after she gave the recommendation.

She texts me straight back.

No and no.
You need to google those names from last night.
I just did.

I pull up a browser window on my phone and type in *parker*. There are hundreds of millions of results and I scroll down the page trying to find one with significance. But it's too vague; too random. I try the same with *barrow* and get a similar avalanche of results, lots of them about Barrow Football Club and the town itself in Cumbria – which is more than a hundred and eighty miles away. This was a needle in an electronic haystack. I type both words together into the search box, *parker barrow*, which yields a mere seven million results. The first dozen links are all about an American rock band from Nashville, Tennessee. Track listings, tour dates, a new album, YouTube videos and other social media accounts. Below that, some corporate entries and more links to the rock band and sites streaming their music.

A single Wikipedia entry nestles among the rest, and I realise suddenly why the surnames had sounded vaguely familiar.

Although they had become much better known by their first names when they had carved a bloody path across Prohibition-era America almost a century ago.

Bonnie Elizabeth Parker and Clyde Chestnut Barrow.

Bonnie and Clyde.

41

I stare at the Wikipedia page describing the spree of robbery, kidnapping and murder committed by Bonnie and Clyde until their violent deaths in a police ambush in 1934. Someone, at some point, had used them as pseudonyms on a dubious 'to-do' list hidden in my house. That person had also used a rudimentary code to obscure the contents of the list, before someone tried to destroy it – without checking whether the flames had done their work.

I send Jess a text.

Bonnie and Clyde??? Seriously?

I know. What's that about?

I'm about to call her when the phone starts ringing in my hand: not my usual ringtone but the high-pitched tinkling sound of a call on WhatsApp. The screen shows an unrecognised number. I offer a cautious greeting to the unknown caller and he responds in kind, his tone clipped.

'Jeremy said you wanted to speak to me about the house,' he says. Almost as an afterthought, he adds: 'I'm Kevin Hopkins, by the way.'

'Right,' I say. 'Yes, thanks for calling back. You're the previous owner's son, is that right?'

'Yup.'

He sounds like he's in his forties. From what I could remember, this guy was an expat living somewhere in Spain. I imagine him in a beachfront café somewhere, sipping an espresso, looking at the ocean, a world away from all of this.

I remember what Shaun Rutherford had blurted out, under questioning from my brother-in-law and me. *He said he lived abroad.* Could the man on the other end of this phone line be the one who had hired him?

'Appreciate you getting back to me,' I say. 'There was something I wanted to ask about the house, it might sound a bit—'

'It's fine.' There is some kind of loud noise in the background. 'Listen, what's this all about? It's actually not a great time, to be honest. And if you've got some sort of issue with the structural survey, I just want to stop you there and tell you to take it up with the surveyors. Reckon you got a very good deal on my dad's house as it is.'

I reassure him that there's no malice in my enquiry, trying to steer him around instead to the topic of when he moved in, and what kind of cosmetic changes might have been made on the second floor. But if he suspects I'm asking about the secret door in the top bedroom, he gives no indication of it.

'I made some changes for Dad,' he says breezily. 'A few modernisations, but he didn't like the idea of doing too much after Mum died. Like I said, if this is some kind of legal claim, if you're thinking of pushing back on the survey or if there's been any kind of bad faith issue, you can forget it.'

I get the sense he's already close to hanging up.

'No, no,' I say quickly. 'It's not that. I'm thinking about some remodelling, but my wife wants to retain as much as possible and I'm trying to convince her that a lot of it is much more recent than it looks. Like, in one of the bedrooms there were some big, fitted wardrobes – did you put those in?'

The traffic noise is getting louder at his end, as if he's right next to a main road.

'What?'

'The big fitted wardrobes in one of the top floor rooms. Right over the top of a wood-panelled wall.'

There is a long pause on the line, a crackle of static as if he's transferring the phone from one ear to the other.

'No,' he says finally. 'I didn't put those wardrobes in.'

I can't help but feel a little deflated. If I could find out when the work had been done, when the hidden door had been blocked off and forgotten about, it would at least give me a starting point to work back from.

'So, they were already there?' I say. 'When you and your parents moved in?'

'That's not what I said. I said *I* didn't do it – I had them done by a guy, a specialist, a joiner or whatever.'

I take a breath. It's a fraction of progress at least, an inch forward.

'Who was the joiner?'

'Seriously, mate? Not a scooby. This was donkey's years ago.'

'Fair enough.' I keep my voice light. 'So, what year would it have been?'

'God, feels like forever.' He sighs with irritation. 'Mum and Dad bought the house in ... summer 2002? Yeah, it was the World Cup, I remember trying to get the TV working in time to watch us get knocked out by Brazil in the quarter-finals, all of us perched on camping chairs in the lounge. Bloody David Seaman cost us that game, he was absolute garbage. Brazil were down to ten men and we still couldn't beat them.'

I can't remember the game at all but it's clearly stuck in his memory.

'So . . . the joiner?'

'Yeah, so, he must have come in pretty soon after that because Mum wanted loads of storage for all her old clothes, all her old costumes from when she was doing am-dram. The old lady they bought the house off was a widower and she'd died suddenly; the place was in a right state when we moved in.'

'Don't suppose you remember her name, do you?'

'What?'

'The owner of the house before your family?'

He blows out a breath. 'Blimey. This is like bloody *Columbo*.'

'Sorry, I'm just trying to fill in some blanks in the history of the place.'

There is more silence on the line, punctuated by the sound of hard footsteps on an echoing floor.

'You know what?' he says. 'I *do* remember. It was one of those weird things but she had the same name as in that TV show. Makepeace. Like, from *Dempsey & Makepeace*?'

'Might have been a bit before my time.'

'Elizabeth, that was it. Elizabeth Makepeace. A right mouthful.'

'And she was a widower,' I say. 'Did she live alone?'

'There was a . . . grandson, or maybe a nephew as well? Or it might have been a godson. Never met the feller.' There is a babble of young voices at his end and his end of the line is muffled for a moment before he returns to the call. 'Look, Alan—'

'Adam.'

'Adam, what is this actually all about? You didn't really track me down to the Costa del Sol for a chat about wardrobes, did you?'

I hesitate, not sure whether to reveal the real reason for my call, whether to share what I've found with a total stranger. But curiosity wins out.

'There's an extra room.'

'A what?'

'An extra room, hidden behind a false wall. A concealed door that leads into a small annexe, looks like it's been undisturbed for a long time. For years. I'm trying to find out why it's there, how long it's been untouched.'

'So?'

'You never saw this room?'

The click of a closing door reaches me from his end of the call, and the background noise finally recedes. His voice, when he answers, is quieter too.

'I don't know what you're talking about. All I can tell you is that it's nothing to do with me, or my dad.'

There is a subtle shift in his tone, a bluntness that suggests his meagre patience is now at an end. For some reason I find myself thinking of the various unsavoury Brits who have washed up on the Costa Del Crime over the years. Was that still a thing, or had it all changed? Was it still a place where you could avoid extradition back to the UK?

Had he concealed the room deliberately, moved abroad to get as far away from it as he could?

The phone is suddenly hot against my ear.

'I don't suppose the names Parker or Barrow mean anything to you?'

There is a moment's hesitation on the line.

'Nope. Who's that?'

'Do you know if anyone else lived there with that name, or nickname? Maybe a lodger, or a friend?'

'No one else lived there apart from me and Dad. And I left years ago, that's why it was all down to me to sort out the house and everything else. If I'm being totally honest, you're welcome to it. He's well shot of that place, I never liked it anyway. It was too big for him to live there on his own.' He clears his throat. 'Look, if there's nothing else? I've really got to go.'

He ends the call and the line goes dead.

42

I leave Callum alone in the lounge and open my laptop on the kitchen table, flicking the kettle on as I go.

Kevin Hopkins was a strange character, helpful one minute and elusive the next, and I wasn't quite sure what to make of him. But he had denied any knowledge of the hidden room and the secret door, and if he'd known it was there, it wouldn't have made sense to simply block it off. Surely if the items in that dresser *meant* anything, if they had sentimental value or were some kind of evidence, he would have done something with them? Removed them, thrown them away, taken them with him to Spain. Perhaps even tried to sell them as I'd done with the watch?

So, either Kevin didn't care what was in there, or he genuinely didn't know about the room at all. Maybe the wooden panelling was too much trouble to take down, too well constructed, too solid, and so he just built over it instead. The passing of two decades had shrouded everything in a thick fog of uncertainty, the half-remembered years of people who had once called this place their home. People who had come and gone, taking their memories with them.

But I *did* have an idea how long the little room had lain untouched: at least twenty-two years, if Kevin was to be believed. The hidden door had been blocked off – either deliberately or by accident – soon after the Hopkins family had arrived in the summer of 2002.

I make another cup of coffee, mulling over what I've just heard from the family's only son. Working backwards, I try to remember what Eileen Evans had told me about her old neighbours too. It's a mixture of old news, local gossip and educated guesswork, but there were some cold hard facts too and I can feel the satisfaction in being able to put a few more of the puzzle pieces in place. Although what the finished picture might reveal, I still wasn't sure.

I go back to the keyboard of my laptop. According to Google, the 2002 World Cup that year had been in Japan and South Korea and had been held from the end of May until the 30th of June, with the England–Brazil game on 21st June. And according to Kevin Hopkins, the new storage had been built upstairs fairly soon after they moved in. Finding a pen in the kitchen drawer, I flick to a clean page in the notebook we use to write the weekly shopping lists and begin to draw a timeline of everything I know so far.

Sep 2001 – Adrian Parish goes missing

2001/02 – death of Elizabeth Makepeace; grandson/nephew/godson goes to live where? Name? CONTACT DETAILS? Find them?

June 2002 – Hopkins family moves in

Jul–Sep (?) 2002 – access to hidden door blocked

2003 – death of Janet Hopkins

January 2024 – we buy 91 Regency Place

I sit back in the kitchen chair and study the timeline, trying to discern any kind of pattern in the dates. It makes for grim reading to see those two deaths and a disappearance in the space of barely two years. Janet Hopkins had died *after* the secret room had been blocked off and hidden, although I couldn't work out if that was significant or not.

But the timing did suggest the wooden-panelled wall and its secret door had already been there when the Hopkins family arrived. Kevin had hired a joiner to put up the fitted wardrobes in that room, he told me, covering the door and most of the wall.

If he was telling the truth.

The name of another previous owner of the house is a new piece of the puzzle; and it's an uncommon name, which should help to narrow it down. But when I type 'Elizabeth Makepeace' into Google and trawl through pages of results, none of them seem to fit. They all seem to be social media pages, LinkedIn profiles for people who are far too young and – more importantly – still alive. A handful of others are historical records going back to the nineteenth century. After fifteen minutes of fruitless searching, I finally admit defeat and acknowledge that an elderly widower who had died around the turn of the millennium was probably of an age, and a time, when she would not feature anywhere online. She was among the last generation that had slipped away before they could become entangled in the internet like the rest of us.

In terms of an online footprint, that twenty-first-century measure of a person's impact on the world, she had barely existed at all.

Eventually, I find myself on the homepage of a website called Deceased Database UK, which announces itself as a central resource of burials and cremations, offered primarily to amateur genealogists researching the family tree. A rudimentary search box asks for first and last name, plus start and finish dates as search parameters. I fill in what I know and hit 'enter', a sand-timer icon rotating on the screen for a moment before it spits out a single result. Five lines of text at the top of the results box.

I read the text and feel a rush of certainty that this is the same person: the former owner of this house had not *quite* escaped the reach of the internet. It had found her – in death.

Last name: Makepeace
First names: Elizabeth Irene
Buried on: 16 January 2002
Recorded in: Nottingham
Date of death: 27 December 2001

The information is tantalisingly sparse and doesn't give any indication of age, next of kin or last known address. I bookmark the page and amend my timeline, then photograph the details and send it to Maxine with a message asking if she's heard the name before in connection with this house or her husband. It doesn't take her long to reply.

Will check but doesn't ring any bells.

I send another message.

Can Charlie find out how long she lived here or when she moved in? Any surviving family?

He will do some digging through RBDM. Will get back to you.

I frown.

RBDM?

Register of Births, Deaths and Marriages.

I stare at the timeline for a moment longer then slide the paper into my back pocket, close the laptop, and go to check on Callum.

*   *   *

Jeremy calls before lunch to ask about the snagging list of small issues that he'd arranged to be sorted out before we moved in – some missing roof tiles, a couple of leaking taps, a boiler service – to make sure they've all been completed to our satisfaction. He's nothing if not thorough and I'm not surprised he's become the most sought-after agent in the city for high-end period properties. Before he rings off, I ask him if he's ever come across the name Elizabeth Makepeace, but the name isn't familiar.

I finally get started on today's decorating tasks.

After a while I find a rhythm with the wallpaper stripping in the dining room, peeling off long sections of the old floral paper in long, satisfying rips. As each thick piece detaches from the wall, the fusty air that emerges from beneath is almost like an exhalation, this room finally breathing out after decades contained behind paper.

I'm starting on the third wall when my phone buzzes again in my pocket. A text from Maxine.

You free to meet today?

It's not quite 11 a.m.; Jess should be back with Daisy before noon. Dom is also due to come over for some uncle-time with the kids, and I won't leave until he's here.

Yes can do when my wife is back. Lunchtime?

12.30 p.m. @NGC. Go to NG1 5JD, section 12 down the hill on the left.

I plug the postcode into Google Maps and it zooms down to a location less than a mile from my house.

Somewhere I've driven past a thousand times but never actually been inside.

43

The entrance to Nottingham General Cemetery is a handsome Victorian gatehouse, a two-storey structure of creamy sandstone and black wrought iron. Walking through the cool shade by the gates gives a moment's welcome relief from the sun before the path emerges into the cemetery itself.

It's huge.

A wide expanse of green slopes gently away from the gatehouse behind me, with thousands – probably *tens* of thousands – of gravestones spread across every piece of ground. Stones of every shade, black, white, grey, some upright but others leaning drunkenly away from the vertical.

Of the living, however, there is no sign. No Maxine or Charlie. The whole place feels deserted. Even when I think I hear footsteps coming through the gatehouse behind me, when I turn there is no one there.

I head down the path and find an information board, scanning the layout plan for section twelve. There is a brief historical panel too which describes the creation of the cemetery in the 1830s and the subsequent interment of more than 150,000 people in this fourteen-acre plot. I go back, read the figure again, trying to take in the enormity of the number. *One hundred and fifty thousand bodies.* All of them here, under my feet. The place had become so full, in fact, that it had been closed to new burials for almost a century.

So why had Maxine asked to meet me here?

I check over my shoulder. Still no one else around. Not a mourner or a gardener in sight . . .

No, there *is* someone else here. Out of the corner of my eye I catch a flash of movement between the stand of trees, a tall, heavy man in a grey coat. But when I stop and stare he doesn't emerge on the other side. Maybe a groundskeeper, or someone using it as a cut-through. It was open to the public, after all.

The path winds first to the right and then splits as it snakes down the hill. I follow the left-hand fork into a more heavily wooded section, with ornate markers, statues of cherubs and ivy-clad tombs standing above ground, flanked by pillars and dark with engraving. This is section twelve of the cemetery – at least I *think* it is. It's overgrown, the grass thick and long around pitted gravestones, the trees above throwing much of it into cool shadow. Some of the graves here are clustered together, enclosed within waist-high iron fences. I stop to peer at one of the plots, which has four grave markers spanning almost a century, a husband and wife, children buried later alongside them. A red admiral flutters to the headstone beside me, wings spreading in a shaft of sunlight.

A rustle of movement close behind me.

I freeze.

The soft sound of footsteps flattening grass and then I'm turning fast, heart jumping into my throat as a figure emerges from behind a statue of an eyeless angel . . .

Maxine emerges wearing a purple T-shirt and jeans, sunglasses perched on top of her head.

'Hey, Adam.'

'Hi.' I let go a heavy breath. 'Sorry, this place is just a bit . . .'

'Deserted?' She holds a hand up in apology. 'Yeah, I know what you mean. Sorry if I startled you.'

'Back up the hill, I thought there was someone following me.'

'I've not seen anyone else. Come on, it's this way.'

She leads me further into this section of the cemetery, between rows of graves stained almost black with age and slanted back at crazy angles. Over her shoulder, she asks me about the picture her son had extracted from the little Motorola flip phone, the enhanced image that had looked very much like the purple scarf wrapped around a pair of wrists.

Both of us agree it's a disturbing image.

But what it proves is unclear.

Eventually, she stops, turns to me and gestures towards a small collection of gravestones grouped together. Like many of the others in this part of the cemetery, it's discreetly separated from the next set of graves with a cast-iron three-sided fence that was once probably black but is now corroded and mottled with rust. Maxine points to a light grey stone engraved in dark, old-fashioned script.

In Loving Memory of
Elizabeth Irene Makepeace
Died 27 December 2001
In her 86th year
Beloved grandmother, mother and daughter
Always in our thoughts

The air is utterly still around us, barely a breath of wind, only the faintest hum of traffic rising up from the city below. Somewhere in the trees above, a solitary thrush sings a high, inquisitive song.

'That's her,' I say to Maxine. 'That's Elizabeth. How did you find her so quickly? You never told me you were some kind of expert hacker.'

'I'm not,' she says with a rueful smile. 'I'm a social worker. It was Charlie who found her – he says you just have to know the right places to look.'

I remember what I'd read near the entrance, about how long it had been since the cemetery had accepted new burials.

'But I thought this place was full, though?' For the first time, I notice there are still open spaces here and there, in contrast to the rest of the cemetery. 'The sign said it was closed to new burials?'

'It is.' She indicates the next stone along. '*Except* in existing family plots.'

I look again at the cluster of headstones enclosed within the rusted iron fence. To the left and behind Elizabeth Makepeace's final resting place are two others, much older, much more weather-beaten and pitted with age.

William John Makepeace
Died 11th June 1964

Besides this one is another, presumably his wife.

Gladys Violet Makepeace
Died 9th February 1980

'There are a couple of others behind them too,' Maxine says. 'But the stones are so old you can't read the names anymore. Reckon they must have bought up this whole family plot back in the day and all those agreements were still honoured by the council for decades. At least they were up until twenty-odd years ago anyway. Looks like no one's been buried here in quite a while.'

I go to stand next to her. On the right-hand side of the family plot are another pair of headstones, these two in dark marble with gold lettering.

Linda Jane Flack (née Makepeace)
13 March 1950–2 June 1986

Besides her is Peter William Flack, whose inscription tells us he was a 'Beloved son and grandson' who had died at the age of twenty-seven. It's clearly one of the newer grave markers here, the clean angular marble a contrast to the time-worn grey stone all around.

Maxine takes a step back, crosses her arms. 'What do you notice?'

'Well ... like you say it's a family plot. I guess there was space reserved here for Elizabeth's daughter, Linda and ... her grandson?'

'Look again.' She gestures at the headstones. 'What do you *see*?'

I study them all again, from left to right, reading each inscription slowly. Going down on my haunches to peer more closely at each one until I end up on the right-hand side again.

Peter William Flack
6 September 1974—27 December 2001
Aged 27 years
Beloved son and grandson

Presumably Peter was Linda's son, which meant the boy had lost his mother at the tender age of eleven. There doesn't seem to be any stone here for a father. Maybe the boy was raised by his grandma? I'm thinking aloud, but when I look back at Maxine, she's still shaking her head as if I haven't grasped the most interesting fact about this little collection of family graves.

'What?' I say. 'I don't see what you—'

And then, all of a sudden, I do.

27 December 2001.

Elizabeth Makepeace and her grandson Peter had died on the same day.

44

'So what does that mean?' I say. 'That they both died on the same day? Some sort of accident, a car crash?'

'It's possible, I suppose.'

Darker thoughts crowd my mind. 'Or maybe they were victims of a crime? An attack, a double murder?'

Maxine shakes her head. 'I don't know if that's possible, is it?'

'Why not?'

'I mean . . . we would have heard about it, wouldn't we? A double murder would have been big news in the local area, right? Maybe even national news. It would have been notorious, the sort of thing that sticks in the memory.'

'So . . . what then?'

'Don't know yet.' She leans down with her phone to take pictures of all five headstones. 'But unless it's just a big coincidence, there must be a story behind it. It must mean *something*.'

'I don't believe in coincidences.'

'Me neither. Two previous residents of your house die on the same day; not long after that the Hopkins family moves in with their son Kevin, and Mrs Hopkins dies the following year.'

'You make it sound like the Amityville House of Horror.'

She gives me an apologetic shrug. 'They're the facts, Adam.'

'You ever heard this name before?' I point at the marble headstone. 'Peter Flack?'

'No. But when you see the date he died ... the first thing I thought of was how close it was to when my Adrian disappeared, in September that year. It was only three months later.'

We agree that she and Charlie will try to find out more about the unfortunate Peter Flack, while I try to find out what happened on that day in December 2001 that took the lives of both Flack and his grandmother, Elizabeth Makepeace. I follow her lead in taking pictures of all the stones, all the names and dates.

Maxine is clearly pleased with her find, and there's a light in her eyes that I've not seen until today. There is an energy about her, perhaps born of the feeling that she might yet discover what happened to her husband – even after all these years. She goes to look at some of the neighbouring gravestones and I open the browser on my own phone, doing a few quick searches for Flack and his grandmother. But nothing comes up. Either 2001 was too early for local news to be routinely posted online, or they're in some obscure part of the early internet that can't be found by Google, or perhaps content that old was behind a paywall to make some money out of family history enthusiasts. I turned eighteen that year and could only vaguely remember pre-internet days; it seems hard to imagine a time when you couldn't just take your phone out of your pocket and find the answer to any question in the world.

'Did you walk?' Maxine is typing on her own phone. 'Need a lift?'

Charlie meets us at the Waverley Street gate in a white three-door Volkswagen and Maxine opens the passenger door for me. *Not a grey Volvo*, I say to myself as I'm clambering into the back seat. The car smells clean, faintly floral, with one of those little flowerpots on the dashboard with a plastic daisy that sways from side to side. It's quite a contrast to my Nissan, with its booster seats and biscuit crumbs and year-old raisins squashed into the upholstery. As Charlie turns onto Clarendon Street and heads towards the city centre, my mind is still in the half-forgotten cemetery, of two deaths linked to our house. A woman and a man. *Bonnie and Clyde?* No, that was ridiculous. She was his grandma, in her eighties and sixty years his senior. I didn't even know *where* they'd died – perhaps it had been somewhere else entirely, nowhere near the place that was now our family home.

It's only as Charlie indicates right and turns across Maid Marian Way, towards the castle, that I realise I haven't actually given them my address.

And yet somehow, we're heading into The Park.

'I've never told you where I live,' I say, leaning forward between the two front seats. 'How do you know?'

Maxine shrugs. 'It was on the death certificate for Elizabeth Makepeace. Thought I'd told you?'

Charlie, who has yet to say a word since he picked us up in town, turns the car smoothly onto Regency Place.

'Anywhere here is good,' I say to him. I don't want them to drop me right at my gate, close to my family home. 'Thanks for the lift.'

'It's no problem,' Charlie says over his shoulder, glancing at house numbers as we pass. 'We're here now. Might as well take you to the door.'

He slows, indicates and pulls across the entrance to the drive. Even now, even though we've lived in it for a week, I haven't got my head around the fact that this house is ours. The imposing red brick, the triple-width chimney stacks, the half-timbered gables and stone-carved date over the front door – it still has the *wow factor*, as Jess said the first time we viewed it.

Maxine gets out and pulls the front seat forward so I can clamber out from the back onto the pavement.

'So this is it?' She turns towards the house, nodding slowly. 'Very nice. Very nice indeed.'

'We're still settling in, really. Finding our feet.'

She lingers on the pavement as if reluctant to leave, taking in the driveway, the porch, the big bay windows and the old oak tree in the front garden. Then she leans down and opens the glove compartment, takes out a clear plastic Ziploc bag and hands it to me. Inside are the dog collar, the little flip phone and the brass key I'd discovered behind a hidden door six days ago.

'Could I . . . see it?' she says. 'The place where you found everything?'

I follow her gaze towards the house. Jess is home with the kids and I still haven't told her about Maxine; Dom's car is in the drive as well. I don't want to get into a whole load of explaining why I've brought two near-strangers to the house.

'Maybe another day?' I say. 'It's still a real mess inside, lots of unpacking still to do. Sorry.'

'I understand.'

'Let's see what we can dig up on Peter Flack and his grandmother. I feel like we're getting somewhere.' I tap the roof of the VW. 'Thanks for the lift.'

She tucks a strand of dark-brown hair behind her ear. 'It's me that should be thanking *you*, Adam.'

'For what?'

'For asking questions. For getting in touch in the first place.' She indicates the Ziploc bag in my hand. 'Most people would have chucked that stuff out and never given it a second thought. But *you* didn't, and it's the first time in so long that anyone has even been bothered to try finding out what happened to Adrian. It's been so long since anyone really cared, apart from me and Charlie.'

We say our goodbyes and she climbs back into the car beside her son. I watch the white Volkswagen pull away, towards the junction at the end of Regency Place, waiting until it turns left and disappears around the corner.

* * *

Back in the house, Dom greets me in the hall where he's busy unloading paint, rollers and dust sheets from his car. He gives me an inquisitive glance.

'So who is *she*?'

'Who?'

My brother-in-law shoots me a disappointed look, as if I'm insulting his intelligence, his sister and the universe in general.

'The mystery woman and her driver,' he says quietly, 'who just dropped you home.'

It's pointless trying to spin him a line. Instead, I hold up the clear plastic bag that Maxine has just given me.

'The address on this ID tag,' I say, 'is her house in Kimberley. Her dog, trained by her husband – who's been missing for more than twenty years.'

I give him a quick summary of my connection to Maxine and the progress we've made so far, leading up to the visit to city's General Cemetery today.

And yet even as I'm explaining it to Dom, something niggles at me like a stone in my shoe. It's only now, as I'm saying it out loud, that I try to give it a shape, a name. Not the fact that Charlie had known exactly where I lived. Something else is bothering me about the last few hours. Something about Maxine. Dom's darkening expression is a mirror for my own thoughts, as I show him the texts she and I have exchanged over recent days.

It's taken me a week of digging into the history of this house, of nosing around, enquiring about the contents of the hidden room. A week of finding my way, like a blind man in a strange new place, finding his bearings by touch alone.

But it had taken Maxine less than an hour to come back to me this morning.

In fact, it was a grand total of forty-two minutes between me texting the information about Elizabeth Makepeace, and Maxine's response with a request to meet at the cemetery. It was *very* quick, a very fast turnaround to find out the information, track down a death certificate, a cemetery and physically locate a family plot in a place with tens of thousands of headstones. Unless . . .

'Unless,' my brother-in-law says, 'she already knew all about it.'

45

Dom keeps his voice low.

'Look, all I'm saying is that you only just met her. You don't know anything about her, she could be a couple of sandwiches short of a picnic for all we know.'

'But why would she already know about it?'

He raises an eyebrow. 'Like you said, she seemed to find that cemetery plot awfully fast.'

'Her son is some kind of computer whizz,' I say. 'I suppose he can track things down.'

'If you say so, Adam.'

'Maybe I'm overthinking this.'

'Maybe you're right to be careful around strangers.' He's always doted on his nieces and nephew, and I can tell he's still particularly bothered by the story of the car that had followed Leah home from school on Thursday. 'Especially at the moment.'

* * *

Unfortunately, what I thought might be a straightforward internet search turns into a long, frustrating hour.

I already know there's virtually nothing online about Elizabeth Makepeace apart from a listing on an obscure website recording her date and place of death, and the date of her burial. I'd hoped there might be something more on Peter Flack, if only for the reason that he had died at a younger age and might have had slightly more of a digital footprint. But searches under his name prove equally futile.

None of the search results relate to the woman who used to own my house, or her grandson.

The discovery that they had died on the same day, more than two decades ago, starts to feel less and less relevant the longer I spend searching for more information. Surely if it *meant* something, if it was significant, it would have made some kind of ripple on the world?

As I scroll pages of unhelpful results, I envisage possible scenarios – each one more outlandish than the last. A fire, flood or family allergy that struck them both down within hours? A car accident? A plane crash? An intruder in the night, a burglary turned violent? Or even ... a murder-suicide? *No.* As Maxine said, that would have conferred a level of notoriety that didn't seem to be in evidence.

I sign up to the General Register Office portal and pay to have copies of both death certificates sent to me but it will be at least four days before they're posted out – it will still be quicker if I can find local news coverage of what transpired on that December day, twenty-three years ago. I email the city's central library to ask how I might access local news archives for December 2001 and January 2002, and it takes me by surprise when a helpful response from a member of staff drops into my inbox barely twenty minutes later.

I find myself smiling as I read the message. There was a lot to love about a local librarian with so much deep knowledge, so keen to help. I reply with thanks and book in to look at the microfiche in the next available slot on Monday morning.

* * *

I take the Ziploc bag into the spare room I've started to use as a study, locking them into a bottom drawer beneath a pile of mortgage paperwork.

The little mobile phone, I notice, is almost out of battery so I plug it back in to charge on the desk. Comparing the original photo on its tiny screen to the enhanced version that Charlie sent on WhatsApp, the difference is even more stark. In some ways it's almost like looking at two different pictures.

Studying the image again reminds me of something else I need to check.

I head upstairs and bump into Jess on the landing, dressed in her decorating clothes. It feels like we've barely seen each other all day and I give her a peck on the cheek, then pull her in for a hug.

'Dinner won't be long,' she says. As if reading my mind, she adds: 'So you best not lock yourself in your man cave again.'

'It's not a man cave, it's—'

'I'm only teasing,' she says. 'Although I did hear about you interrogating Helena on the subject the other day.'

'I wasn't *interrogating* her.'

'You were a bit, according to what I heard.'

'I just wondered if she knew anything about it, that's all. She was being evasive.'

'She was probably trying to be polite. Not everyone is as obsessed as you are, love.'

I shrug. 'I just want to know the truth. Don't like mysteries, especially in my own house.'

'As long as it doesn't end up with you getting hurt,' she says. 'Like it did with MVI.'

'Ouch,' I say, wincing at the memory. 'That was a bit of a low blow.'

She lays an apologetic palm flat on my chest. 'But you know what I mean, love.'

MVI Limited had been several jobs ago, almost a decade ago, a company that had systematically inflated client invoices to cover coding work they didn't need and was never carried out. A tribunal had eventually ruled in my favour but that was long after I'd been fired for asking the wrong questions – and the injustice still stung, all these years later.

'That was nothing like this,' I say. 'And they *were* being over-charged.'

'And it was the first time I realised you had a tendency to get obsessed with things.'

She's right, of course. And maybe I'd allowed myself to focus on the house because it was easier than thinking about my work situation.

'I just want our kids to be safe, for all of us to be safe.'

'I know.' She kisses my cheek, easing herself out of the embrace and turning towards the stairs. 'Let's talk things through with Dom later.'

Coco is curled into a sleepy circle at the top of the second-floor staircase, her tail wagging lethargically as I give her head a quick scratch on the way past. In the small bedroom where this had all started I open the wood-panelled door and then push it shut, doing it twice, admiring the flawless workmanship again even though I've been in and out of here a dozen times already this week. The attention to detail that must have gone into hand-crafting this door means it's still hard to make out, even though I know exactly where it is.

Inside the dusty hidden room, I click on the light and start opening drawers in the dresser in search of the wallet. There were initials on it but I couldn't remember if they were PF – perhaps Peter Flack? – or something different. If they *were* PF then that was another link to another premature death from the same year that Adrian Parish had disappeared. The same year he had died, I correct myself. There didn't seem any real possibility that Maxine's husband was still alive. Not after all this time.

But when I find the wallet in a drawer and open it up again, I see my memory has played a trick on me. The faded silver initials are there but they don't match: not a P, but a D. The initials are DF, not PF.

So it hadn't belonged to Peter Flack. Perhaps a relative?

A faint, muffled voice reaches me through the closed door.

'Adam?'

I stand up from the armchair, banging my head on the swinging bulb above as I grope towards the door.

My brother-in-law's voice comes again. 'Adam? Are you in there?'

I take a step towards the door, catching my shin on the edge of the dresser.

'Hang on a second.'

My fingers find the handle and I pull it open, squinting into the brighter light.

'Jess said I'd probably find you here.' Dom looms into the low doorway, his jeans speckled with white paint. 'So this is where you're spending half your time nowadays – what are you even *doing* in there, with the door shut?'

'Just having another look at the wallet. And . . . I wanted to check if I could hear anything when the door was closed.'

He gives me a quizzical glance. 'Obviously you couldn't hear me shouting for you downstairs. Dinner's ready. And I'm starving.' He turns to go.

I put the old wallet down on top of the dresser and pull the light cord, plunging the little room back into darkness.

Dean

He had enough fish and chips for the two of them.

It was the least he could do, after today. The lad didn't have to help him carry his stuff in, didn't have to wait while the key was sorted, didn't have to hang around until he'd checked the water was on, the electrics worked, the radiator warmed up. The lad – Dean couldn't remember his name – was a volunteer so it wasn't as if he was even getting paid for his time.

But everyone liked fish and chips.

When things got bad, it was easy to forget there were still good people out there. People who wanted to help. The rehab lady, who'd persuaded him to open up about what he'd done, what had been done to him. This lad from the charity who had driven the Transit, helped him unload second-hand furniture for the little bedsit.

The new place was OK. The kitchen floor might be sticky but there was no black mould on the wall, no mouse droppings behind the fridge, not too many stains on the mattress. The little cupboard by the stove was empty apart from half a packet of sugar and a couple of sachets of instant coffee. But Dean still had two ten-pound notes nestling in his wallet, safe in the back pocket of his jeans. He would spend it on food to fill the cupboard, nothing else. And proper food, pasta and vegetables and stuff. No crap. No drugs. No more booze. A fresh start.

It was better than the halfway house, miles better than the last place – although that wasn't difficult. The main thing was that she didn't know where he was. That her new bloke didn't know, that he didn't have to do his psycho routine again just to prove he was the big man.

Dean retrieved the probation letter from one of his half-dozen plastic bags and laid it on the little side table to read later, when he'd had something to eat. That stuff had never come easy to him, the letters always shifting and jumping on the page. He could recognise the shape of his own name printed at the top of the page in black capitals – Dean Fullerton – but only by the angles and lines made by the letters rather than because he could see the order they were in.

He got two chipped plates out of the cupboard, hunted around until he found a knife and two forks that looked clean enough. A first meal to christen the new place. He put one of the paper-wrapped packages – cod and large chips with plenty of salt and vinegar – onto the bigger plate and then began to unwrap his own, grease from the chips already soaking through the plain paper onto his fingers.

'I got enough plates,' Dean said, mustering a hopeful smile. 'You can stay and eat here, if you want.'

The lad checked his watch, looked back towards the door as if he was in two minds about something.

'Thanks,' he said finally. 'I'm starving.'

'You're welcome.'

The lad returned his smile.

'Actually,' he said, moving towards the front door. 'I've just got to fetch something from the van first. Back in a sec.'

46

Dinner is toad-in-the-hole with mashed potatoes and carrots, followed by ice cream for pudding. When we've finished, Dom plays football outside with Callum while I clear up and run Daisy's bath. When the temperature's right, I call her but she doesn't respond. She's developed a reluctance to be the first to go to bed when her brother's bedtime is half an hour later.

I'm about to go looking for her downstairs when her voice reaches me from her own room, soft and indistinct. I push open her door.

'Time for your bath, Daze.'

She continues chattering away to herself, the way she does when she's having a conversation with one of her dolls.

'Come on,' I say, gathering her pyjamas from the end of the bed. 'If you're quick you can have two stories with Uncle Dom.'

She's in the corner, sitting at the little red plastic desk and chair she inherited from her brother last year. The edges of the table are lined with Playmobil figures, every other square inch of it covered with colouring books, pens, bits of Lego and chunky plastic jewellery.

But she's not playing with any of that. Instead, she has one of her toy phones pressed to her ear, burbling away happily in the way she's done ever since she started sitting with Jess and me on our work-from-home days.

'Yes,' she says. 'I have a cat and a dog and my brother has a hamster called Mr Stay Puft and there was a bird on our step but he died.' A short pause. 'I don't know. It was sad.' Another pause. 'No. Don't like it.' Pause. 'Just don't.'

'Daisy?'

My daughter finally turns and I notice something that hits me with the force of a slap.

She's not talking on one of her toy phones.

She has the little flip phone pressed to her ear, the old Motorola I'd left charging on my desk earlier.

'Daisy?' I hold my hand out. 'Give me the phone, please.'

'My daddy's here,' she says solemnly into the mouthpiece. 'It's my bath time.'

She hands me the mobile, its small screen glowing.

'Who is this?' I say. The flip phone is still warm from her hand. 'Hello? Hello?'

But there is only dead air when I hold it to my ear. I study the screen, the blocky visual menu of basic functions arranged in a square, three by three. Pressing the green 'dial' button doesn't seem to do anything.

'Who were you talking to, Daisy?'

'Santa.'

'Really?' When she nods reluctantly, I add: 'Was there really someone there, or were you just pretending?'

'It's secret.'

I kneel down to her level. 'Where did you find this phone, sweetie?'

She shrugs her little shoulders. 'Can't remember.'

'Did you find it on my desk?'

'No.' Her bottom lip juts out. 'It's mine. Callum gave it to me.'

'Callum's had it too?' I scroll through menus, looking for incoming calls or dialled numbers but I can't seem to see anything that's new. Half knowing it was ridiculous – the phone was an antique, it wasn't even on a network so how could it make or receive calls? Unless Charlie had rigged it up in some way so it could make calls again, unless . . .

No. That was absurd.

My daughter seems to have forgotten about it already.

'Do I *have* to have a bath?' She flops dramatically onto her bed. 'Callum doesn't have to.'

I slip the phone into my pocket and lift her up across my chest, her arms and legs hanging loose like a rag doll.

'Callum will go in right after you, Daisy-Doo. Come on.'

* * *

Uncle Dom is chosen by both younger children for a bedtime story and doesn't leave until they're asleep.

He refuses a nightcap, insists a week of night shifts has worn him out but says – with a meaningful look at me – that he'll call tomorrow. When Leah heads up to her room I do a sweep of the house, checking all the doors are shut and locked. Windows in the back reception room and the dining room have been left open to let out some of the spring heat and the clean sharp smell of drying paint, so I pull them shut too before putting supper down for Coco and Steve.

I stand by the front door for a moment, flicking off each of the lights in turn, shadows deepening around me as each bulb goes out. We've been here a week but it still doesn't feel like our house. Like our *home*. It still feels like an Airbnb, a rental property that we're just visiting before going back to our real lives. I hope that will change when we get more of our pictures and books and photos unpacked, put more of our own stamp on the place. When I know I can pay my half of the mortgage again.

When I deal with the threat that still hangs over my family.

I check on each of the kids. All fast asleep. Quiet. Safe. Daisy snoring very softly in the pale blue wash of her night light. In the master bedroom Jess is asleep too, her breathing deep and slow, the Kindle still propped open in its case next to her. I close the cover quietly, put it on her bedside table.

For me, sleep is more elusive.

Reading only seems to make things worse. It's well past midnight when I last glance at the time, the glowing red numerals of my bedside clock mocking me in the darkness. Eventually, I drift in and out of half-snatched dreams, seeing myself high in the branches of a tall tree with no way to get down. Then stuck in a room with no doors, only tiny red lights blinking in the darkness, each one the lens of a camera pointing at me. I jerk awake and Jess shifts uneasily beside me before settling back into her pillow.

Once again, I turn over and try to push the churning thoughts from my mind, to imagine I'm back in our old room, in our old house. Where everything is familiar.

I'm just drifting off again when I hear it.

The creak of a floorboard, old wood shifting beneath weight: a noise that doesn't belong at this time of the night. Not a pet scratching at the kitchen door. Not a child crying out from a nightmare.

This time, it sounds like the nightmare is really here.

Because someone is downstairs.

47

The noise comes again.

Creak. The sound is small and subtle, a floorboard flexing under pressure, but it's loud enough in the deep black silence of this old house.

I feel myself come fully and shockingly awake, as if I've just grabbed an electric fence with both hands, staring into the darkness as if that will somehow make it easier to hear the next noise and figure out where it's coming from. Perhaps it was Leah, creeping to the bathroom? But her room has an en suite, she doesn't need to come down for the toilet let alone down to the ground floor. The younger two would call for me rather than wandering around in the dark at night. And the noise was definitely below.

The front hall was tiled, the kitchen and conservatory too. A creak of wood meant the lounge, the dining room, the back room.

Or the stairs.

I sit up and flick the thin summer duvet off my legs, a pounding red wine hangover already starting its drumbeat in my head. At our old house I'd always kept an old wooden chair leg next to the bed after hearing about a neighbour burgled in the night while his family slept. I'd never needed it, and it had ended up covered in a layer of dust alongside a pile of unread books, but it felt good to have something there. Just in case.

I reach for it in the darkness, my grasping hand finding only the flat cool of the bedroom wall.

The makeshift weapon, I realise, is still in one of the packing crates stacked up in the garage along with most of my books and other bedroom stuff. There's no time to look for anything else – I just have to get to the top of the stairs before they do. Heart thudding against my ribs, I feel my way around the bed, fingers running along the cool metal frame, reach a hand to the wardrobe, the bookcase, the smooth round handle of the bedroom door.

For a moment I wonder whether it will be the man standing on the other side, the ghost that Daisy had seen behind her door. Some wandering spirit come back to haunt us out of his old family home.

Stop it, I say to myself. *Stop being ridiculous.*

With a fist clenched at my side, I wrench the door open.

The landing seems to be empty.

No ghost. No man. No one at all. It's almost as black as the bedroom, only the vaguest of grey lines hinting at the staircase to my right.

I fumble for the nearest light switch on the landing, bracing myself for a sudden flood of illumination from the 100-watt bulb. The breath is coming hot and fast in my throat, every muscle ready to fight, to resist, to do whatever is necessary to stop them getting up here where my family slumbers on, unaware of the danger.

I flick the light switch.

Nothing happens.

Uselessly, I flick it on and off twice more, but the pitch darkness remains. Surely the new bulb hasn't blown already? With my left hand out in front of me, I feel my way across the landing to the bathroom until I reach the light switch beside the door there.

Click. Nothing.

With tentative steps, I feel my way to the next door along, to Callum's bedroom, easing the door open and going close enough to his bed to hear him breathing. Coco is curled at the end of his bed, her old ears oblivious to everything. In the next bedroom along, Daisy's little blue night light has gone dark like everything else but I can just make out her soft snore against the muslin cloth she still takes to bed every night.

At the top of the staircase, I peer down into the shadows below, straining my ears to hear any sound. There is some kind of intermittent noise down there, a soft tapping or clicking. *Just take the car keys and go*, I think. *Take what you want and leave my family alone. Because if you try to come up the stairs, if you cross that line, one of us is going to get hurt.*

I need light, *any* light. With my eyes finally starting to adjust, discerning the blacks from different depths of dark grey, I feel my way back to the master bedroom. Going back around to my bedside table to find my mobile, noticing something else for the first time: the display on my clock radio is also blank. No red numerals. Nothing at all.

Either a circuit breaker has tripped in the cellar, or . . .

Or someone has cut the power.

I feel the way to my phone, the flash of the screen dazzling me as I hold down the power button. *Come on, come on.* I go to my wife's side of the bed while I wait for the phone to boot up.

'Jess!' I call to her in a hoarse whisper. 'Jess! Wake up.'

She doesn't stir.

I call her name again, louder, tapping her shin with my hand. Finally, she moves her head, eyes squinting into the light from my phone.

'What?' She turns her head away from the light. 'Too bright.'

'Jess, listen to me.'

'Turn it *off.*'

'There's someone downstairs and the power is out. I'm going to check, OK?'

'Wait, what?' Her voice is still thick with sleep. 'What's going on?'

'Stay here,' I say again, taking her own mobile from the bedside table and pressing it into her hand. 'Call the police.'

'What . . . Who's here?'

'Just call them. I won't be long. Don't open the bedroom door to anyone.'

I'm pulling the door shut behind me as my phone chimes with the four-note sound that tells me it's booted up, the screen filling with icons over the familiar picture of Jess and the three kids from Christmas last year. I select the torch app and flash it around the landing, wild leaping shadows dancing away from the bright white light. Everything looks different in the dark, in the middle of the night. This house that we've only lived in for a week, that still feels as if it belongs to someone else.

Taking a deep breath, I start to descend the stairs, the night air chilly around my shoulders. I'm wearing only boxer shorts and feel more exposed, more vulnerable with every step, the red-wine throb in my head growing worse by the second.

'Hello?' I pause to pan the phone torch around when I'm half-way down the stairs. Shadows upon shadows, only a weak glaze of light filtering through the front from the old-fashioned gas-lights out on the street. 'The police are on their way.'

I wait for any response, hoping that Jess has already made the call. I strain my ears to hear anything above my own ragged breathing.

Silence.

The tiles of the hallway are ice-cold against the soles of my bare feet.

'Hello?' My voice echoes back to me off the high ceiling. 'I know you're there.'

There is the faintest sound from the sitting room. The shift of fabric against skin, perhaps, or the lightest step on the wooden parquet flooring.

Found you.

I reach out for the nearest hall light switch but it, too, is out of action. Beside it, leaning in the corner, is the golfing umbrella that I take to Callum's football matches. My heart is beating so hard and so fast it feels like it's coming up my throat, my mouth as dry as dead leaves. Brandishing the big umbrella in my right hand, I shine the light from my phone into the sitting room, taking two steps in and scanning wildly around for the intruder, left, right, shadows bouncing and dancing, light flashing off the mirror over the fireplace as I turn back to the left again and there is a sudden movement on the floor . . .

There's no one in the room. Only Steve, his yellow eyes blinking up at me in surprise. The remains of a small mouse are pinned beneath his paw, the tail just visible.

'Jesus,' I breathe. 'Bloody cat.'

He goes back to his prize and I slowly retrace my steps back into the hall. The cat may be roaming around but he wasn't heavy enough to make the noises I heard from upstairs. There *is* someone here, I am sure of it. Someone who wanted to stay in the dark.

In the kitchen I go to the sink, putting the umbrella down and shining the torchlight on the drying rack. *There.* My hand closes on a rolling pin.

The police should be on their way. Although . . . on a Saturday night they probably had their hands full with drinkers spilling out of city centre pubs and bars. The thought brings me up short. What if the police took ten minutes to respond? Twenty? What then?

I had to get the lights back on.

The cellar door is already ajar, and I pull it open further, put out a tentative foot to find the top step. The staircase is dusty cold stone, edges worn smooth with time; the walls are bare flaking brick in this subterranean part of the house that feels untouched, unchanged since the house was first built more than a century ago.

Dank, stale air greets me as I descend. The damp smells of old earth and rust and rot, but also the faintest note of – what? Something sweet, musky, like aftershave. Or perfume? At the bottom of the short flight of steps, I have to hunch over to avoid the cross-beams at head height. The three pitch-black compartments of the old cellar are creepy enough with the lights on but with only the pale jumping shadows thrown by my torch, they look like something out of a horror movie. I shine the light into each one as I pass anyway, the rolling pin gripped tightly in my right hand. But there's only cobwebbed junk, old boxes, tins of paint, rusting metal garden chairs.

The circuit box is in the third compartment, a two-foot panel on the wall enclosed in a clear plastic cover. I flinch as something drops onto my shoulder and runs *tick-tick-tick* down my bare arm.

A spider. Just a spider, scuttling off into the dark.

The master circuit breaker on the panel has been flipped down to the 'off' setting. I flick it back up with a solid *click* to switch the power back on, then reset all other switches one by one, still hunched over to avoid banging my head on the low beams. Everything is still in darkness: the nearest light switch is at the top of the cellar stairs.

I'm halfway up the steps when I hear the scuff of a foot above me, the creak of a hinge.

I shine the torch towards the half-open door at the top of the stairs. In the second before a blindingly bright light shines right in my eyes I can just make out a figure, a mask, a balaclava with only a pale slit for the eyes before the sole of a heavy boot kicks the air from my chest and then I'm falling, a flash of spinning light as the phone tumbles from my hand and the hard brick floor of the cellar rushes up to meet—

PART III

There is so much the so-called experts get wrong. They say we live on the margins, that we all come from broken homes, that we can't manage in day-to-day life. That we will eventually spiral and break under the pressure of what we do, so we can be singled out from the crowd and caught.

Wrong.

Why? Because those theories don't take in the whole picture. They're based purely on a particular subset of people like us: the ones who got caught.

48

The paramedic is shining a light in my eyes.

I do what she tells me, following the movement of the penlight as it swings from left to right and back again. I'm on a kitchen chair, dressing gown bunched at my waist for an examination of the cuts and bruises on my forearms, the sprain of my left wrist, bruising to my chest and angry red abrasions to the skin on my back.

Her main concern, however, is the head injury.

The pain at the back of my skull is a furious, relentless throb that feels as if something is ready to burst. I can remember falling backwards – being *kicked* backwards – down the cellar steps, the sick sensation of being in mid-air with nothing to break my fall, nothing to grab onto, a brief explosion of pain as I hit the solid brick floor and then . . . nothing. Opening my eyes to agonising bright light, dirt and blood sticky against my cheek, all the pain in the world radiating in hot red waves from the back of my head. Jess's desperate voice cutting through everything as she knelt beside me.

There had been no sign of the masked intruder by the time she ventured downstairs, turning on lights and calling my name as she went. Just me, knocked out cold and flat on my back in the cellar. Slowly coming to as she said my name over and over, feeling as if I'd been clubbed with a cricket bat.

The police have already been and gone, two harassed-looking officers arriving in a blur of blue lights and crackling radios, checking the house and garden for signs that anyone was still lurking around. The paramedics were only cleared to come in once the police had told them it was safe to do so, before the officers had been called away again to some kind of incident in the city centre. One of their colleagues from the day shift would return in the next forty-eight hours, they said, to take a statement. In lieu of a police car outside the house, Jess had switched on every single light downstairs – all the rooms ablaze as if illumination alone might frighten away a return visit from the night-time attacker.

Callum stares at the two paramedics, working steadily in their green jumpsuits, as if they are aliens arrived from another planet. Leah sits at the kitchen table beside him, her forehead creased with concern. She was so surprised to be woken that she even forgot to bring her phone downstairs with her. Weirdly, Daisy is the only one of us who seems to have slept through it all; through the arrival and departure of the police; the paramedics hefting their bulky treatment bags into the kitchen; the kettle boiling as Jess made cups of tea, coffee and hot chocolate for everyone.

The paramedic, whose name is Farida, switches off her penlight and stows it in a pocket of her equipment vest.

'Adam?' she says, moving a blue-gloved hand carefully over the side of my head. 'What day is it today?'

'Err . . . Saturday.' I glance up at the calendar on the fridge, the movement sending more sharp skewers of agony through my head. 'No. Wait. No, it's Sunday. Must be Sunday morning now.'

Her colleague is behind me, cleaning the head wound with a brisk efficiency and apologising each time I tense with pain.

He winds overlapping strips of bandage over the wound like a headband, securing it with medical tape.

When he's finished with the dressing, Farida checks the other side of my head, applying gentle pressure with her fingertips. 'And what's the name of the street where you live?'

I blink, groping for the right answer. 'Regency . . . Place.'

She feels behind my ears, looking – I assume – for injury sites other than the gash at the back of my head. Finally, she lowers her hands and sits back in the chair.

'You've had a pretty nasty bang on the head, Adam. I've given you a preliminary examination and we've dressed the external wound but I'd like to get you properly checked at Queen's Medical Centre, all right? So if you want to take a minute to get a few clothes, something to wear on your feet and we'll take you down—'

'No,' I say, shrugging the dressing gown back up onto my shoulders. 'Not tonight.'

She gives me a quizzical look. 'Obviously I can't force you to come with us, but I *strongly* recommend that you do so. They can give you a much more thorough exam, arrange scans if necessary. Better safe than sorry – especially where head injuries are concerned.'

'I'm not leaving my family alone tonight, not after this.' I gesture vaguely at the cellar door. 'And we can't all five of us go together.'

'Adam?' Jess says gently. She hands me two paracetamol and a glass of water. 'She's right. You really should go to QMC with them, get fully checked out.'

I shake my head, the movement setting off a fresh ripple of pain.

'I'll call Dom, get him to come over in the morning and take me down there. But I'm not going anywhere right now, while it's still pitch black outside.' I don't want to mention the obvious, while Callum and Leah are still in the room: that the intruder might come back. 'Besides which, A & E at two o'clock on a Sunday morning will be absolutely wall to wall with crazy drunk people. They will be queueing out of the door and I probably won't be seen until the morning anyway.'

Farida exchanges a glance with my wife as if to say, *What can we do with him?* But she begins to pack away her equipment in the green kit bag anyway.

'It's your decision,' she says with a shrug. 'But I would strongly advise you to get yourself to Queen's, whether it's busy or not.'

'I will,' I say. 'In the morning.'

Jess sees Farida and her colleague to the door, where I can hear them talking in low voices about plenty of rest, painkillers and a sling for my wrist; about symptoms of deterioration that Jess needs to watch for, about *nausea* and *dizziness* and *sensitivity to light*.

Gingerly, I stand up and retrieve my phone from the kitchen side. There is a crack on the screen where it hit the cellar floor, a diagonal spiderweb fracture. Seven missed calls from Jess still showing on the display. I had no idea how long I'd been out cold on the cellar floor – no longer than five minutes, Jess had said – but it was more than enough time for the intruder to make their escape. I check the back door to see if it's been forced or any windows smashed around it. But it looks just the way I left it when I'd gone up to bed a few hours ago. Same for the front door and the patio door, according to the two police officers whose names I've already forgotten. My wallet, laptop and car keys are untouched on the kitchen side.

It's only after the paramedics have gone, after Leah has taken Callum back up to bed, that Jess lets her brave face slip. She stands in front of me with her head down, lips pressed together, suddenly on the verge of tears.

I put a hand on her arm. 'Hey. What is it?'

She shakes her head, cuffing at her eyes with the sleeve of her dressing gown.

'I thought . . .' She tails off.

'Tell me,' I say. 'It's OK.'

'I thought you were dead,' she says quietly. 'I was calling your phone and I could just about hear it ringing somewhere below me in the house, but it sounded so far away, almost like it was underground. You weren't picking up and the police still weren't here, I thought they were never going to come. I kept calling and calling, then I came down into the kitchen, and saw the cellar door was ajar, I switched the lights on and looked down there and I could just see your legs, flat out at the bottom of the stairs. When I got down there you were so pale, there was blood and I thought he'd . . .'

I put my arms around her. 'It's only a bump on the head. Hurts a bit but I've had worse.'

'When?'

'Playing rugby.'

She sniffs. 'Liar.'

'OK, maybe not quite this bad, but I've had concussions before. I'll be all right.'

She puts her head against my chest and we stand like that for a moment in the kitchen, the warmth of her body pressed against mine. The pain, everywhere, receding into the background as we hold each other close.

'What if you hadn't been here?' she says softly. 'What if they'd come upstairs, gone into one of the kids' rooms?'

'But they didn't,' I say, rubbing her back. 'They're gone now. We're all right, we're all OK.'

She looks up at me. 'We're *not* OK. He might have killed you.'

'I don't think that was his plan. I think I just surprised him.'

'I don't understand how you can be so sure about it,' she says finally. She pulls away from the embrace to take a tissue from the box on the kitchen counter, wiping her eyes and nose. 'Is this all about that stupid hidden room, the things you found? A burglar comes into our house in the middle of the night but doesn't take anything?'

'I guess . . . he didn't find what he was actually looking for.'

'Why do I feel like you're still holding something back, Adam?' She leans back against the counter, crossing her arms tightly over her chest. 'What is it you're not telling me? It's all connected, isn't it?'

I look at my wife, at her beautiful face, eyes red-rimmed from crying. The one person in the world I was closest to, who knew me better than anyone, and I had kept things from her. I had not told her the whole truth. But she deserved more than this; she deserved to know all of it.

'Yes,' I say. 'I think it is.'

49

I tell my wife everything.

Sitting opposite each other at the kitchen table, I tell her about Adrian Parish and Maxine, about my visit to her house in Kimberley. I tell her about Elizabeth Makepeace and Peter Flack, about the old Rolex watch and the money I'd made by selling it at the jeweller's shop.

I tell her about losing my job.

She puts a hand over mine, gives it a gentle squeeze. A frown of concern creasing her brow. Sympathy winning the battle against anger – for now, at least – that I've kept such a big secret from her.

'I'm sorry, Adam,' she says. 'That's awful. Those miserable sods never appreciated you anyway.'

'True.'

'But you should have told me when it happened.'

'We were literally all packed to move, all the contracts were signed, the first payment was about to go out on the new mortgage and I didn't want to stress you any more than you already were.' I take a sip of lukewarm tea. 'Wish I'd never found that bloody phone number now.'

'It was me that found it,' she says quietly. 'Me that called it first, remember? We thought it was just a bit of an old curiosity. A blast from the past.'

'Then I wish I'd just thrown the phone away as soon as I found it.'

'Do you think it's someone trying to recover stolen goods, or something?'

'There's got to be more to it than that. Apart from the watch, what could they possibly want with the rest of it?'

She shakes her head, angrily brushing away tears again. 'I hate this, Adam. I *hate* it. Feels like we're being watched the whole time, like we're living in a goldfish bowl. All of this for some stupid wristwatch. Why don't we just leave for a few days?'

'And go where?'

'I don't know. Dom's house?'

'He's only got one spare room.' I say it gently. 'And my parents are two hours away.'

'A hotel, then? Somewhere cheap?'

A bubble of shame expands in my chest, the heat of frustration at my own failure. Most of all, at the danger I had unwittingly brought to our door – danger to the four people who meant more to me than anything else in the world. This had moved far beyond simple curiosity about my new house, far beyond anything that could justify further pursuit of answers about the hidden room. It was time to bring it to an end.

'I know what I have to do now,' I say. 'I know what needs to be—'

'Or we could keep the kids off school for a few days, at least?' Jess says abruptly. 'Until we know how things stand. I'll take some leave, and we can all just stay here, safe together. In the meantime we change the locks, get the alarm fixed and talk to the police about it when they come back to take a statement about what happened tonight. Figure out what to do next. What do you think?'

'I can do better than that,' I say. 'There must be a way to fix it. To make it all go away.'

I had set all of this – whatever *this* was – in motion. And it was down to me to stop it.

Because there was a way to put things right. Of course there was.

* * *

My brother-in-law comes over again first thing on Sunday morning and drives me to the A & E department at Queen's Medical Centre. He barely speaks on the way there and I can tell he's angry, his jaw set tight. Angry at me, at the intruder, at the danger to his nieces and nephew, to his sister – danger that I've been unable to stop.

A & E is busy, shadow-eyed staff still dealing with the overnight backlog of patients sprawled on chairs or laid out on the floor, the vast majority of which seem to stem from drinking, fighting or falling over in the city centre. An underlying smell of bleach in the waiting area is punctured here and there by the sharp tang of vomit.

Dom hands me a cup of machine-brewed tea and I tell him everything, too. All of it. He raises an eyebrow when I tell him what I plan to do next, but doesn't try to dissuade me.

'The thing I don't get,' he says, 'is how they found you in the first place. How they found your house.'

'Jess's phone signal, from when she first called that number? Could they track it somehow?'

He shakes his head. 'Only the police can do that. Or the security services. The place was empty for a while before you moved in, right?'

'A month or so,' I say. 'The previous owner moved into a home and his son cleared it out for him.'

'But ... if there's something in the house they want, this antique watch, or whatever, surely it would have been a lot easier to break in and get it during that month, while the property was vacant?'

I sip my tea. It's strong and bitter, with an aftertaste of hot plastic.

'Which suggests,' I say, 'they didn't know about the hidden room. Not until *after* I got in touch.'

'Exactly,' he says, grimacing as he swallows a mouthful of coffee. 'You know, if they can find you, maybe you can do the same to them. You can give them what they want – or what they *think* they want – and find out where they are into the bargain. Find out *who* they are.'

50

We have a lot of time to kill. It's lunchtime before I'm examined and sent in for a scan, and two hours after that before the wound is cleaned again, stitched up and I'm sent on my way with a pre-scription for strong painkillers and a thin cotton sling for my wrist. On the way back, we make a detour to B&Q where I buy two new deadbolts for the kitchen door and the front door. Tomorrow, I'll call a locksmith in to change the locks as well, and get a couple of security companies to quote on replacing the alarm. I'll figure out how we'll afford it later. For now, the credit card will have to do.

Another detour takes us into the city, where I pay a quick visit to Silverjoy Jewellers. The owner insists she has passed on my number to the person who bought the Rolex – but beyond that, she has nothing more to tell me.

After Dom has dropped me home, I stand for a moment on my drive, looking at our big bay windows, back at the street, up at the tree where the camera had been hidden. The house seems suddenly very exposed, very *open*, very welcoming in a way that I no longer like. Too many trees and hedges, too many ways to be tucked away and private, too many old doors and big windows and semi-deserted streets all around us.

All the things that had attracted us here in the first place. The things that had made us fall in love with the idea of living in The Park.

There are still no curtains in our lounge windows and a stack of cardboard boxes with the black and yellow logo of Robinson Removals are clearly visible from the pavement. The 'Sold' sign was long gone but we had not hidden the fact that we'd recently moved in. If someone had figured out we'd moved to The Park, how long would it take to cruise every street and look for tell-tale signs of a new arrival? It was a relatively small enclave of the city, fewer than a thousand houses in a specific, defined area next to the castle. You could cover every street in a few hours. Maybe less.

The kids are watching *The Greatest Showman* in the lounge while Jess is in the kitchen, sorting through a washing basket full of school uniforms ready for ironing. She makes us both a cup of tea and I tell her about the hospital, the scan, what the doctor had said about rest and painkillers and possible concussion.

She has her glasses on, hair tied back, old jeans and a soft faded sweatshirt, but looks surprisingly fresh considering how tired I know she must be. All seems to have been quiet at the house while I've been away. No visitors. She's been researching hotels, she says, but can't find a decent one at a price we can afford on a single salary, alongside the mortgage.

I measure up the new deadbolts and fit one each to the front door and the kitchen door. They feel solid and substantial, the steel sliding smoothly across to keep both doors securely shut even if someone outside had a key.

'The police didn't come back?' I say as I'm putting the tools away. 'To take a statement about last night?'

'Nope.' She sips her tea, studying the bandage on my head. 'The whole thing is starting to feel like a dream now, like it happened to someone else. Or maybe it's just because I'm so zonked on lack of sleep.'

'Are you OK?' I say. 'Sorry it took so long; A & E was crazy. Too many patients, staff absolutely run off their feet.'

'I'm fine. We're all fine. Lots of questions from the kids, but they seem all right.'

Her phone pings on the counter; she glances at it, touches the screen, smiles briefly before it goes dark again.

Something from a conversation with her brother returns to me, a question he'd asked while we both scrolled mindlessly through Twitter and Facebook as the hours waiting at QMC took their toll.

'I was talking to Dom at the hospital,' I say. 'Random question, but – is your Facebook profile public?'

She shrugs. 'How do you mean?'

'Is it just friends that can see your profile and your posts, or can anyone see them?'

'Just friends. I think.' She picks up the phone and taps the screen, her face darkening. 'Oh. No, it's . . . I opened it up for a school thing, that Easter fete Callum's year group did, so we could sell tickets and promote to parents. I was on the fundraising committee, remember?'

'So it's public?'

'It *was.*' She taps the screen again, selecting and swiping until she finds what she wants. 'Not anymore. Why?'

I take a sip of my tea, keeping my voice neutral. 'When you left the message using the number from that old phone, Daisy and Callum were in the room. They were arguing and I told them to stop, pretty sure I mentioned both their names while you were leaving the message.'

'So?'

'So . . . what if they used Callum and Daisy's names as search terms? Plus you left your first name and somehow that's led them to find your Facebook page, maybe to that picture you posted last weekend? Or it could be any recent post that mentions their names.'

'But that doesn't tell them where we *are*. I'd never post anything about our location, our address.'

She's frowning hard now, two vertical lines between her eyebrows that normally mean she's about to shift from defence to attack. Maybe it's the low, angry throb at the back of my head, the bite of the new stitches, the lack of sleep, the vending-machine food at the hospital, but I keep going anyway.

'I know, I know. Just trying to figure things out.' I stare at the ceiling, trying to drag my thoughts into some kind of order. 'What if . . . they'd found your Facebook profile and really dug into it, checked every post you liked? Cross-referenced with any internal shots of the house you've posted on your feed? Then done some on-the-ground work to identify this specific address.'

My wife is shaking her head.

'The camera in the birdbox, the cameras in the house, they were *already* here when we moved in. Somebody already knew something about this house.'

I rub my temples, at the throbbing headache that has been a constant jagged hum since last night.

'Of course,' I say. 'Sorry. You're right. Feels like my head is full of cement today.'

'You need paracetamol and rest, Adam.' She puts her hands on my shoulders, her expression softening again. 'You need to sleep. You had a lucky escape last night and you need to recover. Why don't you go up now, I'll sort the kids out.'

I nod, my eyes sagging with fatigue.

'Just got something else I need to do.'

'Don't be long.'

She kisses me on the cheek and goes back into the lounge.

I unlock my phone and open the online shopping page I'd found before, checking next-day delivery was still available. Double-checking all the details I could remember to make sure they tallied with the watch I'd found upstairs.

Rolex Explorer
   Genuine replica wristwatch
   A perfect copy of the real thing for only £99 – bespoke engraving available too!

I study the image one last time and click 'Buy Now'.

51

MONDAY

Jess brings me tea and toast in bed in the morning, insisting I take it easy. She leaves it as late as she can before driving Leah to school, telling me she'll try to finish early today. Even though we both concede that the kids will probably be safer at school than at our house. The pain from my head injury has receded to a low background hum, kept at bay by the painkillers. The bruising has started to bloom blue and black beneath the skin of my chest and back, the wrist sprain settled to a dull ache that flares every now and then when I take the sling off.

I drop Callum and Daisy at St Jude's Primary, watching them until they're safely inside their classrooms, then head back to my car and drive straight into town. On the way, I dial Maxine's number, but it goes straight to voicemail. She hasn't responded to any of my messages since Saturday.

My phone buzzes as I'm parking up in the multi-storey on Fletcher Gate. *Finally*. I snatch it up, expecting to see a reply from Maxine. But it's not from her – it's from the unknown number, the first time they've been in contact in a few days.

A needle of ice slides down my back as I read the message.

Next time we bring petrol and matches. Or you can return our property to us. Your choice.

I swallow hard, pushing back a sudden image of the house in flames with my family trapped inside. I resist the urge to respond in anger, or fear: that currency is no longer any good here.

I'm sorting it. Need a little time.

I lock the car and head for the stairs. The car park is busy, and I've ended up on the lower half of level six, where almost every bay is already taken. Above me and to the right, cars are crawling slowly along the higher tier of this level, engine noise growling off the low concrete. Doors slamming, cars beeping as they're locked, drivers hurrying away. A figure catches my eye further down the row. Because I'm below him I can only see his upper body, but I can tell that he's tall and heavy, greying hair and beard and a dark grey coat . . .

There is a cold shock of déjà vu as I realise I've seen him before.

The General Cemetery on Saturday, just before I met Maxine.

I dodge around a car coming up the ramp from below and change direction to head towards him. A van passes in front of him as the phone buzzes again in my hand.

You have until tonight.

For a crazy second I think it must be him who's sending me these taunting messages, who's threatening my family as casually as sending a text on a Monday morning. I break into a run, sprinting up the ramp to the next level, my head pounding, scanning left and right to see which way he went.

But there's only a blonde woman in jeans and a jacket getting out of a Range Rover.

The figure in the grey coat is gone.

* * *

It's a five-minute walk from the car park and I watch for the grey-coated man all the way, doubling back and taking an indirect route to see if he's following me.

I don't catch sight of him again.

The city's central library is a modern glass-fronted building near the train station, with high ceilings and plenty of space between the bookcases. The microfiche reader sits in a corner at the back and looks decades old, cream plastic surrounding a large screen, with a pair of control wheels – one horizontal, one vertical – instead of a keyboard.

A staff member hunts out a cardboard box from a rack behind the desk, sliding out a sheaf of densely printed transparent plastic sheets and checking the tab at the top of the first one: *NEP 1/12/2001– 4/12/2001.*

'Each one of these sheets is about three days' worth of papers,' he says. The screen lights up as he switches the reader on and slides in one of the clear plastic sheets. 'Each page of the city final edition, reduced to four per cent of its original dimensions. The lens magnifies it back up to legible size. Controls here and here for moving the lens from one page to the next.'

He wanders off back to the front desk. I sit down at the reader and flick through the cardboard box of plastic microfiche sheets, the printing impossibly small for the naked eye, tiny consecutive pages laid out in rows side by side.

Elizabeth Makepeace and Peter Flack had died on 27th December, 2001 but both of them had lived in my house for years – or maybe decades – before that. I start with that day's edition, scanning each page carefully for any mention of sudden or unexpected deaths. The type is thick and old-fashioned, the headlines blocky, the whole thing has the feel of a period piece, like something you might discover under the lining of an old carpet.

I scan through pages, slowly at first, moving more quickly as I get the hang of it. The single page of national news on the twenty-seventh is dominated by news of the 'shoe bomber' Richard Reid, who had been arrested after trying to bring down a transatlantic flight with explosives in his shoes. The next day's national story is about the recent invasion of Afghanistan, following the 9/11 attacks.

The first hint of what I'm actually looking for is in the New Year's Eve edition: a few paragraphs on page two. No names, no details, simply that police had been called to an address on Regency Place in The Park after the discovery of two bodies in circumstances the police were treating as 'unexplained'. I take a picture of the story on my phone. On the second of January, there is a longer piece that takes up half a page under the headline POLICE PROBE DOUBLE TRAGEDY. In the article itself, there are quotes from neighbours and friends paying tribute to the pair and describing how Peter, *a doting grandson*, had lived with his grandma since his mother died when he was a boy, his father having long since departed.

I don't recognise any names among the people quoted, and frustratingly it still doesn't give a cause of death.

But it *does* have photos of both victims. Elizabeth is a small, frail-looking woman with a halo of snowy hair, leaning on a walking stick at what looks like a garden party. Her grandson is the absolute opposite in every respect: a broad-shouldered man in his prime, with dark hair and a strong jaw, laughing eyes that brim with confidence and charisma. In the picture he's wearing a muddy rugby shirt, grinning as he holds up a trophy.

I take photos of everything and scroll on through the next day, and the next, each edition comprising dozens of pages. Scanning every article, large and small, for any mention of the mysterious deaths that had happened two days after Christmas. I slot in another of the microfiche sheets and keep going, my head starting to ache as I stare at page after page of black type on the backlit screen. Scrolling, scanning, moving onto the next page. I reach the end of the sheet, then go through the whole of the next one without finding a single mention. Surely there would have been an update, a court report, something from the police? Perhaps I've missed it. I rub my eyes, scan back through again before reaching for the next sheet and slotting it under the lens.

I find the answer on 11th January.

I stop, the breath catching in my throat. Reading every word of a story that takes up most of page five, not quite sure yet what it means or how it fits into everything else. Even as I know in my gut that it's another piece of the puzzle. Because there was no crime, no dramatic incident all those years ago. No attack, no intruder, no murder-suicide. No perplexing mystery still waiting to be solved.

It had been a tragic accident.

52

Elizabeth Makepeace and Peter Flack had died of carbon monoxide poisoning.

Not deliberate, not in the garage with a hosepipe attached to the exhaust of a car, but because of a faulty gas fire turned all the way up on a cold December night.

According to an inquest opened early in the new year, 2002, post-mortems had revealed fatal levels of carbon monoxide in the blood and tissue of both victims. Subsequent testing of an old gas fire used to heat the sitting room had found it was leaking 'significant' amounts of the gas – which had no telltale odour, colour or taste. With the heater on maximum and the hall door closed off with draught excluders to warm up the old room, the build-up of gas had reached toxic levels. Both Elizabeth and her grandson, the coroner surmised, had been watching TV after dinner and had slipped into an unconsciousness from which they never awoke. With a horrible jolt of shock, I realise the story also features a grainy black-and-white picture of *my house*. The picture caption reads: 'DOUBLE TRAGEDY – Victorian villa in The Park where pensioner and grandson died'.

I comb through the rest of the inquest report to make sure I don't miss anything. The alarm had been raised on 30th December by a family friend who stopped by to wish Mrs Makepeace and her grandson a happy new year. The curtains were closed even though it was daytime, and they could hear the noise of the TV but nothing else. By this time the friend had already noticed that a phone call to Elizabeth had not been returned, and that she had missed their regular Friday morning coffee group.

Peter had been out for a lunchtime drink with friends on the 27th and that was the last time he was seen alive, before returning home for what had turned out to be a last supper with his grandmother.

According to the police, there were no suspicious circumstances, or any indication of a third party being involved. Foul play had been ruled out, so there was never a criminal investigation. I wonder, as I reread the article, whether Peter Flack might have had a sibling, a child, some other relative who had come out of the woodwork after all these years to do . . . what, exactly? Was it the watch, had it originally belonged to him? But there's no mention of wider family in any of the articles.

I replace the microfiche sheets in their cardboard folder, switch off the machine and head out, keeping a wary eye out for the grey-coated man all the way up the hill.

* * *

A police patrol car pulls up to the kerb outside my house as I'm putting my key in the front door. And, once again, I find myself sitting in my lounge opposite PC James although he's with a different partner this time, a stern forty-something who introduces herself as Sergeant Okoro, both of them festooned with equipment, cuffs, radios, spray, batons, pouches and body-worn cameras. I take them through the events of Saturday night as James makes notes in a small pad and Okoro listens, asking pointed questions now and again.

'So,' she says eventually. 'Just so I'm clear on the facts: there are no indications of forced entry, no damage to the property and nothing was stolen *from* the property during this power cut.'

'Only because they didn't find what they were looking for.'

'And what was that?'

'Some items that were left behind when we moved in.'

'Valuables?'

'Well . . . no. Not exactly.' I stand up. 'But I can show you.'

She holds up a hand. 'But this individual ignored the laptop, car keys and wallet that were in plain view on the kitchen counter?'

I sit slowly back down on the armchair. 'They weren't interested in any of that.'

'And you've got no exterior CCTV, none of your neighbours saw anything and your wife didn't hear anything either?'

I look from one officer to the other. 'There *was* someone in my house. They kicked me down the cellar stairs, I've got nine stitches in the back of my head to prove it.'

'I noticed the bottles by the front door put out for recycling,' she says. 'Had you been drinking at all on Saturday night?'

'A few glasses of wine,' I say. 'A couple of beers.'

'Anything else?'

'Like what?'

'Spirits?'

'One small whisky before I went to bed.'

She nods slowly. 'And anything else that you might have consumed on a . . . recreational basis?'

'I wasn't high or hallucinating, if that's what you're asking.'

'I'm not interested from an enforcement point of view,' Okoro says. 'Just gathering all the facts.'

'I don't do drugs.'

'But you were intoxicated?'

'Not ... I mean. Maybe a little, yes. But not falling-down drunk. Maybe a bit disoriented at being woken in the middle of the night.'

'And you're not able to give us a description of this supposed intruder beyond the fact that you think they had a black balaclava on.'

'It all happened incredibly fast, and the lights were still off. I was dazzled by the torch, and the next thing I knew I was coming round on the floor of the cellar.'

'I see.'

James flips to a fresh page of his pad and continues to write in his tight, neat handwriting. When he's finished, I show them into the dining room and then the kitchen, where they do a cursory inspection of the doors and windows.

I indicate the door to the cellar. 'Aren't you going to look for fingerprints or something?'

The sergeant gives me a long-suffering smile. 'We'd need to bring in our colleagues from scientific support for that. They would tend to look at areas of obvious entry and exit from a scene, specific areas that a suspect is likely to have had contact with in commission of a crime, that kind of thing. As you can imagine they're very busy boys and girls, and their time tends to be allocated according to the gravity of an offence and whether there is a reasonable prospect of detecting, arresting and successfully prosecuting an offender.'

'Is that a roundabout way of saying no?'

'It's just how things are, I'm afraid.' She holds a hand up. 'I don't like it either, but the staffing rotas are already cut to the bone, they do a hell of a job but there's just not enough resources, not enough staff to go around.'

I blow out a breath. 'Sounds familiar.'

'How about your security system?' Okoro says. 'Could that have logged a breach, or recorded anything downstairs before you were woken up?'

With his biro, James indicates the motion detector dangling from the corner of the kitchen wall, cracked plastic and trailing wires, where Dom and I had levered it off its mount last week.

He says: 'You think the individual did that to evade detection, do you?'

'Oh,' I say, my cheeks reddening. 'No. That was me.'

The younger officer frowns. 'You broke your own burglar alarm?'

'It didn't work, anyway. The main alarm system, I mean. And there were cameras hidden in a couple of the units.'

'Cameras,' James repeats. 'Right.'

'Do you want to see them?'

The two officers exchange a quick glance. James finally puts his notebook away in a Velcro-strapped pouch over his stab vest. Okoro's face is a picture of neutrality but I can see the scepticism lurking just below the surface.

'At this stage we've probably seen enough, sir.'

'I know what you're thinking,' I say. 'You think I was just stumbling around half asleep, half pissed during a power cut and I fell down the stairs in the dark.'

'I didn't say that,' she says. 'But . . . is there a possibility that you fell? I think you mentioned that you've only been in the house a few days, and it can be very disorienting to be in an unfamiliar environment, in the dark, for the first time.'

'The person who came in here,' I say, 'they've already threatened me. Threatened my family. It's not the first time I've had to call the police.'

This seems to get the sergeant's attention. I find the message thread on my phone and show it to her, starting from the first contact on Tuesday last week and ending with today's message: *Next time we bring petrol and matches.*

'I can see why you might be concerned,' she says, scrolling through the texts. 'It may be worth everyone's while if we pay this individual a visit. Have a quiet chat with them, calm things down a little. Have you got an address? Name?'

'No, sorry. They used the name Mason at one point but I think that was probably bogus.'

She hands the phone back to me.

'You've been in contact with this individual but you don't actually know who it is?'

'No.'

'Makes it rather tricky for us to follow up.'

'I know, I just . . .' I shrug. It occurs to me that I've not even mentioned the 'to-do' list under the names of *Parker* and *Barrow*. But I don't think it would make much difference at this stage; they seem to have made their minds up. 'I thought there would be something you could do to help.'

Her radio crackles into life and she has a brief exchange with a brusque male voice at the other end, both she and James standing up and moving towards the door in response.

I follow them out.

'So what now?' I say. 'Is that it?'

Okoro turns, gives me an apologetic look. 'Best thing you can do for now is to remain vigilant, keep all your doors and windows locked and get the burglar alarm back online. If you see anything – *anything* – suspicious, you give us a call straightaway. Until then, you can see why we're struggling, right? There's not a lot that's concrete in any of this, not much for us to work with.'

Her radio crackles again with another urgent voice, and the two of them hurry back down the drive to their patrol car without another word.

53

The fake Rolex is delivered by courier that afternoon, complete with engraved initials and date to match the original.

I lay the watch out alongside the genuine items on the dining room table – the scarf, the wallet, the glasses, the keys, the dog collar and the phone – and explain the plan to my wife and brother-in-law.

'I'm going to hand it all over,' I say. 'Before anyone else gets hurt. Just hope they don't realise the Rolex isn't the real deal.'

My brother-in-law studies the items arranged along the table.

'I've been thinking about this,' he says, looking through the old wallet, empty except for a tightly folded cashpoint receipt. 'How do they know what to expect?'

'They know there are seven items, it was one of the instructions they gave to Shaun Rutherford.'

'But do they know exactly what's *here*? Have they been specific about any of it, about what you're supposed to give them, so they'll leave you alone?'

I scroll through the text thread again. 'Only the watch.'

'So: maybe they *don't* actually know the details. Maybe this stuff has been here so long they've forgotten.'

'I'm not following you.'

'Or maybe they never knew in the first place.'

'Then why do they want it all back?'

'That doesn't really matter.'

Jess crosses her arms. 'Seems like it matters to them.'

'Just humour me for a minute.' Dom lays the wallet down next to the old scarf. 'What if they're not sure exactly what was stashed in that dresser? Then . . . we could give them anything, to get them off your back. They're not going to know, are they? And we get to keep some leverage in case they don't go away.'

'We don't want leverage,' Jess says, frowning. 'We want them to leave us alone.'

I consider his idea for a moment. 'They'll be pissed off if they figure out that we've given them dummies.'

'They're already pissed off,' Dom says. 'It's worth a try, isn't it? You're giving them a fake anyway, so why not give them a few more, retain some bargaining power?'

'I don't know, Dom.'

'They've been smart, these people – not doing quite enough to get the police fully involved, staying anonymous, out of arm's reach.' He indicates the bandage on my head. 'They've shown they're willing to use violence to get what they want. If we can identify them, unmask them, we take away their power and they won't be able to threaten you anymore.'

With my reluctant agreement, we spend a few minutes gathering a handful of items: an old pair of Jess's reading glasses and a wallet from the kids' dressing-up box, one of Coco's old collars, minus the tag. For authenticity, we add the old Motorola phone, the scarf and the brass key with the two rings.

'We need to give them something extra as well,' Dom says. 'Wait here a minute.'

He goes out to his car and returns a moment later, opening his hand to reveal a small metallic disc about the size of a two-pound coin, the familiar Apple logo in the centre.

'What's that?'

'AirTag.' He slips the disc into the lining of the dummy wallet, pushing it in as deep as it will go. 'I keep one in my work bag in case it ever gets lost or stolen.'

'What is it, like a tracker?'

'Kind of,' he says. 'It sends out a passive Bluetooth signal that can be detected by any nearby Apple device. That device sends the location to the Cloud, then you can go to the Find My app and see where your AirTag is on a map.'

I frown. 'But that little thing could end up miles away. Your phone won't be anywhere near it.'

'Doesn't have to be – that's the coolest thing about it.' He grins. Beneath his gruff exterior, my brother-in-law has always been a bit of a Gadget Boy. 'As long as the tag is in Bluetooth range of *any* iPhone, or *any* Apple device, it will be passively broadcasting its location. So as long as it doesn't end up in the middle of the Sahara Desert we should have a good shot at finding it. And the whole thing is anonymous and encrypted.'

'Sounds absolutely perfect for stalkers.'

He gives me a *don't be a spoilsport* look. 'It's perfect for what we need today. We'll be able to track them, see where the bag ends up – find out where this person lives.'

When we're finished getting the items together and he's satisfied the AirTag is pinging its location, I send a text to the unknown number.

OK you can have it all. Tell me where to bring it.

The reply arrives barely a minute later.

*Wollaton Park 8 p.m. exactly, main car park. Put everything
in a black bag. More instructions when you get there.*

Jess reads the message over my shoulder, pulling up Google
Maps on her own phone to study the location. Wollaton Park is
a bit more than a mile west of here, a wide expanse of parkland
with a grand old Elizabethan hall sitting atop its highest point.
It's a popular place for families, concerts are held there in the
summer and deer roam the grounds all year round; but at eight
o'clock on a cloudy Monday evening, it would be fairly quiet.

'It's an interesting choice,' I say. 'For them at least. Lots of
open space, so they'll be able to observe from a distance away.'

We had less than forty minutes. I wrap all the items in a plastic bag and find an old black backpack, zipping it shut as another
text arrives.

*Come alone. Any police and it will be your kids going to the
hospital this time.*

With a chill creeping over my skin, I text a reply to tell them I
understand and show the message thread to Jess.

'OK,' she says grimly. 'I'm doing this.'

Dom turns to her. 'What?'

'Give me your keys.'

'Hang on, sis, I don't think that's a good idea.'

'I'm not standing by, letting you two take all the risks.' She
points at me. 'Adam's already hurt, and you sat down with Shaun
Rutherford a few days ago. For all we know it could be him on

the other end of this phone. They don't know me and they won't be expecting me. Especially not in your car.'

I put a hand on her arm. 'Jess, I don't want you to—'

'They're my kids too, Adam. And no offence to either of you, but you haven't exactly dealt with this problem over the past week, have you? I'd prefer if the two of you stayed here, close to the kids. Besides which, I've run around Wollaton Park a million times, I know it better than either of you.'

'You're sure you want to do this?'

'We're wasting time.' She pulls her jacket off the chair, holds a hand out to her brother. 'Give me your keys, Dominic.'

'Wait a minute.' I hold up a hand. 'Why will they even see the car?'

'Because I'm going to wait, watch the pick-up and follow them. See if I can get a car registration plate or even better, find out where they live.'

'I'm not sure that's such a good idea, Jess. They're going to be watching you, watching everything you do.'

'I know. But there's only two ways out of the park in a vehicle. And one of them is normally blocked off unless there's a concert or a special event. Also—' she holds her phone up '—the gates close at 8.30 p.m., which means they'll have to make a move by then.'

'Unless they're on foot,' I say, pointing to the map on her phone. 'In which case they'll have more options. Footpaths to the south and west, in other directions.'

'Would you be on foot for something like this?'

'Probably not.'

'Me neither. I'd want to get away quickly.'

'Surely you don't need to follow them,' I say. 'We can just let Dom's gadget do its thing, can't we?'

She swings the backpack up over her shoulder.

'This might be the only time they break cover, our only chance to get a look at them. We need to know something about who's doing all this, otherwise we're going to be at their mercy for as long as they want. We need to get on the front foot.'

'I know,' I say. 'But this is my mess, my problem to sort out.'

She shakes her head. 'Bollocks to that. This is my family too. My children.'

'I just don't want you to get hurt.'

'It'll be fine.' She puts an AirPod into her right ear, checks the small white device is connecting to her iPhone and pulls her hoodie up over it. 'I'll be in touch.'

I pull her in for a hug. 'Be careful.'

'You're a fine one to talk about being careful, Adam Wylie.'

'You know what I mean.'

She kisses me, her lips soft against mine.

'I'll be back before you know it.'

54

Dom and I set up camp in the little snug next to the lounge where the Wi-Fi signal is strongest, a tense silence between us.

'We shouldn't have let her go,' he says finally. 'We know what these people are capable of.'

'You know what she's like,' I say. 'Good luck getting her to change her mind once she's set on something.'

'Hmm.'

'Are Daisy and Cal asleep?'

He nods. 'Leah's doing homework in her room.'

While Jess has been driving to Wollaton Park, I've been busy studying maps on my iPad. I've been there with the kids dozens of times over the years but have never seen it as a place of danger before, a place to hide, to observe, to pursue. It was 500 acres in all, including a lake, a golf course, multiple buildings around the main old house and areas of thick woodland here and there, the whole park criss-crossed with footpaths and trails. It was a lot of ground to cover; an easy place to hide. An easy place to lose yourself in.

My phone rings and I stab the screen to answer it, putting it on loudspeaker so Dom can listen in.

'I'm here.' My wife's voice is quiet at the other end of the line. 'In the main car park. Can't see a grey Volvo.'

I check my watch: five minutes to eight.

'Is it busy?'

'Maybe three or four dozen other cars, but the light's fading and there aren't many street lights.'

Keeping the phone line open to Jess, I send a message to the unknown number to let them know we're ready to hand over the backpack.

There is no response.

Eight o'clock comes and goes. My wife gives an intermittent running commentary on what she can see from the car park, from her position – down the hill from the imposing Elizabethan mansion with its high windows and ornate stone balustrades. The natural history museum inside would have shut several hours ago but it seemed there were still a few dog walkers and late picnickers enjoying the warm spring evening.

'I'm going to get out and have a walk around, see what I—'

'No,' I say. 'Not yet. Stay in your car for now and stay on the line.'

At ten past eight, my phone buzzes with another message.

Green roller bin, back of the courtyard café. Drop the bag in there and leave the park immediately. We are watching.

I forward it straight on to Jess, wishing more than anything that I could be there with her, that I could see for myself what was going on. To protect her.

'Talk to me, Jess.'

A rustle of static and the muffled *crump* of a car door closing.

'OK,' she says. 'I'm heading up there with the backpack now.'

There is an interminable silence, punctuated only by the far-away sound of her shoes on the tarmac, the sound of the wind, a car engine passing in the distance. A creeping sense of unease crawls up my arms, the hairs rising as if chilled by a cold wind. Was she walking into a trap?

'I see it,' she says finally. 'No one else around.'

'Nobody watching?'

Her breathing grows a little heavier, the exertion of walking up the incline. 'It's open ground on one side here,' she says. 'But there are trees, bushes, another building, the main house. Like, a hundred places to hide. Putting the backpack in now.'

Over the phone line I can make out the scratching creak of a hinge, a momentary pause before the heavy plastic lid is dropped back into place.

'OK, it's done,' she says, a nervous smile in her voice. 'Feel like I've just dropped off a bag of ransom cash in a movie.'

'Who can you see, Jess?'

'No one. I can't see anyone.'

'*Someone* is there,' I say. 'Somebody must be watching you.'

'I'm going to loop around, take the long way back to the car. See what I can see.'

Dom says: 'Be careful.'

She slips into silence again, only the intermittent sound of her breathing and the occasional dog barking in the distance to prove the line is still open. I'm struck with an overwhelming sense that I should have gone with her, that it should be me taking this risk. Instead, I'm blind, straining to hear what's going on. Only a mile away but it might as well be a hundred.

'All right,' she says. 'I've gone back up and around the visitors' centre. Going to hang here for a minute, see if anyone comes along to pick up the bag.'

'Listen, Jess, I've got a bad feeling about this.' A hard bubble of anxiety is painful in my throat. 'Why don't you head back to your car now? Better than being caught in the open.'

'I'm all right,' she says. 'Don't stress, there's still a few other people around. They're not going to try anything.'

I look out of the window, the evening sky softening into dusk. It's going to get harder for her to see what's going on, and it's not long before the gates will be shut for the night. Unless . . . the person we're waiting for is an employee, right there at the park? A worker at the café, or the visitors' centre? In which case they could wait until all members of the public are gone before retrieving the backpack.

I discuss the idea with Jess while she watches, and waits, answering me in clipped tones.

'Could be,' she says quietly. 'But it would be high risk, bringing us so close to their workplace.'

She spends another five minutes waiting, observing from the shadows. A couple of people emerge into the courtyard but only to go to their cars and drive away. Neither of them goes near the roller bin.

'OK,' Jess says. 'Plan B.'

'Stay on the line.'

She goes back to the car, narrating for our benefit as she drives slowly and conspicuously down the drive to the main gate. Back on Wollaton Road, she pulls into a side street and does a U-turn, positioning herself with a good view of the exit.

It's not long before the silence is broken by her loud exclamation of surprise.

'Bingo!'

I lean towards my phone. 'What is it?'

'Volvo estate, dark colour, leaving now. Pulling out left.' The soft cough of an engine coming to life. 'I'm on him . . . oh.'

'Can you see the driver?'

'I'm not sure . . .' She tails off again. 'Just got a glimpse as it turned through the gate. It might be . . .'

'What?'

'It *might* have been a woman. But it was so quick, it's hard to say. Can't quite . . .'

'Have they seen you?'

'Don't think so. I'm one car back, we're heading west now. Steady as you like, doesn't seem to be in any hurry.'

She narrates the journey as she goes, passing the Admiral Rodney pub on her right before a left turn onto Russell Drive into light traffic. A main street on a quiet weekday evening, then over a railway bridge and up to more traffic lights at a junction.

'Turning right onto Glaisdale Drive,' she says. For a long moment there is only the clicking of her indicator. 'OK, now we're going north-east, back towards Beechdale. Bit quieter here.'

'Keep your distance,' I say.

'Uh-huh. I'm going to try taking a picture of the number plate.' After a moment, she adds: 'Ah, crap. Need to be closer.'

'What's happening?'

'Turning right again now, looks like some kind of industrial estate. Just going to check if the AirTag is showing on the app.'

Dom and I both lean nearer the phone, willing her to break a long moment of silence.

'Jess?'

'Err, OK, yup, it looks like the app is working, it's showing a location.'

'What's the Volvo doing now?'

'He . . . ahh, sugar. Must have turned off into one of these little side roads while I was looking at my phone. It's all warehouses and industrial units here.' She curses. 'Where the hell did they go?'

'Be careful, love.'

'It's a dead end here, it all goes up to the railway line,' she says. 'I'm going to turn around and retrace my steps, it must have pulled in somewhere.'

Dom leans toward the phone's speaker. 'Why don't you just leave it now, sis? We have the tag; you've done what you need to do. Come back now.'

There is a long pause.

'Got him,' she says, almost to herself. 'How the hell did he get that far ahead?'

'Don't take any more risks, Jess, you've done enough.'

'He's stopped at a junction. All right, he's just moving away on a green light now, reckon I can catch up to him and get a picture of his number plate before it goes red again.'

The engine tone in the background rises higher as she accelerates to catch up to the Volvo—

Suddenly overlaid by the roar of another engine revving loud, a piercing screech of brakes almost blotting out my wife's panicked voice.

'Oh crap—'

A thundering crash of metal against metal.

Then nothing.

55

The minute before the call reconnects is the longest of my life.

The first call to Jess's phone goes to voicemail. And the second.

I can't look at Dom.

Heart in my mouth, I dial her number again and whisper a silent prayer for her to pick up, to be all right, just to say something to tell me she's still there. The weight of guilt presses down on me like a boulder.

Please, Jess.

Please.

Just when I think it's about to go to voicemail again, there is a *click* on the line as the call is answered. A rustling sound. Other noises in the background that I can't quite make out.

'Jess?' I say. 'What's happened? Are you OK?'

No answer.

I look up at my brother-in-law, his face as pale as snow.

'Jess,' I say again. 'Are you all right? Talk to me. *Please.*'

The rush of relief that comes next is as powerful as any drug.

'I'm OK,' she says at last, her voice faint and far away. 'I lost him. But I'm OK.'

* * *

It's almost two hours later, after dealing with police at the scene and exchanging insurance details with the other driver, before I can get my wife home. Paramedics treat her at the roadside but the airbags had done an amazing job in absorbing the impact and it was also lucky, they tell her, that the van she'd collided with at the junction was only just pulling out. She's shaken up, with some bruising to her legs, but insists she doesn't need to go to the hospital. Her brother's Skoda is in a rather worse condition and will have to be towed. Fortunately, the van driver was also uninjured and Jess admits straightaway to the police who arrive that it was her fault for going through a red light.

Neither of us mention the Volvo she had been pursuing at the time of the crash.

Back home, she opens up the Find My function on her phone and looks for a location signal for the AirTag. Dom shows us how it works, bringing up a map of the city, zooming in closer and closer onto a blue pulsing dot that I presume denotes the last location of the tiny gadget. I hadn't been sure it would actually work, but there it was – showing on the map as Nixon Street in Bulwell, on the north-western outskirts of the city. A small swell of pride blooms in my chest, pride in my wife settling alongside the guilt over her injuries.

You did it, Jess. You got them.

I take a screenshot of the map and send it to my phone. Seeing it arrive alongside my other photos gives me an idea and I select her camera roll, scrolling through the most recent images. There are half a dozen shots of random people in Wollaton Park, individuals, couples, people walking their dogs. But most of the images are grainy and indistinct, taken from too far away to discern anything meaningful. None of the people look in any way furtive, or suspicious, or as if they're doing anything other than enjoying the park on a warm evening.

The last set of pictures are not from the park. There are a dozen or so, shot through the windscreen of a car, zoomed-in shots of a dark street. It looks as if they've been taken in burst mode, a whole set of pictures shot in very quick succession, all of the same thing. The first ones are slightly blurred, out of focus, but the last ones are pin sharp as the camera found its range.

They show the back of a grey Volvo estate, caught as it crosses a junction.

And a number plate.

*   *   *

I would go and have a look at the location where the AirTag had ended up. That was all. Get an address, a street number – maybe a quick photo of the Volvo if it wasn't in a garage – and pass it straight to the police. I wouldn't knock on the door, or wait around, or do anything that might give the game away. It was very clear what these people were prepared to do, to get what they wanted, and I needed to protect my family.

Jess goes up to bed and Dom insists on staying at our house until I return.

The ring road is quiet as I head towards Bulwell, using the screenshot of the AirTag's location as a guide. There had been no more texts from the unknown number since the drop-off at Wollaton Park, no reference to the backpack or questions about the items inside it.

A police patrol car flashes past me on the other side of the road, blue lights blazing.

Turning onto Nixon Street, I compare the screenshot to the live map showing on my car's satnav screen, heading up and around the long slow curve of small semi-detached houses set back from the road. It was near the end of this stretch, on the left-hand side and towards the next junction, where the AirTag was transmitting its last location. The houses on the left are replaced by a string of three-storey flats, then a small scrubby car park, then an open space before what looked like a pub and a row of shops.

I slow down and check the screenshot again. Maybe another two hundred metres or so: I will drive past first, see if the Volvo is there, then park further up the street and return on foot for a closer look. Quieter that way.

Slowly, I approach the AirTag's location, checking the image against the satnav screen again.

This was it, this was the right place. But there are no houses here, only a row of half-derelict shops, boarded-up windows thickly plastered with posters. Drifts of rubbish piled against abandoned doorways, empty cans and broken bottles, old newspapers and flyers blown together by the wind.

The entire parade of shops seems to be empty. No flats above, no lights on, no signs of life.

I pull over and get out of the car, walk up and down and double-check the screenshot again. This was *definitely* the right place. Across the street is an old petrol station, boarded-up windows heavily tagged with graffiti, pumps standing broken and abandoned in the middle of the potholed forecourt. No CCTV around here, and no people in the immediate vicinity, either. The place smells of rotten wood and oil-soaked concrete.

The black backpack has been discarded like so much rubbish behind one of the pumps.

I shine my phone torch inside – empty.

Apart from a small silver disc nestled at the bottom, with the familiar bitten-apple logo in its centre.

56

TUESDAY

Fatigue weighs down my limbs the next morning. I drink three cups of strong coffee and do the school run on autopilot, while Jess sleeps in, dosed up on paracetamol. She's cancelled her early meeting and will work from home today.

There is still no reply from either Sergeant Okoro or DC Rubin to the message I sent last night with the photo of the number plate and information about the car. *I'm assuming you can trace the owner?* I'd written in the email. *Let me know what you find out.* The AirTag had been a bust but we still had the plate number to go on – so her efforts had not been in vain.

My phone is charging in the kitchen when I hear the familiar buzz of it vibrating against the counter as new messages drop in. But they're not replies from Okoro or Rubin. Instead, I see a string of messages from the unknown number, stacked one on top of the other.

You made a serious mistake last night.
It was also your last chance.
Thought you were a man of your word but obviously you can't be trusted.
Rolex is a fake and the wallet too. Thought you could fool me?
Know what happens when you play with fire?

My stomach lurches as I read down the thread, trying to think of a response that will end this nightmare. But my sleep-deprived brain can't come up with anything convincing.

We got your photo and number plate, have given to the police. Stay away from my family.

As I'm rereading all the messages from the past week, a final reply drops in.

Time for you to learn a lesson, Adam.

Fear kicks beneath my skin as I stare at the screen. I'm jittery, nerves jangling from too much caffeine. But at the same time I feel shattered, wrung out from last night as I go outside to check the front and back gardens, the garage, the street, walking around the house to check all the doors and windows are locked. I text Dom with an update then go upstairs to check on Jess. She's sleeping, the curtains still drawn, and I lie down on the covers next to her.

But sleep will not come. Instead, all I can see when I close my eyes is the image of my wife sitting in the back of an ambulance last night – because of *me*. Because of something *I* had set in motion. The intruder in my house had been bad enough, but last night had taken things to a whole new level.

Time for you to learn a lesson.

Finally, I drift off into a fitful sleep.

I have no idea how long I've been down – it only feels like minutes – when a distant thudding reaches me. At first, I imagine it's Jess, trapped and bloody in a mangled car, desperately hammering on the window to be let out. The thudding continues but I can't seem to pull her free. I'm on the outside looking at her through the window but there is no handle, nothing to grip, no way to open the car door . . .

The distant thudding seems to get louder.

I sit up, suddenly awake, and stumble groggily downstairs where a heavy shape looms beyond the coloured glass of the front door, another solid knock rattling it against the frame. The big wall clock says it's almost 11 a.m. Perhaps DC Rubin has sent a colleague already?

I pull the door open and blink into the mid-morning sunlight, my eyes still gritty with sleep.

The man, in his late fifties, greets me before I can even open my mouth.

'Good morning, sir.'

I blink again, sizing him up. He's heavily built and wearing a grey three-quarter-length overcoat, with a solid gut straining against the waistband of dark suit trousers. A taut white shirt flares open at his bull-like neck, below a neatly trimmed beard flecked with grey.

I recognise him instantly.

'You've been following me,' I say. 'At the cemetery on Saturday. The car park yesterday, in town.'

His face is expressionless. There is an angular black briefcase gripped in his left hand.

'Have I caught you at a bad time, sir?'

'It's true, isn't it? Who are you?'

'I was hoping we could have a chat, Mr Wylie.' His voice is officious, a deep, penetrating bass. 'Inside, if you don't mind.'

'How do you know my name?'

'If you give me five minutes of your time, I can explain.' His small blue eyes, sharp as flecks of ice in the fleshy folds of his face, stay fixed on mine. 'If we could just go inside.'

A flare of alarm pulses in my chest. There is no one else here apart from Jess, asleep upstairs. The street is deserted. My mobile is charging in the kitchen, the landline out of reach. I remember the text from last night: *Time for you to learn a lesson.*

'It's really not a good time. Sorry.'

I start to push the door closed.

He puts a big palm flat against the coloured glass, stopping it dead.

His voice is low and flat. 'I need to talk to you, Adam.'

'If you don't leave, I'm going to call the—'

'About this.'

He reaches into his jacket and takes out a Rolex watch.

57

The stranger introduces himself as retired Detective Constable Gordon Webber, formerly with Notts Police and now a civilian investigator serving with something called the East Midlands Special Operations Unit.

He has some sort of official ID but it looks unconvincing and my instincts are still tingling: there is something about this man that doesn't feel quite right, something in his manner, the tension in his shoulders. The sharp movements of his eyes. Although the Rolex looks like the real one – the one I had found upstairs – not the fake I'd bought online a couple of days ago.

'We can talk out here on your drive if you want,' he says. 'But I don't think you'll want your neighbours to overhear what I'm going to tell you.'

'How long have you been retired?'

'A few years.' His expression remains blank. 'Like I said, you have to surrender your warrant card when you finish. Otherwise there would be a million retired coppers all running around, using their IDs to stick their noses into God knows what.'

'Just like you're doing now?'

'Give me ten minutes and I'll tell you why I'm here.'

He takes his phone from his pocket, taps the screen a few times and holds it out to me. The display is filled with an old story from the *BBC East Midlands*, the layout blocky and basic in the style of an old web page. I can't see the date but the image seems to be of him reading a statement outside a large concrete-clad building – albeit a younger, leaner, less grey version of him. The caption says: 'Detective Gordon Webber made a public appeal for information'.

'That was me,' he says. 'Back in the day.'

I hand the phone back to him. I've had enough strangers in my house for one week, but there is still that old familiar itch of curiosity to hear what he's got to say.

'They do really good coffee at the Trip,' I say. 'And I could use the caffeine. If it's all the same to you?'

Webber shrugs his big shoulders. 'Fair enough.'

He doesn't seem to have a car, so I drive us down the hill onto Castle Boulevard, then pull a left and park outside the Olde Trip to Jerusalem pub. We pass the couple of minutes' journey in silence and he follows me into the garden seating area, past the familiar claim on the white-painted wall – *the oldest inn in England* – to a table in the far corner. It's not busy, still a bit too early for the lunchtime crowd, but it feels better to be in a public place.

I get the drinks in and bring them out to the table, where he sits with his back to the wall puffing on a small black vape. The smoke has a sickly sweet cherry tinge to it.

He gives me a nod of thanks, taking a long pull on his pint of bitter. 'Been a few years since I was in here.'

'It never changes,' I say. 'Apart from the staff getting younger.'

He takes the Rolex from his jacket and lays it on the stained wooden table between us. As when he'd first shown me on the doorstep, the watch is sealed inside a clear plastic bag.

'So,' he says quietly. 'Where did you get this, Adam?'

'It's not stolen, if that's what you think.'

He gives me a strange look. 'Not recently, anyway.'

'What does that mean?'

'Did you buy it from someone?'

I take a sip of my Americano, relishing the instant dark hit of caffeine.

'I take it you got my details from the manager of the jeweller's shop in town?'

'Correct.'

He had been looking for this particular watch, he says, for years – setting up online alerts on all the big internet trading websites, registering what he called an NIPC advisory – a Notice of Interest in the Proceeds of Crime – with jewellers and pawn-brokers all over the Midlands. Checking in with them all every so often in case they had come across a Rolex Explorer with a very specific engraving on the back.

'I knew it would surface sooner or later,' he says. 'A valuable piece like that, it was only a matter of time before someone decided to cash in.'

'Seems like an awful lot of trouble to go to for a wristwatch. No matter how fancy it is.'

'I'm interested in why you suddenly wanted it back,' he says, 'only a few days after getting rid of it. I'm guessing it's some-thing to do with the cuts and bruises on your arms? Those fresh stitches in the back of your head?'

Feeling suddenly exposed, I lean back in my chair.

'Tell me,' I say. 'What sort of police work did you used to do?'

'A mixture. Thirteen years in uniform then CID. Ended up on major crime, retired when my thirty years was up. But this was always the case that stayed with me, the one that I could never let go of. So when they offered me the gig as a civilian investigator with the Special Operations Unit, I jumped at the chance.'

'What case? A stolen wristwatch?'

He shakes his head, taking another deep puff on the vape and blowing a thick stream of grey smoke above my head. 'You're not in any trouble, if that's what you're wondering.'

'That's a matter of opinion.'

This seems to get his attention. He studies me over the lip of his glass, small blue eyes holding me with an unblinking stare.

'How *did* you get that bang on the head, Adam?'

It's on the tip of my tongue to lie, to skirt around what had really happened rather than open myself up to this man, this stranger who had found his way to my door. But then I think of Jess and the children, of the threats to burn down my house, the seeming inability of the police to do anything to protect us, and can't see what else I've got to lose by just telling the truth.

'Someone came into my house,' I say. 'On Saturday night. They cut the power and when I confronted them, they kicked me down the cellar stairs. I was knocked out cold for a bit.'

He sits up straighter in his chair, setting his pint glass down hard on the table.

'I see,' he breathes. 'So they found you already? Did they take anything?'

'Who is *they*, exactly?'

'In a minute. Tell me everything first – start from the beginning.'

I drink more of my coffee and briefly run through the other events of the past ten days, including the pursuit and crash last night.

He taps the plastic-wrapped watch that lies between us.

'So it wasn't just this?' he says. 'You found other items too in this chest of drawers? It would help if I could examine all of it.'

'Hold on,' I say. 'You've barely told me anything about your interest in all of this. Your turn to give *me* something, I think.'

'You're right. And it's also my round.' He points to my nearly empty coffee cup. 'Same again?'

I nod and he stands, lumbering off between tables towards the side entrance of the pub. The black briefcase, I notice, he's left behind next to our table. But the watch had disappeared back into the pocket of his voluminous suit jacket.

The pub garden has started to fill up a little now it's gone past midday, office workers from Castle Wharf bringing drinks out to occupy more of the tables in the warm spring sunshine, a handful of tourists comparing selfies taken with the Robin Hood statue just up the hill. After spending half an hour with Webber, I'm still not sure whether I trust him, whether he's telling me the whole truth, and he's still not *really* explained why he's taken the trouble of tracking me down after acquiring that Rolex.

He re-emerges into the garden with a fresh drink in each hand, sets the steaming black coffee down in front of me and eases down into his own seat with a second pint of bitter.

As before, he takes the watch from his jacket pocket and puts it carefully on the table. But this time he lays it face down, smoothing out the plastic so he can point to the finely tooled inscription on the back of the casing: *EJS 29–11–75.*

'This Rolex,' he says, 'belonged to a man called Edward John Stiles. It was given to him on his eighteenth birthday, in November 1993, a gift from his maternal grandfather. Quite the favourite grandchild, Edward was, from what we could glean later. And he wore this watch on special occasions. Never replaced it, always took good care of it and had it serviced every year. Does the name Edward Stiles mean anything to you?'

'It's not familiar.' I shake my head. 'Should it be?'

'Perhaps not. It was a long time ago.'

'Was he a . . . suspect in a crime you were investigating?'

'No. Not a suspect.' He studies me for a long moment, taking a slow drink and wiping a film of beer froth from his moustache when he's done. 'Edward Stiles was murdered. And his killer was never caught.'

58

It's a cold case.

Edward Stiles had gone missing in the spring of 2001. A single man, he had been a keen hiker, often spending long weekends wild-camping in the Lake District, Snowdonia and the Yorkshire Dales. Sometimes he would walk on his own and it wasn't uncommon for him to be out of contact for a day or two while he was 'off on one of his adventures', as his parents had told Webber all those years ago.

In the first few days, the ex-detective explains, his parents assumed Edward had simply taken an extended trip and not come across a payphone. After he failed to turn up for work the next week, they involved the police, who began to develop a theory that he had fallen while hiking alone. Subsequently there was speculation that he may have deliberately harmed himself, or even taken his own life.

There is an uncomfortable echo in his words, a reminder of Adrian Parish and the police theories that he too had come to harm by his own hand.

Webber unfolds a creased sheet of paper from his briefcase, four images photocopied onto the same page: a young-looking guy with a shy smile and wavy dark-blond hair. In two of the pictures he's wearing a yellow waterproof jacket, a rucksack on his back.

'It was five months before his body was found,' Webber says, 'in a shallow grave in woodland north of Derby. Decomposition made the autopsy more difficult, but cause of death was eventually determined as a single stab wound in the back. Most likely with a serrated hunting knife. No defensive wounds that they could find. It was one of the first cases I was put on when I made the murder squad, one of the cases we never closed. The unit I work for now, we do what's called "historical review" of specific unsolved crimes.'

'Cold cases.'

'Exactly.'

I think back to my own life in 2001. I had been finding my feet in my first year at university in Aberdeen, when life revolved around new friends in my hall of residence, around sport and music and nights out at the students' union, with a few lectures on the side. A fairly typical self-absorbed eighteen-year-old.

'I was a teenager when he died,' I say. 'But I don't remember ever hearing about it.'

'It was a strange one, right from the off,' Webber says. 'There was no obvious motive, the victim didn't appear to have any enemies, no criminal record, no prior contact with police that we could find. The body was fully clothed when they found him – his wallet was there, cash, credit cards, car key, all untouched. The only thing missing was the watch. Never recovered from the scene, from his house, his car, his work. We searched everywhere.'

'And you've been looking for it ever since?'

He nods. 'I had a feeling it would turn up sooner or later, a piece like that is too fine to just throw away. And yet it hadn't surfaced in more than twenty years,' he says. 'Not until you strolled into that jeweller's shop last week.'

I swallow, the coffee suddenly bitter in my mouth at the full, stark realisation of what I had done, what I had set in motion.

'But this means something, doesn't it? A lead – I mean, you can talk to your former colleagues in CID, right? Refer it on to them.'

He shifts uncomfortably in his seat. 'When the time's right. Not yet. I need to establish some of the wider context first.'

'Surely you can just give them a ring? Have an off-the-record chat?'

'It's not as simple as that,' he says, eyebrows drawing together in frustration. 'I need more to justify a full reopening of the investigation.'

'But surely—'

'And I need the rest of it too,' he says, more forcefully. 'I need *all* of it, to make a compelling case. Everything you found in that room. Anything short of that is not enough – you know that as well as I do. You've already tried to get the police involved. Have they shown the slightest interest in reopening anything from twenty-three years ago?'

I put my coffee cup down and push it away. 'Well, no, not exactly.'

'They're barely treading water as it is, dealing with the workload they have day to day let alone restarting an old case that's been stone cold for more than two decades. Have they even come back to you on that number plate you gave them?'

'Not yet. But it was only last night.'

'Let me see what I can do,' he says. 'I've still got a few contacts, could pull in a favour or two.'

I select the camera roll on my phone and show him the image of the Volvo's registration, which he jots down in a small black notebook.

There is an intensity in his eyes, a look that I've recognised all too often in myself: a desire to know. To find the answer. To solve the puzzle.

'Why this case?' I say. 'You say it was your first murder, that it was never solved, but why this one in particular?'

He takes another hefty swallow of his pint, which is already almost half gone. Putting it down on the table between us, he glances over at the other customers.

'Because it wasn't just one case, it was only the tip of a very dark iceberg.' He leans in closer. 'What I'm about to tell you is confidential, for background only. It was never official, never confirmed.'

'OK.' Unconsciously, I find that I've leaned in closer too, my arms crossed against the warm wooden table.

'There was circumstantial evidence linking this case to others.' He lowers his voice. 'Fibres found on Stiles's body that potentially linked him to the death of another man the year before, a 39-year-old recovering alcoholic by the name of Dean Fullerton. Then there was an eyewitness that *possibly* linked Fullerton's death to the case of a teenage runaway nine months before that. But it was never enough; it was all circumstantial, like I said. Nothing that we could use to identify a suspect in those or a number of other disappearances and unsolved murders over a thirty-four-month period between 1998 and 2001.'

'I don't remember ever hearing about any of this.'

'That's because they were never formally linked, not by us, not by the media, not by anyone. I always believed there were connections but the top brass didn't want to go there, didn't want to frighten the public with talk of a serial killer on the loose. Of course, it didn't help poor old Edward Stiles that his body was found not long after 9/11, when people's attention was elsewhere. He never really got the attention he deserved, poor bugger. None of them did, if I'm honest.'

'And no one was ever even arrested?'

His features cloud for a moment. 'Plenty of arrests. Never a conviction.'

'And your colleagues never accepted there was a link between the cases?'

'The killer was way ahead of us for a long time. He was smart. A couple of victims here in Nottinghamshire, then Stiles over the border in Derbyshire plus at least one on the coast in Lincolnshire, Fullerton down near Market Harborough. No pattern in place or weapon or motive, minimal forensics, no real similarity between the victims that we could ever establish. Basically, your worst nightmare as a detective. Different police forces, different teams and trying to get cooperation just slowed everything down to a crawl. Fullerton's death was prosecuted as a domestic situation, his ex-wife's new boyfriend got fourteen years, served two before the conviction was overturned on appeal. Another one was treated as a suicide at first and by the time it was reinvestigated months later, the cremation had already taken place and any leads had gone stone cold.'

I tell him about Adrian Parish while he takes notes, a glimmer of excitement in his eyes.

'So what happened?' I say. 'With your theory? Your boss wouldn't listen?'

'He was more interested in toeing the party line. You have to understand that it took a long time to connect the dots, start linking these killings. I was on my own – my colleagues thought I was wasting my time. By the time Stiles's body was discovered, by the time I'd finally made some progress, I started to realise something else about the killer.'

'What?'

'At a certain point not too long after that,' Webber says, 'he just stopped.'

59

It took a while, Webber explains, before he began to believe that the killer had stopped his murderous three-year spree around the region.

'At one point I even thought he might have emigrated,' he says. 'So I went through visa applications and passport data for everyone from the East Midlands who left the country in the year that followed. Took me the best part of six months on my own time to plough through every single one of them, profile them and eliminate them all.'

I shrug. 'Perhaps he went to jail for something else?'

'No. We'd have linked him through DNA recovered from a couple of the scenes. We'd have picked him up on *something* in the last twenty-three years.'

'Or maybe he just changed,' I say. 'Realised the suffering he was causing.'

'People like that don't change: it's in their nature, right at the essence of who they are. It's like saying the colour of your eyes could change, or your fingerprints. It's an impossibility.' He swirls the remaining beer slowly in the bottom of his glass, before taking another swig. 'No. It's far more likely the pattern was disrupted in a fundamental and permanent way: that the person in question is dead. And that's why the killings stopped. I started working through the death records too but you're talking thousands across a large swathe of the Midlands and I was reallocated to other cases before I could really get anywhere.'

I reach for my own drink again, remembering too late that the coffee is almost cold as it slides unpleasantly down my throat. What I've just heard is starting to make a horrible kind of sense.

'But . . . if this killer is dead, why are we even having this conversation? Why bother with the watch after all these years, why take the time, why come to my house? Just to give Edward Stiles's family some sort of closure?'

He shakes his head slowly. 'No. His parents are both dead. No children. Not much other family to speak of.'

'Then what? Professional pride? I mean, I get it. I understand that you want to solve this case, prove your theory was correct all along. But if your killer has been dead for twenty years, surely the chance of actually proving his guilt is infinitesimally small?'

More to the point, I think to myself, *who has been coming after me and my family for the last ten days? Who followed Leah home from school? Who broke into my house? Who was Jess following last night?*

Even though I think I already know the answer.

He sits back in his chair, the wood creaking under his weight, and crosses his arms over his big chest. He looks at his almost-finished pint, then glances towards the entrance to the pub before seeming to think better of it. Finally, his small, sharp eyes settle on me again, as if coming to a decision.

'I was a police officer my whole career,' he says quietly. 'Always took pride in trying to do the job right, to the best of my ability, no matter how much it went against the received wisdom. I still do. Even if most of my colleagues thought I was crackers by the time I handed in my warrant card. What I'm about to tell you has never been disclosed to any civilian outside the force. It was never widely shared internally either and I shouldn't be sharing it with you, really. But here we are.'

I nod, waiting for him to continue. He takes a puff on his vape, streams of pale grey smoke issuing from his nostrils.

'Like I said, we got a lot wrong with those cases. We never really got close. And there was one thing in particular that we didn't grasp at the time – it's only in the years since that I figured out what it was. But fundamentally we made too many assumptions without even realising it.'

'Assumptions about the killer?'

'Yes and no. I believe we made a fundamental mistake at an early stage which skewed everything that came afterwards. You see, we had no name, no physical description, no convincing forensics to hang an ID on. So, I gave him a nickname, a shorthand to use when I was talking about the case, trying to convince people.'

'Kind of like the *Yorkshire Ripper*?'

He frowns. 'That sort of thing, yes. I started calling the suspect the *A52 Killer* because the first two victims that I linked were on either end of that particular road, one in Derbyshire and one on the coast, and there was hardly anything else to connect them. But it sort of stuck from then on.'

I had been on the A52 a thousand times myself. It was a main road, one of the region's arteries running east to west from Stoke-on-Trent to the Lincolnshire coast at Mablethorpe.

'That's a long stretch of road,' I say. 'A lot of towns along the way where your dead guy could have come from.'

'A hundred miles or more,' he says. 'But I've long had a suspicion there was a more basic problem with the nickname. A suspicion that's been proved correct, from what you've told me. From everything that's happened since you discovered that room at the top of your house, in fact.'

I look at him, a cold loosening of terror low down in my stomach.

A confirmation of all my worst fears over the last week, gathered in one place.

Bonnie and Clyde.

My voice, when I reply, is so quiet that I can hardly hear it.

'There were two of them, weren't there?'

He looks surprised, almost impressed. Gives me a slow nod of approval.

'Yes. I believe it was a pair, working together.' He takes another deep drag on his vape. 'The A52 Killer was actually two people, not just one individual. Two of them, hunting as a team. And one of them is still out there.'

PART IV

You learn to recognise them, the ones who are like you. Recognise the 1 per cent that sets you both apart from everyone else. Because we're 99 per cent normal. We're not broken, if anything we're more efficient, more effective, more alive to the world than regular people.

You learn to recognise targets too – the ones who were always destined to end up as victims, one way or another. The plain, the unremarkable, living life on the periphery. The ones who aren't photogenic, or rich, or anything other than just slightly below average. The runaway. The secretive single man, living alone. The ex-junkie fresh out of jail.

But just because you recognise each other, doesn't mean you always agree. Especially if one of you starts taking unnecessary risks, stupid risks. Taking pictures. Acting like they want their moment in the sun. Acting like they want to get caught.

60

An ice-cold wash of fear rolls over me and my first thought is for the kids. For Jess.

One of them is still out there.

The kids should be safe at school for the time being, but I need to speak to my wife. I ask Webber to give me a minute, taking out my phone and half turning away.

'Hi, Adam,' she says sleepily after four rings. 'What's up?'

'Hi,' I say, relieved just to hear her voice, to hear that all was still normal in her world. 'Nothing, just wanted to check in. Everything OK?'

'Yup, all fine. Where are you?'

'Just talking to . . . someone. I'll fill you in when I get back.'

She rings off and I put the phone back in my pocket, a measure of relief washing over me that I know is only temporary. She had been right all along – I should have left things well alone. Cleared everything out of the house, taken it all to the tip and got rid of it without a backward glance. Without opening Pandora's box and looking inside.

Without stirring up the past.

But now all that mattered was keeping this threat as far away from my family as possible. Better still: try to find a way to neutralise the threat.

Another thought, elusive and indistinct, is bubbling at the back of my mind. An echo of something else I've heard, but I can't quite bring it into focus.

'Two killers,' I say to Webber quietly. 'How did you figure it out?'

He looks around at the increasingly busy pub, the table in front of us now taken up by a trio of suited office workers, jackets off and ties loosened. Next to us, a family of four with two young children have settled onto the wooden bench seats with soft drinks and bags of crisps.

'Now's probably not the time,' he says, his voice a low rumble. 'But there are aspects of the victimology, the selection of targets, the psychological profiling work I've done that point very strongly to a pair working together. I've had this case in my head more than twenty years, I know every detail of every incident, inside out and back to front – and I'm *absolutely convinced* that's why we never caught them. You'll have to trust me.'

'What, so one died and the other one went to ground? Blended back into everyday life, carried on as if nothing had happened and still hasn't been caught, all these years later?'

He nods. 'I've got a proposal for you, Adam.'

I don't like the sound of this. 'Go on.'

'We work together to catch this person, once and for all. You and me.'

'Surely it's the regular police that need to—'

'I can help you, we can help each other, we both want the same thing. And, first of all, I need to see that hidden room in your house.'

'Or . . . I could buy the watch back off you, hand it over and forget we ever had this conversation. How much did you pay for it?'

'It's not for sale.'

A beat of strained silence passes between us.

'Had a feeling you were going to say that.'

'I'm keeping it until this case is finally closed.' There is an edge to his voice now, a hint of consequences. 'It needs a full, comprehensive forensic examination, along with everything else you found – I'm not going to just give up evidence that could help nail a multiple murderer.'

'So you've got me over a barrel, basically? I can't give them what they want, unless you give me the watch.'

He shrugs. 'We work together to find this person, we finally get justice for the victims and put a stop to all of it. For good.'

We leave the Olde Trip to Jerusalem and walk to my car for the short drive back to the house, back up the gentle incline of Peveril Drive, taking a left turn before the tennis courts and passing almost no other traffic on the way to Regency Place. Parked up on the drive, we sit for a minute, both of us looking up at the big red-brick house with its high roof and tall windows, its wide chimney stacks and ornate Victorian detailing around the front door. It's been my home for more than a week now, but it still doesn't *feel* like home. If anything, it feels less and less like a family home with every passing day.

'Don't build 'em like this anymore,' Webber says. 'Did you meet the previous owners?'

I describe what I knew about the Hopkins family, the widowed father, the son who lived abroad. It's only as I'm telling him, passing on what I'd heard from Mrs Evans, that the elusive thought finally snaps into focus. The connection lands with the force of a punch as I remember Webber's words in the pub. *He just stopped.*

'Oh, God,' I say.

'What is it?' Webber turns to me, shifting his bulk in the passenger seat.

'Did you ever have a suspect called Peter Flack?'

'Who?'

'He died suddenly, unexpectedly in his late twenties.' *Could it have been him? Could he have been part of this?* 'Carbon monoxide poisoning in the front room of the house.'

'When was this?'

'December 2001.'

He makes another note in his small black pad.

'Any idea how long he'd lived here?'

'Not sure, but I get the impression his grandmother owned it for a good long time.'

He fires more questions at me about the previous owners and the next-door neighbour who seemed to know everyone's business. At Webber's insistence, we walk around to number ninety-three and rap the heavy brass knocker of Mrs Evans's front door. But there's no answer and no sign of life through the opaque porch window, so we return to my house and I show him into the hall. He takes it all in silently, shaking his head when I offer him a drink, the black briefcase still clutched in his left hand.

He's wheezing by the time we've walked up the stairs to the second floor, standing on the last step for a moment to catch his breath and take in his surroundings. Back when it was first built in the 1880s, I assumed that this floor would have been the servants' quarters. Many of these houses had been built for the wealthiest men of the county, the mill-owners and coalmine bosses who had paid some of the most notable architects of the time to make each residence distinctive and unique.

The landing runs in two directions from here: right, to Leah's bedroom and the small shower room next to it; and left to two more irregular-shaped small rooms, one with its long-defunct fireplace and damp stains in the pitted plaster above it, the other with a single wood-panelled wall, the planks and panels of the old fitted wardrobe still piled in the corner where I had taken them down.

This was the room at the very end of the corridor, the furthest away from the front door, from the outside world. The room where all of this trouble had started.

'Still a bit of a mess up here in the two small rooms,' I say. 'Need to watch your step.'

He nods and follows me down the corridor, his bulk almost filling the doorway from side to side, eyes roving over the interior. The room has become a bit of a dumping ground for boxes, ornaments and picture frames that we're not sure where to place, all of it piled haphazardly on the floor and leaning against the walls. Webber is taking care, I notice, not to touch the door or the frame or any other surface.

'Tell me again,' he says. 'How many items in total?'

I count them off in my head. 'Six. Plus the phone.'

There are three left, I tell him – the glasses, the wallet and the pet collar. The unknown caller has the rest, part of the failed bluff that we had tried with the drop-off at Wollaton Park. The watch remains in the pocket of Webber's suit jacket.

'So what are they?' I say. 'Keepsakes? Souvenirs?'

'That's what we're going to find out.'

'By getting the police to examine them, right?'

'Yes,' he says, 'but I need *all* of it first, every item – we'll only get one chance at this, and there's no sense going off half-cocked.

So I need background, context, *we* need to build a compelling case for the police to reopen this as a live enquiry. You know how much it costs for full forensic profiling of multiple pieces of evidence?'

I pull two heavy boxes of books away from the hidden door, sliding them across the bare floorboards until they're under the small, square dormer window.

'Have to keep it blocked during the day,' I say over my shoulder, 'so my kids can't get inside. I've told them it's out of bounds but you know what children are like – you might as well put a sign above the door daring them to come in.' I push a third box out of the way. 'Have you got any yourself?'

'One of each,' he says. 'Grown and gone now, though.'

Running my hand over the dark wooden panelling, I feel slowly from side to side until my fingers brush the join in the wood that is all but invisible to the naked eye. Even now, after going through this door countless times since we moved in, I'm still impressed with the craftsmanship, with the skill of the person who had built this hidden door and made it virtually impossible to detect. I push the rectangular panel, and with a soft *click*, the door pops open a centimetre towards me.

'It's a low doorway,' I say. 'So watch your head. And be careful inside the room, there are some nails sticking out of the roof beams and a few other places that have drawn blood on me a few times.'

I pull the door open and duck my head to fit through the low doorway, standing back up to snap the light on with the pull-cord swinging next to my head. Everything is just as it was when I last set foot in here, the dresser pushed up against the wall on the left, the old armchair, the side table, a thick layer of dust disturbed where I have walked across the floorboards, sat down, opened and closed the small drawers in the dresser. The air is still stale with the smell of old bricks and slow decay.

A moment later, Webber follows me in and I sense him standing silently behind me, his bulk crowding the space in this small room. I'm still talking, explaining how I came to find the key hidden in the back of the dresser's wooden frame, when the shadows deepen and I realise he's pulled the door fully shut.

When I turn back I notice two things: first, he's snapped blue surgical gloves onto his hands, the latex straining taut against fleshy knuckles.

In his gloved left hand, he's holding the pair of tortoiseshell-framed glasses with the broken lens.

And in his right hand is a hunting knife.

Pamela

He was married. She had known that almost from the start.

It was why he was so secretive – because he was terrified of being found out. Hence the lonely hearts ad. Hence the pseudonym and the codes they used, the way he always insisted they meet in a neutral location so the neighbours didn't see her at his house, and he wasn't spotted at hers. The way they promised to each other that they wouldn't send letters or cards that might fall into the wrong hands, or the way he always called her from a payphone when he was out and about, never from his home phone. He'd talked about getting each of them one of those new mobile phones but she didn't really see the point in those things.

The secrecy made it more exciting at the beginning, like a passionate forbidden love affair in a film or a novel.

But now Pamela was eager to move things forward.

And so was he.

It wasn't surprising: as an Aquarius she was highly compatible with his best Leo traits. It was truly a match made in the stars and it had been missing from her life for so long that she had almost grown used to its absence, like a missing tooth that you no longer notice. It was only when he'd shown her what they could have together that she realised what she'd been lacking all these years.

He was young too, could almost have been her son if she'd had any children. She got the sense that his other half was very controlling, very jealous, that they had married far too young, before either of them really knew what they wanted out of life. He was looking for more in a relationship, for the maturity and wisdom he couldn't get from someone his own age. He didn't even like to acknowledge his wife's existence, but at their third rendezvous he'd forgotten to take off his wedding ring and he couldn't very well deny it then, could he?

They'd been taking things slowly so far, because of his job as well as his wife.

But now he'd shown her he was ready to move to the next stage.

She straightened her best jacket and looked at herself in the mirror one more time, pushed the new tortoiseshell glasses up her nose and checked her hair was just right. Excitement bubbled in her stomach, an unfamiliar tingle of nerves and anticipation that made her smile to herself – a little secret smile – every time she thought of him. She'd even woken up smiling, knowing that today was the day.

Pamela pulled the front door of the small terraced house shut behind her and picked up her small overnight bag. She'd memorised his instructions, just like he'd told her. Not even writing them down, just repeating them over and over in her head until she had them off by heart:

- Leave your car at home.
- Don't take a bus or taxi either.
- Walk the fifteen minutes down to the lay-by on the other side of the railway bridge.
- Be there at 7.25 p.m. exactly, not a minute earlier or later, and he would arrive to pick her up.

Checking her watch one last time, Pamela set off into the gathering dusk.

61

The hunting knife has a wide, shining blade that curves to a wicked point.

Clutched in Webber's big fist it looks small, almost like a child's toy, but it's still six inches of razor-sharp serrated steel and I have nothing – absolutely *nothing* – with which to defend myself. I straighten up slowly, taking one step back away from him until my heel bangs against the end wall of the annexe. No way out. It's incredibly claustrophobic in here and we're barely three feet apart. He's taller, bigger, heavier than me, and I'm completely boxed in, away from the door.

My limbs flood with adrenaline, a surging electricity of fear as an overload of signals all rush to my brain at once – *fight or die, fight to live because if he beats you then Jess and the kids will be next* – my eyes flicking between his face and the blade, watching for the first hint of movement in either one.

I was an idiot. And I was probably going to die because of it. *Time for you to learn a lesson.* Somehow he had lured me back here, had appealed to my curiosity with his spiel about cold cases, forgotten victims and a serial killer's sidekick who had never been caught. Because *of course* he knew all those details. Of course he did. How could I have got him so wrong? But it didn't matter now. It was too late for any of that: I had woken something up and now it was here, in my house.

We stare at each other for a moment, his blue eyes unblinking above the thick greying beard, the perfect black of his pupils like two pinpricks in the harsh light of the bare bulb. The slim metallic pull-cord for the light switch hangs down from the ceiling between us, just within my reach. If I can grab that, plunge the room into darkness, I might have half a chance of getting around him, behind him, disarming him somehow. Or maybe even escaping, trapping him in here.

'Gordon,' I say, 'what are you—'

'What do your instincts tell you to do now,' he says evenly, 'in a situation like this?'

I roll onto the balls of my feet, ready to lunge for the pull-cord.

'What?'

He raises the knife towards me, light flashing off the blade.

'What's your instinct in this situation?'

The adrenaline is screaming through me now, an overwhelming urge looking for violent release, to wrench the light switch with my right hand as hard as I can, rip the cord free, use my left to push him away from me, go around him, keep away from his knife hand, loop the cord around his neck.

Fear coats the back of my throat, making it hard to swallow. *Fight or die.*

'You can take whatever you want,' I say. 'Just take it and go.'

'What? No. You're not listening, or maybe I'm not asking the right question.' He waves the knife again. 'Try this: what's the most interesting thing in this room right now?'

'The knife.'

'Almost hypnotic, isn't it? Hard to look away.'

'That's one way of describing it.'

I'm about to launch myself towards the pull-cord when he lowers the knife.

'Edward Stiles,' he says slowly, 'was stabbed once in the back, remember? No defensive wounds. Probably because all his attention was on the threat in front of him. So, you see how much easier it is, if you have two killers working together? One is the distraction, the lure, the shiny decoy; the other one makes the kill. There's a real multiplier effect when you have two suspects working together. That's how I first started developing my theory.'

He takes a black leather scabbard from his jacket and slides the blade into it, drops it back into the pocket.

'Jesus,' I breathe. 'Seriously?'

'Are you all right, Adam?' He flashes me a grin. 'You look a bit pale.'

'What the hell is wrong with you?' My voice rises. 'Scared the living crap out of me, thought you were going to stab me right here.'

'Why would I want to do that?'

'You pulled a knife on me!'

He grunts a half-hearted apology. 'Just trying to make a point.'

'Thought I was going to have a heart attack.'

'All right, fair enough,' he says. 'So, are you going to show me where you found the watch?'

I blow out a huge breath, the jackhammering of my heart starting to ease. With a shaking finger, I point at the old Welsh dresser squatting against the wall beside us.

'In there, with everything else. Each item in a separate drawer.'

'And I take it you've already touched all this, previously? With ungloved hands?' When I nod an affirmative, he hands me a pair of blue latex gloves from his jacket pocket. 'Better if you wear these from now on, if you're handling anything in here.'

I pull the gloves on, the cool latex snapping against my wrists, and retrieve the small brass key from its hiding place before taking the remaining items from the drawers: the dog collar with its tag and the wallet. I show him the note too, the to-do list for *Parker* and *Barrow*. He has me slide each item into clear plastic bags that he produces from his briefcase – sealed to preserve DNA and other forensic evidence, he says.

And then he gets up close and simply stares at them, shines his phone torch onto each one in turn as if they are ancient artefacts newly recovered from an Egyptian tomb. Leaning over the dresser, examining them, turning each one carefully in its plastic bag to study it from another angle. He takes half a dozen pictures of each one on his phone, then more pictures of the room, the door, the drawers in which they were found.

When he eventually speaks again, his voice is low, almost reverent.

'We're going to get them, Adam.' He leans forward. 'Me and you. After all these years, we're finally going to get them.'

'How?'

'If you want to catch a wolf, you have to set a trap.' He holds up the cracked glasses in his gloved hand. 'And now we have the perfect bait.'

62

'So, this *supposed* investigator,' Jess says, sitting cross-legged on the sofa. 'He could be anyone. Did he show you his warrant card?'

'He said he was a civilian investigator now, working with some regional cold case unit.' I describe the webpage Webber had shown me on his phone, the old news story with his picture.

She shrugs. 'Easiest thing in the world to fake. What about a car, what was he driving?'

'He just turned up. Said he got a taxi.'

'Or maybe he didn't want to bring it because it's a grey Volvo. Please tell me you didn't hand over the rest of the stuff, the last of the things you found?'

'Gave him the glasses. Kept the other two things.'

'I don't like the sound of this guy,' she says. 'Something about him doesn't ring true. And that whole thing with him waving a big knife around – that's just messed up.'

'He was quite strange. But maybe the job does that to you, working on the murder squad for years.'

'What if it *is* him though? What if Webber is the sidekick, the one who's been hiding in plain sight all these years?'

'Then why didn't he stab me up in that room today, when he had the chance?'

'Maybe it's all about recognition for him now, maybe he's craving the "credit" that he never received at the time. The point is, how do you know he isn't just burrowing his way into our lives, to find out what you know as part of some sick plan to go down in a blaze of glory?'

'He wants to solve this case, Jess. He wants the same thing as us.'

She gives me a look as if I'm being hopelessly naive. 'I don't think you should trust him. I don't think you should trust anyone.'

* * *

Exhaustion from the last few nights of broken sleep overtakes me and I fall into a deep, dreamless sleep in the late afternoon. When I wake up and head downstairs, there's a car in the drive I've never seen before. A battered white Toyota pickup with a dirty green tarpaulin stretched over the cargo bed at the back. I look around the front garden. No one seems to be here, no one is *supposed* to be here, as far as I know. Jess was picking the kids up from school and working from home this afternoon, but she'd not mentioned anything to me about a visitor.

The dashboard of the pickup is littered with fast-food wrappers and other rubbish, the seats tattered and stained. I shift the tarpaulin off the cargo bed to find a set of aluminium ladders, a chainsaw, various spades crusted with soil and a thick stack of heavy-duty refuse sacks. Lying next to them, a sledgehammer and two black-handled axes.

A figure emerges through the gate from the back garden and I feel a sudden jolt of alarm before I realise it's Tobias, in jeans and a grey sweatshirt. Three bulging garden waste bags in each of his hands. He nods a greeting to me as he heads over to the green bin at the side of the house.

Jess's words are still fresh in my mind. *I don't think you should trust anyone.*

What was the other thing she had said? *He doesn't really like being shut in, he prefers to be outside.* Maybe that was because he'd spent so much of his life under lock and key, behind prison walls? Was that why the killings had stopped, all those years ago? I summon the memory of Saturday night, trying to picture the intruder in my house during the power cut. Was he the one who had broken in, the one who had been at the top of the cellar stairs? This stranger who had access to my garden, my house?

'Hi,' I say. 'Tobias, isn't it?'

He dumps the first bag into the green bin and I notice a dirty bandage around the palm of his left hand.

'That's me.'

'What happened to your hand? Car accident?'

He doesn't look at the bandage. 'Barbed wire.'

'Right.' I turn and head for the house, reaching for my keys. 'Wait there a minute, will you?'

His voice, behind me now, takes on a harder tone. 'Is there a problem?'

I ignore him. In the house, the tiled floor of the hallway and the kitchen are wet, as if they've just been mopped. I call out but there's no answer, eventually finding Helena upstairs in the spare bedroom wiping glass cleaner off one of the big leaded windows.

The last stranger I'd confronted up here was Shaun, who had knocked on my door with some story about his grandfather's old watch, and I'd had to march him out of the house after finding him rooting around in the master bedroom. She has the same yellow Marigolds and pink housecoat as the last time she was here, same outfit, hair clipped up in the same way, but all I can think of is the conversation with Webber from earlier.

One is the distraction, the lure, the shiny decoy; the other one makes the kill.

Helena was in her mid- to late forties, so around the turn of the millennium she would have been in her early to mid-twenties. She was an attractive woman now, with fine, delicate features, and I'm sure she had been as a younger woman too. And at least two suspected victims of the A52 Killer – Edward Stiles and Adrian Parish – had been single men who might have been easily taken in by a woman like that.

The distraction, the lure, the shiny decoy.

My heart starts to thud painfully in my chest and suddenly the only thing I can think about is getting her out, getting them *both* out, off my property, away from here. The idea of strangers being here makes the small hairs stand up on my bare arms.

There's a real multiplier effect when you have two suspects working together.

'Nearly finished in here,' she says breezily. 'Your wife asked me to take the dog for a walk around the block as well. Coco, isn't it? She seems very friendly.'

'You have a key from Jess, do you?'

'Yes.' She is completely calm. 'Back door.'

Of course. I kick myself for not thinking of it sooner. She's had access to the house since before the weekend – that's why I'd never heard a break-in on Saturday night.

'Listen, I'm really sorry but there's been a bit of a . . . misunderstanding,' I say. 'I'm going to need your key back until we can get some more sets cut.'

'Oh?'

'I need to give a set to my brother-in-law and we just don't have enough to go around just yet. Sorry.' I hold my hand out. 'Do you mind?'

She reaches into a pocket and drops the key into my out-stretched palm.

Quietly, she says: 'I was glad to hear your wife was OK, after last night.'

There is a sudden chill at the back of my neck, as if cold fingertips are resting there.

'Thank you. She's a tough one.'

'Sounds like she was lucky,' she says. 'Thank goodness.'

Is there the ghost of a smile at the corner of her lips, or am I just making her nervous?

'You know what?' I say. 'It's actually not a good time right now, the kids are back from school soon and Daisy's still not really settled in yet. She gets very anxious around strangers so I wonder if you could just finish up now? Obviously we'll pay you the full amount.'

She gives me an odd look but doesn't argue, pulling off the rubber gloves with a shrug and heading downstairs to find her cousin.

As their battered Toyota is crunching up the gravel drive, Jess's car appears on the street. She waits for the pickup to indicate and pull out onto Regency Place before turning in and parking up behind my Nissan.

She gets out and goes to the rear door to unstrap Daisy from her car seat.

'Hey, what's up with Helena and her cousin?' she calls over to me. 'Just saw them leaving but they were supposed to be doing three till five today.'

'I sent them away.'

She frowns, as if she's misheard me. 'You did what?'

'It's not a good idea to have lots of strangers in the house right now. Lots of people we don't really know.'

'They're not strangers. She came recommended on that WhatsApp group, the Park Estate neighbourhood chat.' Her voice is laced with disbelief. 'You didn't *actually* tell them to go, did you?'

'I didn't know you'd given her a key.'

She helps Daisy to climb down from the back seat onto the drive while Callum clambers out the other side, swinging his school backpack from one strap.

'Quite difficult for her to do the job without a key,' she says. 'So you're going to pick up where she left off, are you?'

'I don't trust her,' I say. 'Or him.'

'This has gone far enough, Adam.' She slams the car door with a little more force than is needed. 'I'm worried about the effect this is having on you, as well as the head injury. You're not being rational and you need to stop, this *all* needs to stop so the police can deal with it.'

'The police aren't interested.'

She checks over her shoulder to make sure Callum and Daisy are not in earshot. But they are both momentarily distracted by a squirrel sitting on the garden wall.

'That fall in the cellar could have killed you,' she says under her breath. 'I got lucky last night. Who knows what they're going to do next? Enough's enough. This *has* to stop.'

'That's the whole point,' I say. 'It's not as simple as that anymore. Whoever's doing this, they're not going to stop or leave us alone. Not unless we stop them first. And until then we have to protect ourselves, which means keeping strangers away.'

She stares at me a moment longer, frustration hardening her features. Then she simply shakes her head again and stalks into the house, Callum and Daisy trotting along close behind.

63

DC Tanya Rubin finally calls me back later that afternoon, while I'm trawling the internet for other unsolved murders from around the turn of the millennium. The detective is brisk and business-like on the phone, as if she's doing me a huge favour just making the call. But I feel a small bubble of hope when she tells me she has an update on the number plate that Jess had photographed as she followed the Volvo out of Wollaton Park on Monday evening.

'We sent an officer to the address,' she says. 'That vehicle has been reported stolen.'

'Seriously?'

'According to the owner.'

'When exactly was it reported stolen?'

I can hear her flicking through notes, pages turning. 'Monday afternoon, sometime between two and five p.m. The owner says they spent the evening at home and that's corroborated by two witnesses.'

They had covered their tracks well: a bogus report backdated to a few hours before Jess had followed it from Wollaton Park. The bubble of hope bursts.

'And where do they live, the owner?'

'You know I'm not able to divulge information like that, sir.'

I try a different tack, telling her about a possible link between Edward Stiles and Adrian Parish, asking if she'd been able to discover anything else about Parish since we last spoke. She tells me there *is* a file on the system archive, that Parish was still listed as an outstanding missing person – but it was not currently an active investigation and had not been for a long time.

'Isn't there a national database, a system, some way for you to access their case files? I found things that belonged to both men in an attic room of my house, hidden away in the same place.'

'In that case you should bring the items to us, and we'll take a look. But it would need to be significant new evidence relating to either case for us to open a new line of enquiry.' Her voice is tight with impatience. 'Now, is there anything else, sir?'

I can feel her interest, her attention, slipping away from me.

'I don't suppose,' I say, 'you've ever crossed paths with a detective named Gordon Webber? Became a civilian investigator after he retired, but he was on the murder squad from around 2001 onwards.'

There is a short silence at the other end of the line.

'Doesn't sound familiar.' Her tone tells me she's about to ring off. 'Then again, in 2001 I was still at primary school.'

*   *   *

My earlier argument with Jess smoulders all evening, like glowing embers just waiting for a breath of wind to catch the bone-dry kindling all around. It's only when we've put the younger two children to bed that I broach the subject again, going over the conversation with Webber and the cold case he had been investigating for so long, his theory about a pair of serial killers who had hunted together more than twenty years ago.

But before I've even finished, she's already shaking her head at me in disbelief.

'You've got a nerve,' she says. 'Having a go at me for getting a cleaner in for a couple of hours when you're giving a house tour to a total stranger who just happens to knock on the front door this morning.'

I take a bottle of red wine from the rack and two glasses from the cupboard. It's only Tuesday evening but it feels like it's been a long week already.

'The point is,' I say, 'it's worse than we thought. Webber thinks there were two of them operating in the region back in the early 2000s and one of them was never caught. One of them is still free and it's that person who is trying to recover the stuff from the hidden room. Because it's evidence of what they did.'

'Right. There's just one tiny flaw in his theory.'

'What?'

'The fact that there was never any serial killer on the loose back then, no string of unsolved murders in the city, no hue and cry in the media about a Yorkshire Ripper or a Fred West. We'd have known about it, wouldn't we? We both grew up here, and that's the sort of thing you remember.'

I fill both wine glasses and put one on the counter next to her.

'But the police never linked them,' I say. 'They were all treated as separate, individual cases.'

'OK,' she says. 'Let's say, for the sake of argument, that there are these unsolved crimes from goodness knows how long ago. Has it occurred to you that this supposed detective might be more involved than you think? That he might be implicated himself?'

'It's possible, I suppose. But it doesn't seem likely.'

'Because it seems to me that Helena is just a pleasant, efficient person who was recommended by our neighbours and who came here because I asked her to.'

'All I'm saying is we don't know for sure about Webber *or anyone else*. We just need to be extra careful until we do know, so I was thinking we should probably cancel Helena for the next few weeks.'

'After you sent her away today, I'll be surprised if she wants to come back at all. Have you any idea how mad and paranoid you're starting to sound? And don't imagine it's not affecting the kids too, because they've definitely picked up on it. Takes ages to get Daisy settled down at night now because she's convinced that the bad man's going to come back in the middle of the night. Callum's been a bit tearful too and I know it's affecting Leah's revision for her GCSEs.'

I take a sip of my own red wine.

'We need to protect ourselves.'

'By cutting off all contact with everyone else?'

'Does it not seem like a coincidence that we get a gardener in last week, we have no real idea who he is and he's working out there unsupervised, right under our noses, and then we find a surveillance camera in the garden, spying on us?'

As soon as the words are out of my mouth, I wish I could pull them back.

Jess's expression darkens. 'What's that supposed to mean?'

'He could be anyone, he could have his own agenda for all we—'

'Just say it,' she says, cheeks flaring red. 'This is just like what you said the other night, isn't it? That it's all my fault, all of this?'

'All I'm saying is that we need to be careful about who we invite to the house, who we give a key to.' I reach into my pocket for the kitchen door key. 'This is the one you gave to Helena, right? Just hope she hasn't made copies.'

My wife is shaking her head.

'Don't you dare put this on me, don't you *dare!*' She's shouting now. 'You're the one who started all of this with the bloody phone and the watch and all the other crap from that stupid room on the top floor. If you'd bagged it up and taken it to the tip with everything else we wouldn't even be having this conversation!'

She takes an angry swallow of wine and for a second I think she might throw the glass at me. But instead she slams the glass down on the counter so hard that Merlot sloshes over the counter.

'Jess—'

'This has got to stop, Adam! Do you hear me?'

I'm about to reply when I realise the kitchen doorway is pushed half open and Daisy is standing there in her pyjamas, thumb clamped in her mouth, muslin cloth held tight to her cheek. Her blonde hair is tangled, her pale face streaked with tears.

'You shouted,' she says to me in a small voice. 'You woke me up. Why are you being mean to Mummy?'

I have no idea how long she's been standing there, how much of our row she has witnessed. Before I can reply, Jess holds out her hands and scoops our youngest into her arms.

'Sorry, baby,' she says, making for the door. 'No more shouting. Come on now, it's bedtime.'

64

WEDNESDAY

If I want to check into Helena's background, there's an obvious place to start.

Daisy and Callum are both subdued when they wake for school and I have to cajole them through every part of the morning routine from the moment they roll, grumbling, out of their beds. They both perk up a little by the time we arrive at St Jude's and once they're dropped off I go back to my car, sitting with my phone as all the other parents drive off and head to the office, or back home, or wherever else they were going on this cloudy spring morning.

By ten past nine I'm pretty much the only car parked on this suburban street but I'm not going home – not yet. Instead, I dive back into the neighbourhood WhatsApp thread again, scrolling back until I find it again: a request from Jess, posted soon after we moved in and had just been added to the group, to ask if anyone could recommend a cleaner and gardener. The rapid response from user Sarah@84GT with a glowing recommendation for Helena and Tobias.

Helena, who would have been in her early twenties at the turn of the millennium; and Tobias, the supposed 'cousin' who had some kind of claustrophobia. There was something about those two that had not rung true right from the start.

Webber answers his phone after the first ring.

'Adam?' He doesn't sound surprised to hear from me. 'I was going to call you.'

'Two questions for you,' I say without preamble. 'Something I should have asked you yesterday.'

'Go on.'

'The surviving partner of this serial killing pair, the sidekick, the follower, whatever you want to call them. More likely to be a man, or a woman?'

He exhales heavily, as if he's puffing on his vape.

'Good question. Typically, in a relationship like this you'd have a dominant partner who calls the shots, and a secondary or subservient partner seeking their approval. And so in this case, when the dominant partner died, the follower just stopped. Without the motivation, cunning and aggression of the dominant half, they didn't have the drive to continue on their own. They can't operate alone.'

'So, basically there's an active leader and a more passive follower.'

'Exactly. Both feeding off each other: the charismatic, dominant partner to show his control while the role of the submissive is to encourage, to praise, to enable. In some cases to copy the other partner. You'll also see the secondary partner sometimes being used as a lure, to make that first contact with the victim – either because they're female, or younger, or less physically imposing than the alpha.'

'Like . . . Ian Brady and Myra Hindley?'

He gives a grunt of approval. 'You see something similar in the partnership of Fred and Rose West, various examples of the same thing across the pond. Charles Starkweather and Caril Ann Fugate, Debra Brown and Alton Coleman, the list goes on.'

'Bonnie and Clyde.'

'Sure. You get the picture.'

I compile a quick mental list of all the women over forty who had come into our lives since we moved in. Eileen Evans, the next-door neighbour who could easily have had a key to our house in the past. Maxine, whose husband had vanished. But it was Helena who fit the profile most closely, who ticked more of the boxes than any of the others. Being a cleaner was the perfect cover, with access to the house and time to look around in the course of her work.

'So,' I say, 'we're looking for a woman?'

'I think it's more likely to be a female, yes. With the Moors Murderers, Brady was the dominant partner but it was Hindley who lured many of the victims into the car – because they didn't perceive a threat from a young, attractive female. And yet, on her own, it's possible she might not have gone down a criminal path at all. It was only when she came into Brady's orbit that that side of her was unlocked.'

'You think if Brady had died before they were caught, Hindley might have gone back to some kind of normality? She might have just resumed a normal life, like a switch being turned off?'

'Hundreds, thousands of concentration camp guards did exactly that in 1945.'

'But that was different, that was—'

'Was it? It was still murder. The same rationalising process, justification for it, dehumanising of victims. And then some-how, they slotted back into their old lives, despite what they'd done, what they'd seen, all the crimes in which they'd been complicit.'

'Lots of them were caught, eventually.'

'Not enough.' He pauses to take another drag on his vape. 'Just to be clear, I believe it's more likely to be a male–female dynamic but I still wouldn't rule out other alternatives, either.'

'Two men?'

'Or two females,' he says. 'The psychology works in a similar way in any two-person partnership. You said you had two questions – what's the other one?'

I picture Tobias, an unremarkable man who Helena *claimed* was her cousin.

'I might be completely off target here,' I say. 'But might this person potentially seek out another partner to try to recreate that relationship again? Only this time, they would be in charge, the alpha?'

'Hard to say. It's possible, if the circumstances were right. Have you got something to tell me, Adam?'

'Not sure yet,' I say. 'Maybe.'

'I'll be in touch in a few hours. I'm putting a plan together.'

I ring off and switch back into WhatsApp.

On Sarah@84GT's profile there is nothing else except for a phone number and a grainy picture of a baby propped on someone's shoulder. The adult's face is hidden from view and there is nothing else recognisable in the image. I select the group description, which has the phone numbers of the admins and a list of a dozen streets where members live. Second from bottom on the list, I find the corresponding initials that I'm looking for.

Grandfield Terrace is only a few streets down from us, running east–west rather than north–south, and it's easy enough to find in the car. I keep my speed down as I turn into a long, tree-lined street that is much like many of the others on the estate although there are also some low-rise flats slotted in here and there, a few post-war two-storey blocks that look incongruous alongside the grand Victorian villas that characterise so much of this part of the city. I've started at the wrong end, I realise, where the low-numbered houses are. There's hardly any traffic; everyone has either gone to work or school already, or they're working from home. I keep the car in third gear, counting house numbers, looking for number eighty-four. Formulating a rough plan in my head of what I'm going to say to the WhatsApp messager who goes under the tag of *Sarah@84GT*. *How do you know Helena? Does she live locally?*

It's only when I get to the end of the Grandfield Terrace that I realise I've missed it. The street across the junction is called Stanswick Grove. I pull the car in a wide circle across the road and go back the way I came. The end house is number ninety-eight. I keep my speed at a crawl until I get to a house with number eighty-six on a stone pillar at the head of the drive, then pull over and park.

Next door is a set of squat, red-brick flats occupying the full width of two plots, presumably where the original old houses had been knocked down and replaced with more affordable accommodation. The communal front door is heavy, dark wood, with a panel listing six flats, A to F, and a buzzer next to each. Above the door in faded chrome lettering is the shared address: *Eighty-Two Grandfield Terrace*. I walk back to the house next door: definitely number eighty-six. Returning to the flats, I start pressing buzzers at random and asking the same question of the three residents who answer, asking them how I can find number eighty-four.

All of them give the same response.

Eighty-four Grandfield Terrace doesn't exist.

65

Back in my car, I send a private message to Sarah@84GT on WhatsApp.

> *Hi, thanks so much for recommending Helena – she's great. My wife brought some chocolates to thank you and asked me to drop them round to you – can you let me know where? Adam*

If the address was a fiction, then perhaps 'Sarah' was a fiction too.

And if my instincts were right, I didn't imagine that this person – whoever was actually behind the Sarah@84GT account – would be in a hurry to reply to me. I tap on the menu to bring up more options, selecting 'Group Info'. There were 217 members in total, all listed by name and phone number, spread over a range of streets in our little corner of The Park. The size of the group helped to explain two things: why it was so busy, and how a bogus account could hide in plain sight. All you had to do was get someone to add you, and no one paid too much attention to whose friend or acquaintance or neighbour you were. I'd bet that most of these people had never even met in real life.

There are six members listed as admins, nominally in charge of the group. I pick three at random and send them private messages asking if they've used Helena and who recommended her; and asking for any more information on who might have added Sarah to the group.

Next, I send a message to Jess, apologising for last night and asking if she's had any other contact from this person who had connected us with Helena and Tobias. We've not spoken since the row and I know it was my fault, I know I overstepped the mark. I want to speak to her rather than texting but I know – from the few rare times we've had spats in the past – that she'll hold me at arm's length for at least a few more hours, not picking up my calls or returning messages until later. She's due to pick Callum up from tag rugby at four, but I don't imagine I'll hear from her until then.

Almost straightaway, my message has the two blue ticks to show it's been delivered and read.

I stare at the screen, willing my wife to message me back. Even if it's angry, a response is better than silence.

She doesn't reply.

*　　*　　*

Webber rings me, his voice taut with excitement.

'OK, it's on. Five o'clock today.'

He explains his plan to me. I will message the anonymous number and say I'll deliver the last three items personally, to a location of their choosing. I will relay that location to Webber and he'll descend on the rendezvous with enough police officers to subdue and arrest whoever comes to meet me.

'So I'm the bait, am I?'

'One of us needs to go. If he sees me, it'll spook him – he'll know it's a set-up.'

'Alright,' I say. 'I'll do it, on one condition: you give me back the last three items, so they know it's for real. Including the watch.'

He hesitates, but only for a moment. 'Deal.'

'Just keep everything away from my house.'

I send a message to the unknown number.

I've got the Rolex, the real one. And the rest of it. I'll bring it to you, wherever you want to meet, 5 p.m. today. No police. Just us. And then you'll never hear from me again.

I press 'send' and wait for a response, imagining the satisfaction of seeing them in a few hours, handcuffed and surrounded by police.

Because I already have a pretty good idea of who it is.

*   *   *

There's a letter on the welcome mat when I push the door open. No stamp, no address, just my name in block capitals on a plain white envelope. I take it into the kitchen and tear it open, pulling out two A4 sheets, each folded twice.

It's a colour printout from a local paper, dated 29th October, 2009. The first page has a big blocky headline under a tabloid masthead, and for a second I think it's a copy of the same story I'd found at the library on Monday. But everything else is unfamiliar and it doesn't have the distinctive tone and shade of a printout from a microfiche transparency; this looks more like a photocopy of a well-preserved original.

The main picture is a candid shot of a man in a dark rain-coat, caught in profile on the street, looking over his shoulder as if talking to someone behind him. A man who'd come to my door yesterday, telling me his name was retired Detective Gordon Webber. In the image he's younger, his beard still fully black. But it's definitely him. There are five words handwritten in biro, blocky black capitals at the top of the photocopied page.

THIS IS WHY HE QUIT

Below it, the text of a story that takes up most of the front page and runs onto the second sheet of A4 behind it. I read further, a sick dread curdling in my stomach. It outlines the sensational collapse earlier that year of the trial of Janusz Makowski, a 33-year-old labourer who had been wrongly accused of the 2001 murder of Edward John Stiles. Makowski had been cleared of all charges after a judge halted the trial over concerns about police conduct.

A subsequent case review by a team from a neighbouring force, Leicestershire Police, uncovered 'significant violations of procedure' related to the handling of evidence, tampering with key prosecution exhibits and coercion of witnesses involved in the case. I read on to the bottom of the article, which outlines the findings of a hearing that had looked into every aspect of the trial that had collapsed.

Just like the scribbled words said: former Detective Gordon Webber had left out something rather important from our conversation yesterday.

He had been demoted for misconduct and quit the force not long after.

66

The headline sums it up: MURDER COPS RAPPED AFTER CASE PROBE.

Reading between the lines, it seemed fairly clear that Webber had been doing absolutely everything he could to get a conviction, even if it meant trying to frame an innocent man. But the judge had seen through it and halted the case, triggering Webber's suspension and an internal investigation. The resulting firestorm of blame had ended the careers of three senior officers, and seen four others disciplined, demoted and kicked off the murder squad – including Webber.

His career had crashed to earth in public disgrace.

Webber, of Stapleford, Notts, was described as 'falling far below the standards of professional behaviour expected of a serving officer' by the chair of the misconduct hearing.

So my first instincts had been right about him, after all: he had lied to me. I hear my wife's voice, almost as if she's whispering in my ear. *I don't think you should trust him. I don't think you should trust anyone.*

How he had managed to return to a civilian investigator role years later was anyone's guess. Perhaps the police were so desperate for experienced staff that the bar had been lowered to allow it. I google Janusz Makowski and find a small piece a year later about a compensation payout he had received after his wrongful arrest and detention on remand for almost a year before the trial that had collapsed. And then – nothing. No hits on Google after 2009 that relate to the same man. I guessed he might have changed his name. I probably would have done the same, in his shoes.

As to who was trying to warn me off the ex-detective, I didn't have a clue.

My phone buzzes with a FaceTime call from Maxine. She looks different on the little screen: older, more businesslike.

'Finally,' I say. 'I've been leaving messages, trying to get hold of you.'

'Been busy,' she says breathlessly. 'Following up leads. That's why I need to talk to you.'

'Did you send me the note?'

She frowns. 'What note? What are you talking about?'

'This.' I lay the pages flat on the kitchen table and point the phone at it, give her a brief description of the contents. 'Someone hand-delivered it to my house this morning.'

'Not me.'

'Do you know Webber?'

Something passes across her face, then it's gone.

'Forget about that for a minute. I've found something you need to see.'

'Can you show me?'

'The quality's not good enough to look at on a small screen. You need to see the original – up close.'

* * *

We meet back at Stapley's Tea Room, off Market Square, in the middle of the city. Maxine is already there at an upstairs table when I arrive, sitting with her back to the wall, coffees ordered for both of us.

She's on her own today.

'Good to see you.' I give her a quick update on Webber's theory. 'What have you got?'

'Charlie's been busy digging up what he can find on Peter Flack. From what we've gathered so far he studied at Trent High School, started work at eighteen, bounced around a few different jobs before an apprenticeship as a joiner. Ended up working for one of the biggest companies in the city, at their national head office.'

'But stayed living at home with his grandma.'

'Yup.' She reaches into her bag for a green cardboard folder, sliding out a single sheet of paper from the top but keeping it face down. 'So the place he worked had thousands of staff – still does – and before the turn of the millennium, some poor bastard there was tasked with a special project. A hardback yearbook, featuring pictures of every single UK employee. Every team, in every shop and warehouse.'

I take a sip of my coffee. 'Sounds like a nightmare assignment.'

'I know, right?' She turns the sheet over, spins it round so it's facing me. It's a colour photo of a group of people, standing in front of a large industrial building. It's formal, posed, a few dozen people in four tiered ranks, each one higher than the one in front. The building in the background has a large corporate logo over its entrance. 'Take a look at the back row.'

I scan the faces. It doesn't take long to find the handsome, square-jawed profile of a man in his early twenties with a passing resemblance to a young Zac Efron.

'That's Flack, isn't it?'

'It is.' She points down to a figure on the right, a slim man with thick glasses and an awkward smile. 'And this guy here, do you recognise him?'

It takes a moment for the penny to drop, for a memory to slot into place. The picture that Webber had showed me yesterday, at the pub: a young man with wavy dark-blond hair and a shy smile.

'Shit.' I stare a bit closer at the image. 'That's Edward Stiles, isn't it?'

She points her index finger at me as if she's aiming a gun. 'Gold star for Adam.'

'So . . . they worked together at this place? There's a direct link between Flack and Edward Stiles, they maybe knew each other?'

'Or at least Flack knew enough about Stiles to know that he was a loner, struggling with his own issues, who might not be missed straightaway if he dropped out of sight. An easy target. An ideal target. That's probably why the Rolex ended up in your house.'

A chill flows over my skin, like a cold draught. 'You think . . . Flack killed him?'

'Flack plus his sidekick, if your disgraced ex-copper is to be believed.'

I don't tell her I've already got a decent idea who the side-kick is.

'Exactly.' I nod. 'The two of them.'

My phone buzzes with a message from *Alissa@14BG*, one of the admins in charge of the neighbourhood WhatsApp group.

Hi Adam, sorry for delay getting back to you, have been at Pilates. Helena's with me now if you want me to ask her about Sarah?

I stand up from the table.

'Sorry,' I say. 'Got to go. Thanks for the picture, can I keep it?'

She hands the sheet to me. 'Stay in touch, Adam.'

I give her a thumbs up as I hurry to the stairs.

67

I spot the battered white Toyota just as it's pulling out of the driveway of number fourteen Blenheim Gardens, and follow it on a brief journey to the other side of The Park. The driver is slow and careful, cautious at junctions and respectful of cyclists and pedestrians – as if they're on their best behaviour.

They pull over on Valley Terrace, in front of another big Victorian house with another big drive.

I guess Wednesday must be a busy day for them, with one booking after another.

Tobias gets out of the driver's side of the pickup truck and goes to the tarpaulin at the back, lifting out a shovel and a chain-saw from the cargo bed. Helena gets out of the other side and fetches a small carrier of cleaning supplies, checking on bottles of spray and polish.

I park up close behind them and get out. Need to do this now, before she disappears inside the property.

'I know it's you,' I say as I walk up to her. 'I know what you've been doing.'

She looks up in surprise. She's wearing the same pink house-coat she'd worn at our house and seems smaller, somehow, standing on the pavement.

'Hello, Adam,' she says hesitantly. 'Can I . . . help?'

'I know how you got into my house.'

'Sorry, I don't know what you're talking about.'

'You invented a fake profile on the WhatsApp group, didn't you? Sarah@84GT? Pretend you're a resident so you can recommend yourself to other people, get inside their houses. That's right, isn't it? So you can get keys cut and look around, scope them out, find your next target?'

She shakes her head. 'I'm sorry, not sure what you're—'

'Or in my case, steal evidence from the crimes you took part in twenty years ago.'

'What?' She looks around for Tobias, who was carrying his tools around to the side gate but has now stopped and turned around to stare. He begins to walk back towards us.

'When did you meet Peter Flack?'

She frowns, her face a picture of confusion. 'Who?'

'Were you a couple, was that it? You were seeing each other?'

'I don't know that family; I've never worked for them. I don't know what you're talking about.'

'I want you to stop, OK? Stop all of it, the text messages, the harassment, following my daughter home from school. Cameras, dead animals, threats, the burglary. I know it's you and Tobias, I've got the police involved and I'm not going to let you do it anymore.'

'I don't know about any of that.'

'And I don't believe you.'

A heavy red blush is creeping up her neck.

'Honestly,' she says quietly. 'We didn't do anything bad.'

'You're lying.'

A tear brims in her eye.

'It was just . . .'

'It was just what?'

'I needed the work. We used to live here but it got too expensive. Then we were on the outside and we had to have a way in, a way to get recommended to people who can still afford a cleaner or a gardener and there aren't many of those nowadays. It's so hard to get enough hours, enough clients, to keep our heads above water. Please don't tell anyone. *Please.* We won't come back to yours but we need the work, we need all the clients we can get.'

The tear spills and she cuffs it quickly away, embarrassed.

'Please,' she says again.

Tobias, wearing a black hoodie, lays the spade and the chainsaw on the lawn as he walks up to me. He puts a hand on Helena's shoulder, whispers something in her ear then throws a quick look back towards the house, another glance up and down the street.

Then he steps in and hits me with a clubbing punch that comes out of nowhere and catches me just under the eye. It's a short jab but there's a lot of power behind it and I stagger back down the kerb as pain explodes in my cheek. He drops his hands to his sides as if nothing has happened, checks the street again and leans in close.

'I don't like you upsetting her,' he says quietly. 'Time for you to go. Unless you want me to really do a number on your face.'

'I know who you are, who *she* is,' I say, pointing at Helena. 'What she's done.'

'You're deluded.' He takes me by the arm, his grip like a steel gauntlet, and walks me to the driver's side door of my car. 'And I'm not going to warn you again.'

The two of them stare at me from the kerb as I drive away.

* * *

At the school pick-up at St Jude's, the darkening bruise under my eye attracts curious stares, not least from Mrs Pett, Daisy's reception teacher.

'Looks like a sore one,' she says, watching each of her children out of the classroom door. 'How did that happen?'

'DIY accident.' I give her my best grin. 'Too clumsy for my own good.'

Daisy is also extremely curious, insisting on studying the bruise close up and discussing at length how it had happened. At home, this extends into a lengthy game of doctors and nurses, in which she's the doctor and I'm the poorly patient who has to go to hospital and *have horrible medicine that tastes yuk but will make you better, Daddy.*

A reply from the mystery number arrives while we're in the middle of the game.

OK. The old RAF base at Newton. Main hangar. 4 p.m. not 5.
If you're a minute late or if you're with anyone, your house gets burned to the ground instead with everyone inside it.
This is your last chance.

I check my watch. I'd never been to the old abandoned airbase at Newton, east of the city. I had no idea what was even left there. It's only a few miles away but a twenty-five minute drive at least, at this time of day. The meeting being an hour earlier means I'll only just make it if I leave straightaway.

I send a response, then write a message to Webber with the meeting location, a stab of hesitation as I remember the anonymous note put through my door only a few hours ago.

Could I trust him?

Did I even have any other choice at this stage? And there was no time.

I press 'send' and forward the message to the ex-detective, adding,

I'm on my way now.

We were going to set a trap for a wolf.

Leah is in the dining room absorbed in her phone, school textbooks arrayed across the table in front of her.

'Leah?' I say. 'I have to go out for a little while, OK? Can you look after your sister for a bit? Your mum's going to get Callum from tag rugby after school.'

She nods without looking up from her phone. 'Where are you going?'

'Something I have to ... drop off. Should be back in about an hour.'

She's asking another question, but I'm already heading out, grabbing my jacket and keys and going to the car. My head is a whirl of theories and facts, of cold cases and new dangers, the bruise throbbing under my eye.

* * *

The old airbase is little more than a collection of old huts, a decaying control tower and half a dozen hangars overgrown with weeds and moss and every type of greenery. From what I could remember it was an old Second World War base that had been out of commission for decades. There is no gate and the fence is torn down in a dozen places.

I drive in and park near the biggest hangar with barely two minutes to spare before the 4 p.m. deadline. The ground is a patchwork of asphalt squares, with thick weeds growing through the gaps. It is utterly desolate and deserted. I take the small grey backpack from the passenger seat and walk towards the hangar, looking around for any signs of life.

I message Flack's accomplice.

I'm here.

Webber and his colleagues in uniform have done a good job of concealing themselves. I can't see any sign of them at all.

I pull up his number and fire a message to him too.

At the airbase. Where are you?

I walk into the biggest hangar, a mess of rusted machinery and overgrown concrete, everything thick with the smell of rot and the ancient stink of spilled aviation fuel. There are large, jagged holes in the roof and the end wall. Apart from the signs of a few small fires on the concrete, it doesn't look as if anyone has been in here for years.

My phone rings, loud and tinny in the echoing cavern of the old hangar.

'We're stuck in traffic,' Webber shouts. 'It's total gridlock here, we haven't even moved in twenty minutes. Don't go in on your own. Do you hear me? I've got three officers with me, do *not* go in there alone.'

I end the call without replying.

With his voice cut off, the silence in the old hangar is even more profound. A deep, dull nothingness that seems to absorb sound and light, deadening even the faint sound of traffic from the A52 over the hill.

I check my watch. Five past four.

My phone buzzes with a new message from the unknown number.

Didn't really think I'd be there, did you?
I've always loved the smell of petrol.

I reply to tell them that I'm here at the meeting place, I've got everything they asked for. I open the grey backpack and take a picture of the Rolex inside, send it. But they don't even acknowledge it. Instead, another three messages land one after the other.

Change of plan.
You were going to double-cross me.
So now I'm going to make you pay.

The horrible realisation of what I've done lands with a sick jolt in the pit of my stomach. We thought we were setting a trap, but the wolf had seen us coming from a mile away.

I've always loved the smell of petrol.

My house isn't safe anymore. I call Dom but his phone rings out without being answered. Jess's goes straight to voicemail and I leave her a message telling her not to go back to the house when she's picked Callum up.

'Go anywhere,' I say breathlessly into the phone. 'Next door, to your brother's place, anywhere – just don't go home.'

I stab at Leah's number next, shouting at her to pick up.

'Hey, Dad.'

'Leah! I need you to take your sister and get out of the house, OK? Go next door, stay with Mrs Evans and don't let anyone in, all right? No one.'

'Dad, what are you talking—'

'Just do it!' I'm shouting now, but I can't help myself. 'You're in danger. Get out and don't go back until I've told you it's safe. Do it now.'

I ring off and sprint for my car.

68

My phone rings as I'm weaving through stop-start traffic on the dual carriageway back into town. The display shows it's Mr Sedgewick, the teacher who oversees tag rugby after school.

'Just checking on pick-up arrangements for young Callum,' he says, failing to keep the annoyance out of his voice. 'He's the last one.'

'My wife's picking him up today.'

'Any chance you can do it? She doesn't seem to be here. Must be a crossed wire somewhere.'

'One of us will be there, very soon. Sorry.'

'As I said, Mr Wylie, all the other parents have already collected—'

I hit 'end call' to cut him off and ring Jess but she doesn't pick up.

She must be running late, but it's not like her to be out of contact. And however annoyed she was after what I said last night, she would never take it out on the kids.

Another call to Jess's mobile goes unanswered, and a cold wash of dread starts to turn in my stomach.

As if on cue, my phone buzzes with another text and I jab the screen with a sudden lurch of hope that is instantly dashed.

It's not from my wife.

Heart rising up into my throat, I click on the message.

It's five seconds of looping video: Jess's unconscious face, her eyes closed, black tape over her mouth, a line of blood snaking down from her temple. Below it, a brutal succession of texts drop in one after the other.

You made me do this.
Bring everything that belongs to me. No police.
She has maybe fifteen minutes of life left.
Or you will never see her again.

I type a rapid reply with one shaking hand, steering with the other.

Will bring it all to you. Where?

Further instructions to follow.
GPS says you're heading in the right direction.
But if you're late, she dies.

Fifteen minutes was barely any time at all but I had to get to her.

I push down harder on the accelerator, flashing through a gap between a truck and a bus pulling away from the kerb. On the other side of the carriageway, traffic is gridlocked and at a total standstill. In my head, I can't stop seeing that five seconds of looping video of Jess, unconscious and helpless, at the mercy of a psychopath. The ultimate confirmation that my family would never be safe until Peter Flack's partner in crime was off the streets for good.

I dial Webber's number again.

'My kids are in danger,' I shout over him. 'You need to send police to Regency Place, they've gone to my neighbour's house but they're in terrible danger.'

He doesn't seem to have heard me. 'Listen, Adam, that name you gave me, Peter Flack? I put it into the system, but he was never on our radar, no criminal record at all, he was absolutely clean as a whistle.'

'JUST SEND THEM!' I repeat the address and hang up, weaving around the cars in front and accelerating through a traffic light as it goes red to a chorus of honking horns behind me.

Thirteen minutes. It was going to be incredibly tight.

Another call to Dom's phone goes straight to voicemail.

I'm overtaking into oncoming traffic when the FaceTime app on my phone shows a new video call. I stab the green icon to accept, almost crashing as I swerve lanes and dive back into a gap. The screen opens up on an image of a dark ceiling, moving as the camera pans down onto my wife's motionless body.

'Jess?' I shout it, the word catching in my throat. 'Where are you? Are you OK?'

But she can't hear me. She can't speak. The black tape that had been covering her mouth is gone but her face is pallid, her lips starting to turn blue as if she's slipping away. A trickle of blood crusting at her chin. The call cuts off abruptly and a message drops in a moment later.

You better hurry, she doesn't have long left. You know where.

I blink, suddenly realising that I *do* know where. I recognised the room, the desk, the wooden panelling on the wall. I recognised all of it.

Because the call was coming from inside my house.

PART V

Betrayal. It's a sharp-edged word. An ugly word. And so you find a way to guard against it. A guarantee of mutual loyalty so you both keep the secret, or you both go down together. A blood pact, written in the blood of others. And it meant those hidden souvenirs served a double purpose.

Not just to remember each victim, but an insurance policy too.

It was foolproof, a tried-and-tested system of mutually assured destruction. There was just one flaw, one tiny problem that never occurred to me back then, when I decided he had to die.

I had no idea how well hidden his little insurance policy would turn out to be.

69

I run every red light on the way back and almost crash twice. A grey Volvo is parked on the drive when I get home, pulled up close to the porch.

The front door is ajar, the house silent. I grab the grey backpack from the passenger seat of my car and race up the stairs two at a time, resisting the urge to call out to my wife.

The first floor landing is empty.

Halting for a second to catch my breath, I realise the house is not *quite* silent. Up here, I can hear something above me, a steady mechanical hum that is too vague to make out.

The phone buzzes in my pocket again. But I'm here now and I know what I have to do.

I run up the second staircase into the smallest of the three bedrooms on the top floor, the place where all of this started. Still a mess of boxes and bags and old broken furniture, a desk pushed hard up against the hidden door. I haul it away and wrench the door open, smashing it back on its hinges, a wall of heat hitting me as I step over the threshold into the small, enclosed space.

Jess . . .

She's there, lying sideways in the dark, in her work clothes but with no shoes, her bare feet tied with thin rope. Her wrists are bound in front of her.

Her eyes are shut, skin beaded with sweat.

The noise is coming from a portable diesel-powered heater in the corner of the room. It looks ancient, paint flaking with rust as it chugs away, pouring hot air into the enclosed space.

Not only hot air.

I reach over and snap off the generator, then grab the pull-cord for the overhead light. Nothing happens – and I realise why as shards of the broken bulb crunch beneath my feet. My wife is breathing but only just, her pulse weak and fluttery. She needs air, she needs oxygen, she needs to be anywhere but in this room with these toxic fumes.

'Jess?' I carry her unconscious body out through the doorway, before laying her down as gently as I can and patting her cheek. 'Can you hear me? Wake up, love. *Please* wake up.'

I take out my phone to call for an ambulance and see there are now two missed calls and two picture messages from Maxine's number.

I dial 999 and minimise the screen as I wait for the call to connect, selecting the first of the picture messages. The text below it is only three words.

Charlie found this.

The screen fills with what looks like a photo of a photo.

It's a group of teenage boys and girls in skiing jackets and salopettes. They're on the balcony of a restaurant, against a backdrop of snow-covered mountains and a perfectly blue Alpine sky. An elaborate school crest on the cardboard mount features a Latin motto and a gold-embossed heading that reads 'Trent High School, Chatel, 1992'.

The phone continues to ring.

Two faces on the photo have been circled in red. The first one I recognise instantly: in the centre of the group, as if surrounded by adoring acolytes, is the movie-star handsome face of eighteen-year-old Peter Flack. He reclines in his chair like a king, tanned, relaxed, a predatory smile full of toxic confidence. The very definition of an alpha male.

The 999 call is still ringing. I put it on speaker with an impotent shout.

'Come on!'

The other face circled in red is on the periphery of the group, the edge of the picture, turned slightly towards Flack as if they can't take their eyes off him even for a second.

I pinch the image with my fingers to zoom in closer.

It looks like . . .

Oh, shit.

Finally, my 999 call connects.

'Operator,' a young female voice says. 'Which service do you require?'

I'm about to answer when a shadow falls over me.

As I turn, there is a shattering, clubbing pain in my left temple.

Then another.

Then everything goes black.

70

I wake up in a fog of pain but it all comes back to me in one sickening, tearing rush.

I had been wrong.

Wrong about so many things.

Wrong about the people who had done this.

Not a man and a woman, like Brady and Hindley or Bonnie and Clyde. Not a female at all.

Another partnership that was just as toxic.

Instead, an alpha male – the pack leader, the top dog – with the beta male very much in his shadow, smaller in every respect. In courage, in confidence, in physical stature. A beta male who had finally emerged from that shadow all these years later, to take up the mantle of the master. The picture Maxine has sent me is still on the screen of my phone, the faces circled in red blurring in and out with each throb of pain in my skull.

Jeremy Swann, the estate agent, leans over me.

He picks up my phone off the floor, cancelling the emergency call.

Through the pain in my head, I hear him rummaging in the grey backpack I carried upstairs.

'I'll have these, I think,' Swann says calmly. 'To complete my collection.'

My hands are tied behind my back. He drags me into the hidden room, grunting with the effort, and lays me alongside Jess. She looks worse than ever, a greyish tinge to her skin that makes my heart clench with fear and love and grief for how badly I've let her down.

Swann turns the diesel generator back on with a gloved hand, pulling a small respirator up over his mouth and nose. In his other hand he holds a short, thick wooden club with a grooved handle and a leather strap around his wrist.

'Thought carbon monoxide poisoning would be a nice touch,' he says. 'Wouldn't be the first *tragic* accident this house has seen. Appropriate, no? Considering what I had to do to Pete and his poor old grandma in the end.'

'You were at school with him.'

He nods, smiling behind his mask. 'Two years and about a million miles below him in social terms. We lost touch after school and I was twenty-one before I bumped into him again. But as soon as we saw each other, as soon as we started talking, we both just *knew*. It's hard to explain to an average Joe like you. But we recognised each other as if we were looking in a mirror. We saw something in each other that we'd never seen in anyone else.'

'That you were both psychopaths.' I couldn't help myself. Despite the fact that I was breathing in carbon monoxide with every word I uttered.

He shrugs. 'If you like. If you want to put a label on it. Pete, he was . . . free. The only *truly* free person I've ever known. We were the same. And yet at the same time he was an absolutely extraordinary man, like a young god, a young Achilles. One of a kind. I've never met anyone like him, even *close* to him, before or since.'

'Didn't trust you though, did he?' I flex my arms, ball my fists, trying to work some movement into the knot around my wrists. 'Otherwise he would never have kept his little stash of compromising evidence on you. To make sure he always had a hold over you.'

Swann studies the Rolex with an air of detached interest before putting it in the gym bag with everything else.

'Obviously I didn't know exactly where he kept his "insurance policy", as he liked to call it.' He zips the gym bag closed. 'That was the whole point of it, the little souvenirs with their traces of blood and DNA were insurance against betrayal from the other. We weren't supposed to know where the other one lived, where they worked, who they socialised with. There was nothing to link us together – that was the safest way. We just met up to . . . to do what we did.'

'To hunt.'

'Yes.' He smiles. 'To hunt. Best days of my life.'

'Until it went sour.'

'It was his fault. After a while he started to get . . . reckless. Almost as if he wanted to get caught, wanted the world to see how clever he was, how many he'd killed. He was always in charge when we were together, always the leader, but that was never *my* plan. We were never supposed to get caught. So I had to work out a contingency plan instead, found out he lived in this posh house in The Park, and that his dozy grandma never used to lock the back door, made it easy enough to get inside and make a few *adjustments* to the old gas fire. I broke in once after he died too, when it was empty, but couldn't find anything. Thought maybe he had a safety deposit box somewhere instead that would get thrown away when he stopped making the payments. But I had to be *sure*.'

'He'd hidden his stash so well you couldn't find it.'

'After I took care of him and old grandma Elizabeth, the house went on the market and *that's* when I had the idea. Got myself a junior's job with the estate agent that was handling the sale. Thought I'd get a set of keys and be able to wander around whenever I liked, turn the place upside down if I had to.'

'And why didn't you?'

He snorts. 'I was *so* naive back then. I was the new junior agent and they gave me all the crap jobs, viewings on the low-end properties, they never let me handle the expensive stuff. I never even got *near* this place while it was on the market in 2002. It sold to that old fart Mr Hopkins pretty quickly, and all of it was handled by the branch manager because it was top-end value.'

'You missed your chance.'

'Yeah, but then something weird happened. I got a taste for it, the house-selling business. And I was *good* at it, too. Enjoyed it, seeing how people lived, having access to all of it. And I thought, what better way of keeping an eye on this house, having a reason to drop by, to be in the neighbourhood with a full set of copied keys. To have an interest in what was going on. Eric Hopkins was old, I knew sooner or later it'd be up for sale again, that one day it would be empty again – and that would be my chance to check it thoroughly from top to bottom. To make absolutely sure I was safe. I just had to be patient. Even got some cameras set up in here to keep an eye on everything in case some idiot eventually stumbled across Pete's stash of souvenirs. Some idiot like you. Tried to make it easy for you, but you wouldn't listen. I tried to warn you off Webber with a little note about his chequered past, but you didn't listen to that either.'

Greyness clouds my vision. The gas.

'Please . . . let my wife go. She doesn't know anything.'

He notices me fighting to keep my eyes open.

'What you're feeling now? That's because carbon monoxide is replacing the oxygen in your red blood cells, preventing it from getting to your tissues and organs. It's quite painless, not a bad way to go, all things considered. You'll just slip away. Together.'

'Let Jess go. Please.'

He shakes his head, raising the wooden club.

'Sorry, Adam,' he says. 'You really should have left the past alone. If you'd just let it be, none of this would have happened.'

He swings the club down again and the pain knocks me flat, a paralysing, thundering blow above my ear.

Unconsciousness claws at me and I start to surrender to it, closing my eyes.

Darkness waiting to take me on one last journey.

71

I sense Swann standing over me, staring down like a hunter trying to decide whether to administer the coup de grâce. The noise of my own ragged breathing drifts in and out. Receding, nearing, receding again.

I lie perfectly still.

Playing dead.

Motionless.

Seconds pass, days, months, years . . .

I hear the *snick* of a blade as my wrists are freed, the rope pulled away, and I search my fogging brain to figure out why. Letting my hands flop lifelessly to my sides, trying to work out why he would do that.

So it looks like we came up here of our own free will. So it looks like an accident.

There is a click as the door is closed and we're plunged into impenetrable darkness. A scraping noise, a thud, as the heavy desk is pushed up against the door. Steps receding as he leaves the room.

I count to ten. Then again. When I can no longer hear footsteps, I lift my head from the floor with a grunt of pain.

It is pitch dark. *Perfectly* black.

Biting back the nausea threatening to rise up my throat, I crawl on my hands on knees towards the noise of the diesel-powered heater, burning my hand on the edge of the vent before I can find the switch to kill the engine. The air is still thick with fumes, a little voice in my head saying, *Lie down, just lie down for a moment and close your eyes, rest a minute, take it easy and catch your breath, sleep . . .*

But I know if I close my eyes now I will never open them again. With a hand outstretched before me in the darkness, I crawl back to where Jess is lying.

The rope binding my wife's hands and feet is gone too, I notice. I call her name desperately, pat her cheek with my palm but there's no response. A cough sends a hacking jolt of pain through my head. There is another smell creeping through the floorboards, rising through the brickwork to add to the poisonous mixture that has already driven out most of the air in this room.

Smoke.

Curling up through tiny gaps where the floor met the outside wall. Rising invisibly between the floorboards.

Swann had finally made good on his promise, made all those days ago.

Next time we bring petrol and matches.

The carbon monoxide filling this room was also flammable.

I realise something else with a sick jolt of panic. By the time the fire brigade are called, even if they get here in time, if they break down the front door, put out the flames, search the house, it won't matter.

Because they'll never find us in here.

They'll never find the room in time.

This is going to be our tomb.

Our children, orphans.

Unless I can save us both.

I haul myself to my feet, staggering with dizziness, feeling my way to where I think the door must be. Lift the lock and push.

Nothing.

It doesn't even move a millimetre.

I take a step back and throw myself against it once, twice, pain exploding in my shoulder as I smash against the frame. But it is utterly solid. The old desk pushed up against it, perhaps other heavy furniture too. I feel around on the floor for anything that I can use as a lever or a battering ram, anything to give me purchase on the door.

A jagged pain pierces my hand as a piece of the broken bulb presses into the heel of my palm.

The sting is sharp as I pull out the fragment of glass and it prompts a flare of memory, trying to break the surface of my clouded brain. What is it? *Broken glass.* But not the only thing broken in this place. The first day we moved in, the day I found the door, the room, the first time I saw the dresser. I was going to break it open, rather than waste time looking for a key. Snapped the blade of that old chisel right off—

The armchair.

Under the armchair.

I reach out in the dark, feeling my way with a shaky hand through the dust and cobwebs, the old carpet rough beneath my palm.

There.

The tools.

The tools I'd brought up on the first day are still here, where I'd kicked them under the armchair and forgotten about them. The screwdriver. The old chisel with its broken blade. And – *please be there* – my fingers close around the smooth heavy steel of the crowbar. A foot long, with its distinctive hook shape and flattened ends.

I climb to my feet, feeling my way in the dark, reaching out towards the wall. Tearing down the rug nailed against it, bloody fingertips groping for the bare brick, finding the distance as more smoke doubles me over with coughing.

With all the strength I have left, I start to batter the wall with the sharp end of the crowbar, wielding it with both hands like a spear in the hope that I can gouge a way through. Looking for a single weakness, a single piece of loose mortar, just one gap to drive the hard steel into the wall as chips of brick are hurled back into my face. Battering and smashing until I feel something start to give—

—hitting it harder, focusing all my anger and fear on that one point until I can prise a single brick loose with bleeding fingers, smashing the crowbar into those around it, breaking another, pulling a third free in a cloud of choking dust. Throwing all my weight against the gap and the wood behind, a shout of pure rage bursting from me as I charge against the gap, agony blooming again in my shoulder, but I can barely feel it, smashing again with the heavy crowbar, levering more bricks out, the steel making a new noise now, a resonating thud of metal against wood.

I smash the blade into it again, feeling the last of my strength start to leave me, acrid smoke from below filling my lungs, the pain in my head as if it's going to burst, swinging the tool hard against wood with everything I have left. Again, and again, and again.

A splintering of wood, a cracking, and then—

Light.

72

Lungs burning, eyes stinging, I carry Jess out through the front door.

The drive is in a state of chaos: drifting grey smoke, an ambulance, people moving in slow motion. Some standing, others sprawled on the ground. Firefighters on the street running hoses towards the house burning behind me. My vision is blurry, streaming with tears from the smoke, my head pounding, every muscle in my body alive with pain.

I can't see Swann among the mill of activity.

A figure appears in front of me: a green-uniformed paramedic ushering me away from the door and helping me to walk to a waiting ambulance, to lay Jess on a stretcher. An oxygen mask is put over her mouth and nose, another paramedic hooking her up to a machine. My wife's eyes flutter half open, her head turning towards me.

The first paramedic is leaning over her, talking loudly. 'Jess, is it? Can you hear me, Jess? We're giving you oxygen now, you're going to be all right, just give me a nod, OK?'

She gives the smallest of nods and I feel my heart filling, expanding, as if it might burst out of my chest.

Someone else is trying to speak to me. A stubble-cheeked firefighter, the strap dangling from his helmet.

'Is anyone else inside, sir?' he says for the second time. 'Anyone left in the property?'

'No,' I say, my throat raw. 'My kids are . . . next door. I think.'

Then he's gone and I see, through the drifting smoke, another group of figures coming slowly down the drive. Eileen from next door and Mr Sedgwick from the school with the three children between them, Coco on a lead clutched in the teacher's hand. The two younger children stare up at the house, the smoke, the firefighters, with a mixture of terror and curiosity and overwhelmed awe.

Leah breaks free and runs across the drive, throwing herself into my arms in a tearful hug.

'Dad!' She clings to me in a way she hasn't done for years. 'What happened? Are you hurt?'

'I'm all right.'

'Your hands are bleeding.' She looks horrified. 'And your head. Uncle Dom's been calling me, said he couldn't get hold of you.'

Callum and Daisy look as if they might follow their big sister across the drive but I hold a hand up.

'It's OK,' I call across to them. 'We're safe now, we're both all right. Just stay there with Eileen and Mr Sedgwick while the firemen do their work.'

Leah releases me and leads me away from the house and the drifting smoke to where a figure is lying prone on the gravel, with two others on top of him.

Swann, his face twisted with impotent fury, is pinned to the ground.

Blood is running down from his hairline into his right eye.

Maxine sits across his legs while Charlie is on his back, a knee up between Swann's shoulder blades.

The young man brandishes his metal walking stick in Swann's face.

'You want me to hit you again? Because I will if you don't lie still.' He leans down closer. 'You deserve much worse for what you did to my dad.'

Maxine raises a hand to me as I approach. 'Are you all right, Adam? You look terrible.'

Despite the pain, I find myself smiling. 'You caught him.'

'You didn't respond when I sent you that picture. I was worried, thought I'd come by and check you were OK.' She indicates the dazed figure of Swann beneath her. 'We saw the smoke when we pulled up, and then who should come hurrying out the front door but the man himself. Took him by surprise when Charlie whacked him.'

'Good job,' I say. 'Both of you. Thank you.'

There is a squeal of tyres from the street, the heavy crunch of running boots as two uniformed figures emerge through the smoke.

'Cavalry's arrived,' Maxine says.

Sergeant Okoro goes to confer with one of the firefighters while PC James approaches us with one hand on his baton, trying to take everything in.

Everyone else seems to move at once, as if all of us have been released from some spell.

Callum gives a sudden shout of delight and breaks free of Eileen's hand.

'Mr Stay Puft!'

He runs over to the flowerbed under the oak tree, where the hamster is chewing something he's found, oblivious to everything.

Above him, on a low branch of the old oak, Steve sits and surveys the whole scene with wide amber eyes.

Daisy slips free of Mrs Evans's grip and rushes towards her mother in the ambulance.

There's a scramble of movement to my left, and when I turn back, Maxine and Charlie are sprawling in the gravel as Swann rolls away from their grasp, rising to his feet again, staggering forward, shifting into a run, angling towards the narrow gap between the ambulance and the hedge. He's surprisingly fast, each step kicking up sprays of gravel, darting past my outstretched hand and sidestepping Leah in a headlong sprint towards the street.

At the last second, PC James – all six feet three and sixteen stone of him – pivots into the gap and drops his shoulder.

Swann cannons into the young officer and bounces back onto the gravel like a rag doll flung against a brick wall.

James is on him in a second, a knee in his back pinning the smaller man to the ground.

'Sir?' He takes the handcuffs from his belt, unsnapping them with a practised flick. 'You're under arrest. You do not have to say anything, but it may harm your defence if you do not mention when questioned something which you later rely on in court. Anything you do say may be given in evidence.'

He closes the cuffs around Swann's wrists and hauls him to his feet.

73

SIX MONTHS LATER

The house will survive. Swann actually set three fires that day, one on each floor, but fortunately they didn't take hold properly before the fire brigade arrived. The repair work's only just finished but the damage wasn't structural. It wasn't permanent.

The police investigation is moving slowly because of the sheer number of cases the new task force has had to reopen. Swann stonewalled all questioning at first, until the forensic results came back on the items I had found in the dresser in the hidden room.

Since then, he seems to have changed his tune.

According to what I've heard from DC Rubin, he's now insisting he was coerced by Peter Flack, that he was in awe of him, swept up in his slipstream during their three-year killing spree around the turn of the millennium. Flack used him, for the very reason that he was a small and unassuming man, the kind of person who could put potential victims at their ease because he was clearly no threat. I'm not sure that will help Swann much when his trial starts. Each of the items from that room – with the exception of the old flip phone – contained viable traces of both his DNA and traces from the victims. The cashpoint receipt in the wallet didn't belong to a victim, but it gave investigators a precise date, time and place that put the account holder within a quarter-mile of another victim's bedsit, on the evening he went missing. The account holder's name was Jeremy Swann.

All of it had been insurance – so Peter Flack could keep his acolyte in line.

Until Swann turned on him, and Flack himself became a victim.

I hope the families might finally find answers; be able to find some kind of peace after all these years. Swann has already led detectives to human remains in a shallow grave in Sherwood Forest. Those remains have been identified – using DNA from Charlie Parish – as those of Adrian, his father.

The trial is not scheduled to start until next spring.

From the work the police have done so far, the case will revolve around the deaths of six people. Six men and women who never knew each other in life, who had disappeared or died in unexplained circumstances over a short span of years. Whose families had come to believe they might never have any answers – until now. The media coverage has been steady over the past six months, as each new name has been added to the grim tally of those who fell victim to a pair of ruthless serial killers more than twenty years ago.

Edward Stiles, twenty-five.

Adrian Parish, forty.

Carys Neill, thirty-two.

Dean Fullerton, thirty-nine.

Sian Stott, eighteen.

Pamela Roy, sixty-one.

I've kept in touch with Maxine and Charlie and we've met for lunch a few times. To me, the two of them seem changed in ways that are both subtle and profound; a liberation from the past, perhaps. Finally able to lay old ghosts to rest. Webber, too, seems to have found some redemption at last.

The hidden room was fully dismantled in the end, all of it carted away by the police for further examination. Every other inch of the property scoured and searched by boiler-suited forensics teams, floorboards pulled up here and there, the attic thoroughly searched, the cellar examined in minute detail, sections of the garden dug up and ground-penetrating radar used to find various items they won't even tell me about.

Now, it's pretty much back to normal. Back to how it was – except one top floor bedroom that's slightly bigger than before. Like I said: 91 Regency Place was built to last, it was built solid and strong, with good bones and deep foundations. Built to be somebody's forever home. Somebody's dream home.

I hope the new owners will be very happy there.

As for us, those eleven days were enough: we never spent another night under that roof again.

Dom put us up at his house for a couple of days while we recovered and found somewhere to rent. It was strange – Jess and I never discussed it but we both came to the same decision: that we would sell the house and figure out everything else afterwards.

It's only bricks and mortar, after all. A house is only a home because of the people in it.

That's why I find myself driving out here after work every so often, to see how things are going. To chat to the builders, the site manager, the surveyor, to see our new house take shape as it rises from the ground. We decided to move out of the city – not too far, just enough to breathe a little easier – to a place on the edge of a lovely village. A small development of half a dozen purpose-built new houses, with views out across the open fields.

They've given me a full set of floorplans and architectural drawings so I will know every room, every corner, every inch of the property by the time we move in.

It may not be a Victorian villa, but it will have everything we need.

It will be a clean slate, a blank page on which to write a new story. A place without secrets.

A place where we can start again.

Acknowledgements

First and foremost I'd like to thank our family friends Claire and Tom Grimble, for the real house-moving story that inspired this novel (even if they didn't have any idea at the time that I'd weave it into one of my thrillers). Thankfully, their real-life story was very different to this one – but it planted the seed for a book.

Thanks to *you*, for picking up *The Dream Home*. I hope you enjoyed sharing the story of Adam, Jess and family as they slowly discover the dark secrets of 91 Regency Place. If this is the first book of mine that you've read, I hope you might be inspired to pick up another. And if you've read all eight . . . an extra thank you. It means the world to have such dedicated, loyal readers and I'm immensely grateful to each and every one of you.

The character of Shaun in this book is named for reader Shaun Couldstone, who made a very generous bid in an auction run by the charity Young Lives vs Cancer as part of their 'Good Books' campaign. Young Lives vs Cancer do great work to support young people and their families dealing with a diagnosis and I was glad to be able to help.

Thanks to our friends Mark and Liz Rice, who told me about the hidden rooms that used to be found in old houses where men would hide from the Royal Navy's pressgangs. My friend Anthony Round kindly shared his professional knowledge about Rolex watches and I'm also grateful to Neil White, former news editor of the *Nottingham Evening Post* (and my boss when I was a reporter there), who helped me with queries about online news content back in 2001. Thanks to Brenton Smith, estate agent with eXp UK, for answering my questions about the house-moving process and what happens to property left behind.

I read Ken Brand's excellent publication, *The Park Estate, Nottingham* (published by Nottingham Civic Society) for historical background. I've taken a few liberties with the geography of the Park, but the essence of it is real. There is no street named Regency Place within its boundaries, but there's a great deal of fantastic nineteenth-century architecture that provided inspiration for this story. It was lovely to see some of those historic houses up close as part of the Park Garden Trail in summer 2023 – thank you to the homeowners and the organisers of this biennial event.

The East Midlands Special Operations Unit is a real police body, doing valuable work to tackle serious, organised and violent crime across the region. The old airbase at RAF Newton, however, has been subject to a little fictional licence for the purposes of this book.

I'm delighted to have signed with my brilliant publisher, Bonnier Books, for three more novels (which will be books nine, ten and eleven). There are still days when I have to pinch myself that I'm able to write stories for a living and I know how lucky I am to have found a home at Bonnier. Huge thanks in particular to my editor, Sophie Orme, and also to Perminder Mann, Sarah Benton, Rachel Johnson, Holly Milnes, Ellie Pilcher, Eleanor Stammeijer, Emilie Marneur and Isabella Boyne.

Thanks, as ever, to my agent Camilla Bolton and to the awesome team at Darley Anderson Agency and Associates, particularly Jade

Kavanagh, Mary Darby, Rosanna Bellingham, Salma Zarugh and Georgia Fuller. Also to Sheila David for her tireless work in bringing my books to the screen.

And thanks to my wife, Sally, who hears my ideas first and always gives great feedback and support. This book is dedicated to our children, Sophie and Tom, who have grown into a pair of smart, kind, funny, thoughtful and wonderful adults. I'm beyond proud to be your dad – this one's for you.

Enter the world of

T.M. LOGAN

Master of the up-all-night thriller

Sign up to the newsletter and get access to:

Regular giveaways

Cover reveals

Exclusive writing

Plus, download a free deleted scene
as soon as you join

Join today at
geni.us/TMLoganNewsletter

Hello,

Moving house can be a step into the unknown. There's a sense of discovery, of trying to make a new place your own even as you discover more about its quirks – or perhaps about the people who lived there before you. I wanted to capture that feeling with *The Dream Home*, the feeling of secrets slowly revealed, of the history contained within those walls.

The initial idea for the story was sparked by a conversation with some friends, Claire and Tom, who moved into a house some years ago and found a long-neglected space behind a false wall. It was not on the estate agent's plans for the property and they found it quite by chance. But it got me thinking . . . what if you moved into a house with the very darkest secrets? What if you inadvertently stirred up old ghosts, old crimes? And what if the perpetrator of those crimes was still out there?

I'm also a fan of the Netflix show *Mindhunter*, which is about the early years of the FBI's Behavioural Science Unit and its research into serial killers. I kept thinking about a single line from an episode in season two: that most of what we know about such killers is *from the ones who got caught*. In other words: perhaps there are some out there who have never been identified, who have managed to stay under the radar, beyond the reach of the police.

That was my starting point for *The Dream Home*.

My next thriller will be coming out in early 2025 and if you'd like to be the first to hear more about it, you can sign up to my free newsletter at www.tmlogan.com. Just click on the yellow 'Sign up' button, it only takes a moment and I promise I won't spam you with lots of emails.

My publisher Bonnier Books will keep your information private and confidential, and it will never be passed on to a third party. I'll get in touch now and again with news about my books, cover reveals, competitions and more. When I have news, my newsletter subscribers are always the first to know – so sign up if you'd like to become a member (you can unsubscribe at any time).

And lastly, a quick favour . . . if you have a minute, please do rate and review *The Dream Home* on Amazon, Goodreads or any other e-store, on your blog or social media accounts, talk about it with friends, family or reading groups. Sharing your thoughts and views helps other readers, and I always enjoy hearing what people think about my books.

Many thanks again for reading *The Dream Home*, I appreciate it.

Best wishes,
Tim

Read more from
THE MASTER OF THE
UP-ALL-NIGHT THRILLER

T.M. LOGAN

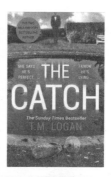

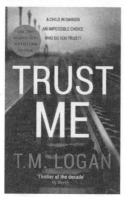

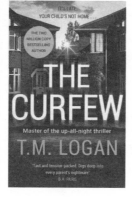

Can't get enough?
Sign up to T.M. Logan's newsletter for exclusive content and regular updates.
https://geni.us/TMLoganNewsletter